श्री राम श्री राम श्री राम श्री राम श्री राम श्री राम श्री राम श्री राम श्री राम

CITATION

K. K. Birla Foundation presents its twenty-first Saraswati Samman for the year 2011 to Dr. A. A. Manavalan for his Tamil work *Rama Kathaiyum Iramayanankalyum* published in 2005.

Dr. A. A. Manavalan is a scholar of Tamil, English, Hindi and Telugu with literary theory, comparative literature and translation studies as his special area of interest. He believes that the Ramayana and the Mahabharata, as perennial custodians and corpus of the Indian culture, have exerted immense and ineluctable influence on the literary outlook and development of the Indian languages.

Born in 1935 at the village Mosavadi, Tamil Nadu, Dr. Manavalan did his M. A. in English from Jamal Mohammed College, Tiruchi. M. A. in Tamil from S. V. University, Tirupati and Ph. D. in English from the University of Madras. He held the post of Professor and Head of the Department of Tamil in the University of Madras till his retirement in 1996. During 1988-89 he won the Fulbright Fellowship and visited six American Universities including Indiana, New York and Chicago as Honorary Professor of Comparative Literature.

Dr. Manavalan has so far published 13 volumes of literary criticism and four volumes of transactions, apart from editing five books of literary theory. Among his better known works are *Epic Heroism in Milton and Kamban* (1984), *Twentieth Century Literary Theories* (1995), *An anthology of Tamil Bhakti Poetry* (2004), *Comparative Studies in Literary Cultures* (2010) and others.

Irama Kathaiyum Iramayanankalyum, the book for which the Saraswati Samman is being conferred on him is Dr. Manavalan's magnum opus. The result of his interest and experience in the area of literary cultures, this work is a comparative study of 48 Ramayanas in the languages of Sanskrit, Pali, Prakrit, Tibetan, Tamil, Old Javanese, Japanese, Telugu, Assamese, Malayalam, Bengali, Kannada, Marathi, Hindi, Odishi, Persian, Malaya, Burmese, Maranao, Thai, Laotian and Kashmiri. This study being geographical, linguistic and cultural in approach, it brings out the Ramakatha's influence over the South-East Asian cultural splendor during the last two millenniums and more.

The Foundation wishes Dr. A. A. Manavalan a long life in the name of Goddess Saraswati.

Shobhana Bhartia
President
K. K. Birla Foundation

N. K. Bhattacharjee
Member Secretary
Chayan Parishad

R. C. Lahoti
Chairman
Chayan Parishad

New Delhi 19 September, 2012

RAMAYANA
A Comparative Study of Ramakathas

A A MANAVALAN

Translated into English and edited by
C T Indra & Prema Jagannathan

Vitasta
LET KNOWLEDGE SPREAD

Published by
Renu Kaul Verma
Vitasta Publishing Pvt Ltd
2/15, Ansari Road, Daryaganj
New Delhi-110 002
info@vitastapublishing.com

ISBN 978-93-86473-71-4
© C T Indra, Prema Jagannathan
First Edition 2021
MRP ₹995

All Rights Reserved.
No part of this publication may be reproduced, stored in a retrieval system, or transmitted in any form, or by any means—electronic, mechanical, photocopying, recording or otherwise—without the prior permission of the publisher. Opinions expressed in this book are those of the original Tamil author. The publisher is in no way responsible for these.

Editors: Papri Sri Raman, Kanagam King
Cover and layout by Somesh Kumar Mishra
Printed by Gopsons Papers Ltd.

RAMAKAATHAIYUM RAMAYANANGALUM

in Tamil
by
A A MANAVALAN
Former Professor and Head
Department of Tamil Language
University of Madras
Chennai

Translated into English
and edited by
C T INDRA
Professor and Head (Retired)
Department of English
University of Madras
Chennai

and

PREMA JAGANNATHAN
Associate Professor (Retired)
Department of English
Stella Maris College for Women
Chennai

Contents

Publisher's Note — ix
Setting The Book In Perspective — xi
Translators' Note — xv
Foreword — xvii
Preface — xix

Preface to the Scheme of Research — 1
Origin & Development of Rama's Story — 11
Bala Kaandam — 73
Ayodhya Kaandam — 157
Aranya Kaandam — 227

Glossary — 367
Bibliography — 373
Translators' Acknowledgements — 385
About Professor A A Manavalan — 389
Translator-Editor C T Indra — 391
Translator-Editor Prema Jagannathan — 393

Publisher's Note

Ramayana: A Comparative Study of Ramakathas is an English translation of Professor A A Manavalan's Saraswati Samman-winning critical study in Tamil titled *Ramakaathaiyum Ramayanangalum*. It takes up for analysis Bala Kaandam, Ayodhya Kaandam and Aranya Kaandam from the perspective of the discipline of Comparative Literature and explores in a meticulously structured manner the parallelisms and divergences in the representations of kernel events in these three kaandas in the various narratives on the Ramayana in different regions and their languages.* The ideological issues presented in the book are fascinating to the reader. The author leaves issues, especially gender issues, open for the reader to judge. We hope to bring to English language readers a bit of the richness of flavour, the delicacy of nuances and romance of the many Ramayans that straddle Asia, through this translation of Professor Manavalan's epic work in Tamil.

---

* Vide map of Rama's journey added on page 384.

SETTING THE BOOK IN PERSPECTIVE

What is Comparative Literature? It was a Western European academic phenomenon rising in early twentieth century. Of course, much before its institutionalisation, Goethe had talked of 'World Literature'. Rabindranath Tagore (1907) used the term '*Visva-sahitya*', but translated it as 'Comparative Literature' and not as 'World Literature'. Analogy, contrast, reception and influence are the nodal points of comparison in a systematic juxtaposition of phenomena from different literatures. These are exactly what we find Professor Manavalan looking for in his magnum opus in Tamil, *Ramakaathaiyum Ramayanangalum* (2005), which was awarded the prestigious Saraswati Samman by the K K Birla Foundation in 2011. It is a critical treatise on the re-renderings of Ramayana in India and South East Asian countries.

A product of 'Reception Study', it enquires into the convergences and divergences between the Indian Ramayanas and other language Ramayanas without placing the different poets in a hierarchy.

Intellectually engaging are the analyses of the symbiotic interaction of the northern and southern cultures which have impacted the various Indian Ramayana versions. A couple of riveting instances may be mentioned.

Agastya is a sage who came down the Himalayas, subdued the Vindhya mountains and went South to settle down. Professor Manavalan shows, through meticulously compiled comparative lists, that the greatness of Agastya as one who fostered the Tamil language, performed miracles and caused river Cauvery to flow, is brought out only in the Ramayanas of South Indian languages, following Kamban, whereas the Northern versions simply mention that he came from the Himalayas and that Rama met him.

A more interesting feature is the horoscope of Rama, based on the planetary positions at the time of his birth, as well as the representation of the hero as an incarnation or as an ideal or even at times as an imperfect human being. It is a paradox that the idea of celebrating Sri Rama Navami originated in the South, especially the Tamil country where a famous poem rejects faith in planetary influences. How Rama Navami has become a pan-Indian festival is an example of cultural diffusion.

The idea of Bharat as a cultural continuum does not call for obliterating sharp variations in perceptions governing the respective semiotic systems of each region or community. Professor Manavalan argues that the cultural and literary commerce has not been a one-way traffic.

Hence a later text alters the so-called original because the 'original' Valmiki itself is a palimpsest, thanks to the 'counter-influence' from the South. This, he claims, alters the very concept of 'influence' in Reception Studies.

Discussion of some critical deviations from traditional narratives of the story of Rama engages the attention of the reader interested in gender issues. The comparatist is at his best in unravelling the variations in the treatment of the Ahalya episode. In *Kamba Ramayanam*, a later text, Ahalya is cursed to turn into a stone. Absorbed with the task of tracing the genealogy of concepts, ideas and episodes, Professor Manavalan locates the source of Kamban's version in Tamil Sangam poetry. This version of the Ahalya legend was already in circulation in Tamil society and literature. Where in the Northern Recension of Valmiki there is just the curse, in the Southern Recension she turns into a stone. So we ask, which Valmiki says so?!

Various accounts of Manthara as an incarnational being, her grudge against Rama, and her secret sexual attraction towards Bharata emerge in Professor Manavalan's explorations, provoking the interest of the reader. The Buddhist and Jain Ramayana texts do not narrate Tataka's (Taraka's) killing. In Aranya Kaanda, the motivation of Surpanakha as represented by different Ramayanas deserves to be highlighted in keeping with their respective religious, social and literary conventions. South Asian Ramayanas like *Ramayana Kakawin* briefly refer to Surpanakha's complaint in general terms whereas the Laotian Ramayana *Gvay Dvorabhi* does not present a character called Surpanakha at all. In the two Buddhist Ramayanas, *Dasaratha Jataka* and *Dasaratha Kathaanam*, the incident of the abduction of Sita has not been narrated.

Similarly, the parallel study of the pre-marital days of Rama and Sita in folk literature and in the mainstream literature offers good scope for Professor Manavalan to highlight the transaction between *grand récit* and *petit récit*. Discussion of the altercation between Maricha and Ravana is also an instance of nuanced comparative study.

Thus, Professor Manavalan focuses on the genealogy of the core events as traceable to the ideologies governing the various rewritings of the Ramayana.

The aim of the English translators of this award-winning Tamil work is to show how it deftly participates in the critical debates in recent years about the Ramayana being an ethical text or an ideological text. Professor Manavalan avoids the Scylla of debilitating piety and the Charybdis of irreverence and directs his critical gaze steadily at the rich tapestry of the many Ramayanas we are fortunate to have as our cultural legacy.

— **C T Indra**

Translators' Note

The English translation, as it stands now, is a more compact one than it was in its earlier version. The length has been reduced without injury to the text and its reading. Since it is a study driven by comparative literature and its focus is on the influence and reception of the source work, we have kept, in the case of the crucial events, the elaborate accounts in the original Tamil book while deleting or abridging the summary sections in some cases.

- Indian words and terms have been retained as suits the context with English explanation in footnotes and parenthesis.
- The footnotes in languages other than English have been transliterated, indicating whether a footnote is in Hindi, Tamil or Sanskrit.
- Tamil and other Indian language titles have also been given in transliteration both in the footnotes and in the bibliography.
- As far as possible the translation of the book has been kept

close to the source text in Tamil. Where it was felt necessary, syntax and tense have been altered to make the reading more comfortable.

- The preliminary sections in the Tamil text such as the publisher's note and the Preface to the Tamil original by R Parthasarathy of the Institute of South Indian Studies have been left out of this translation.

- The maps have been included as they appear in the Tamil text.

- The bibliography in the original Tamil text has been reordered. In the present edited version of the English translation some footnotes have been omitted although the bibliography shows them under Works Cited.

- The term *vanmikam* has been retained as it is consistently used in the source text following the Tamil textual and hermeneutical tradition of the epic to refer to the corpus of lore/versions/renderings that go in the name of Valmiki Ramayana.

- The titles of South Indian Ramayana texts have been spelt with a final 'm' as is common in these languages.

FOREWORD

The story of Rama began, perhaps, in the collective unconscious of the ancient Indian tribes who inhabited India in the distant past. The story might have remained as an oral tradition for a long time and later found expression in a written form in the Buddha Jataka Tales (fifth century BCE). It was an essential part of the spiritual mythography of Buddhism. It was a simple and straightforward fable, wherein Rama represented one of the evolutionary stages of Gautama, the Buddha, before he attained Nirvana. There was only one twist in the story, the self-exile of Rama to the Himalayas to avoid the wrath of his step-mother. The Buddhist versions scrupulously avoided war and violence, befitting the sattvic traditions of that religion.

Valmiki, hailed as *Atikavi* (the first poet or Aadikavi in Sanskrit), collected the various myths and legends of his time, obtained from different parts of the Indian subcontinent and integrated them with the Rama story. He thus created a narrative and thematic continuity, set on a vast canvas that spread from

Nepal to Sri Lanka down below. Because of this inclusive setting, all the regions identified themselves with the epic, each one in its own distinctive way, so that when it was rendered in the language of the specific region, the impact and diversity helped to give the story a pan-Indian character. Thus Ramayana became an intrinsic aspect of the Indian cultural psyche.

India is a synthetic fabric of many-coloured threads, each thread having its own distinctive hue and identity but remaining inseparable from the fabric. So the same Rama story is retold in almost all the languages of the country with variations but without deviating from the main thematic content. Each version justifies the genius of the language in which it is told and also the culture of the region. Professor A A Manavalan, an eminent scholar in the field of comparative literature, has painstakingly made an intensive and analytical study of the Rama story in forty-eight languages not excluding the folk tradition. He wrote this brilliant book in Tamil and it won the prestigious Saraswati Samman. Professor Manavalan does not make any judgmental remarks with regard to the various versions, but his main focus is how the receiving language's rendering could make a greater impact than the original in the popular imagination of the people. Professors C T Indra and Prema Jagannathan have elegantly translated this book into English for a wider reach. This translation captures the thematic purpose of the Tamil original and creates a forum 'to discuss whether Ramayana is an ethical text or an ideological text'.

— **Indira Parthasarathy**

Indira Parthasarathy is a renowned writer and critic in Tamil. He was a professor in the Modern Languages Department in Delhi University, the first professor of Theatre in Pondicherry Central University and the first professor to hold the Tamil Chair at Warsaw University, Poland. He has won several awards including the Sahitya Akademi Award, the Saraswati Samman and the Hindu Lifetime Achievement Award.

Preface

Professor A A Manavalan was my respected senior colleague in the University of Madras, teaching in the Tamil Linguistics Department. Several years after he retired he suddenly dropped in at my home one day towards the end of 2012 with his award-winning work on Rama's story *Ramakaathaiyum Ramayanangalum* (Volume 1, covering the portions up to the Aranya Kaandam, published in 2005 by the Institute of South Indian Studies, Chennai). He insisted that I translate it for him into English. Taking one quick look at the contents and bearing in mind my domestic situation at that time, I was unsure if I would be able to undertake the project. I essayed a few pages and found what a daunting task it was going to be. My poor knowledge, inadequate language abilities and lack of technical skills dissuaded me from continuing. But Professor Manavalan was sure it could be done. It is said faith can move mountains and it is his faith in my abilities that has sustained me till the end. I had just finished the first draft of the introductory chapter of historical and theoretical discussions as well as Bala Kaandam, when he was taken ill and my hope of having periodical sittings with him to get clarifications and approval was gone.

Hearing 'at my back...Time's winged chariot hurrying near' I sought the collaboration of Prema Jagannathan. With her versatile knowledge of Tamil literature and language, although a practising English teacher, Prema stepped in and shouldered the burden with resolve and an amazing repertoire of technical skills. She could uncannily and effortlessly gloss unfamiliar terminology and concepts. Thus, together, we pulled the story of Rama to Ayodhya Kaandam. I must also mention how she single-handedly rough-drafted the longish Aranya Kaandam. Of course, I took a long time editing it with Uma Rajagopal's help because of the complex nature of the Tamil narrative syntax. I record here my deep sense of appreciation of Prema's professional commitment and support at all times. I also wish to record my grateful admiration for Malini Ravindran, my neighbour for long years who now became our saviour. With infectious enthusiasm she plunged into the task given and elucidated many recondite grammatical and cultural aspects of Tamil for me.

Professor Manavalan's Tamil work was selected for the prestigious Saraswati Samman by the K K Birla Foundation, Delhi, for 2011. My association in the 1990s with that organisation in various capacities was also partly the reason why I accepted the task of translating the book into English. Besides that, Professor Manavalan's discussions of the Ahalya episode and its various versions, and of the Surpanakha episodes, not to mention the role of Manthara and Kaikeyi in the unfolding action set me thinking as a woman scholar and an Indian. Today, scores of writers in various Indian language works are debating these issues. Professor Manavalan is a trained comparatist and hence has approached in this book the source and derivative texts avoiding value judgement per se, though he does not rein in his partiality for Kamban. The book's ideological interests, though deliberately occulted by the erudite Professor, also fascinated me much. They are not new, but they refuse to die. I hope this English translation helps to site the Tamil original within such discourse.

— **C T Indra**

Preface to the Scheme of Research

THE COLLECTION OF stories named Ramayana has been in vogue all over India long before historicised times, existing in various forms such as myths, *Purana*s and orature or oral literature. There is an opinion held among anthropologists and social scientists that even before it took a literary form through Valmiki, this compendium of stories had spread in all the regions of India in the shape of myths and folk songs. Even so, it is only in Valmiki's Ramayana that we find it taking, for the first time, the shape of a written epic.

Since the emergence of Valmiki's narrative, Ramayana has attained the form of an epic and has been in existence in more than twenty odd Indian languages starting with Sanskrit. Among them, depending on differences of religion, even in the same language we find that many epics have appeared. The objective of this study is to identify, on a comparative basis, how the various epics in different languages and religions have similarities with regard to many aspects of the story of Ramayana and how they vary with regard to others, and what the agencies or factors – social, cultural and literary – are, which have effected such changes.

Although the living aspect of a culture sustains the continuous flow of life of a country as a subterranean spring, it is but natural that the mechanics of existence driven by politics, history, society and external cultural mixing or blending should radically transform it on the surface, modifying it in such a way that it appears to be an entirely different set of cultural features. Accordingly, it is obvious that though the India of today was from time immemorial called Bharata Kandam, and referred to as a nation – geographically speaking, its Southern, North-west and Eastern regions underwent a few changes from time to time owing to external factors such as language, climate, food, dress, habits and arrival of outsiders impinging upon them sporadically now and then from the central Gangetic plains.

In view of this, the objective here also stems from the keen interest to do comparative research into how the various Ramayana epics, which have come up in different Indian languages, reveal these transformations in artistic forms. Given this situation, depending on the data available, Laotian, Malaysian, Siamese, Indonesian and Burmese Ramayanas have also been subjected to study.

This research has been conducted based on Reception Studies. That is, this study involves enquiring into how and where the Indian Ramayanas and other language Ramayanas which have blossomed forth by receiving the original story or the primal text of Aadi Ramayana, conform to the original or diverge from it. Hence it does not deal with topics which otherwise mark comparative research such as the salient features of character creation in the Ramayana texts, the poet's power of imagination, poetic style, and rhetorical features; nor are such features subject to any comparison. Hence no attempt is made to evaluate and place the poets in a hierarchy.

The differences discerned through this study are not used as criteria for evaluating the relative superiority or inferiority of the linguistic, literary and cultural variations. Comparative research is not interested in individual valuations; on the contrary, it is marked by the tendency to formulate, 'This is of such nature', by studying its contribution to the totality of the subject.

It may be unavoidable for a reader to identify himself/herself with one work arising from a particular language and its distinguishing cultural features as discerned in this study, or view them negatively. It must be made clear, however, that all such subjective responses are the reader's and this researcher does not share them.

Ramayana Texts

Although myriad Ramayanas have appeared in virtually every Indian language, only some texts have been included in the list that follows, taking into view their provenance and literary merit. Following this list, maps of regions where the Ramayana texts appeared are also given.

Moreover, important Ramayana texts which have appeared in Southeast Asian countries such as Tibet, Burma, Malaysia, Java, Laos, Thailand, Philippines also find a place in this study.

Apart from these texts, folk tales in Tamil, Telugu, Mythili, Bhojpuri, Braj, Hindi and Bengali as well as some songs from

North Indian popular literature have also been used in this study, some of them deeply and extensively, some briefly, as a note, as a reference, or as just a citation.

— **A A Manavalan**

In Table 1 some columns on Religion left blank by the Tamil author have been filled in by the publishing editor.

Publisher's notes have been provided in several places to relate to the contemporary debate and facilitate understanding of the context of statements for English language readers.

Table 1
Ramayana Works

Sl. No.	Name of the text	Author	Period/ Century	Language	Religion
1.	Dasaratha Jatakam	Unknown	5 BC	Pali	Buddhism
2.	Anamakam Jatakam	Unknown	3 BC	Pali	Buddhism
3.	Valmiki Ramayana	Valmiki	4-3 BC	Sanskrit	Hinduism
4.	Bharatam	Vyasa	4-3 BC	Sanskrit	Hinduism
5.	Dasaratha Kathaanam	Unknown	1 BC	Pali	Buddhism
6.	Raghuvamsa	Kalidasa	4-5 AD	Sanskrit	Hinduism
7.	Pauma Chariyu	Vimalasuri	4-5 AD	Prakrit	Jainism
8.	Vasudeva Hindi	Sankha Dasa	5 AD	Prakrit	Jainism
9.	Narasimha Purana	Unknown	5 AD	Sanskrit	Hinduism
10.	Ravanavaho, or Setubandha	Pravarasena	6 AD	Prakrit	Hinduism
11.	Bhagavata Purana	Unknown	6-7 AD	Sanskrit	Hinduism
12.	Bhattikavya or Ravanavadha	Bhatti	7 AD	Sanskrit	Hinduism
13.	Janakiharan	Kumaradasa	8-9 AD	Sanskrit	Hinduism
14.	Uttara Purana	Gunabhadra	9 AD	Prakrit	Jainism
15.	Tun Huang	Unknown	9 AD	Tibetan	Animism, Buddhism*
16.	Kamba Ramayanam	Kamban	10 AD	Tamil	Hinduism
17.	Ramacharita	Abhinanda	10 AD	Sanskrit	Hinduism
18.	Ramayana Kakawin (Indonesian Ramayana)	Yogheswara	10-11AD	Old Javanese	Hinduism

19.	Sambo-ekotoba (Japanese Ramayana)	Minamotono Tamenori	10 AD	Japanese	Buddhism*
20.	Champu Ramayana	Bhojaraja	11 AD	Sanskrit	Hinduism
21.	Ramayana Manjari	Kshemendra	11 AD	Sanskrit	Hinduism
22.	Bhusundi Ramayana	Unknown	12 AD	Sanskrit	Hinduism
23.	Padma Purana	Ravisena	12-15 AD	Sanskrit	Hinduism
24.	Udara-Raghava	Sakalya Malla	12-14 AD	Sanskrit	Hinduism
25.	Hobutsushu (Japanese Ramayana)	Tairano Yasuyori	12 AD	Japanese	Buddhism*
26	Tibetan Commentary Ramayana	Dmar-ston Chos-rgyal	13 AD	Tibetan	Buddhism*
27.	Ranganatha Ramayanam	Gona Budda Reddy	13 AD	Telugu	Hinduism
28.	Bhaskara Ramayanam	Bhaskara and three others	13 AD	Telugu	Hinduism
29.	Assamese Ramayana	Madhava Kandali	14 AD	Assamese	Hinduism
30.	Kannassa Ramayanam	Rama Panikkar	14 AD	Malayalam	Hinduism
31.	Adhyatma Ramayana	Unknown	14-16 AD	Sanskrit	Hinduism
32.	Krittibasi Ramayana	Krittibas Ojha	15 AD	Bengali	Hinduism
33.	Molla Ramayanam	Aatukuri Molla	15 AD	Telugu	Hinduism
34.	Ananda Ramayana	Unknown	15 AD	Sanskrit	Hinduism
35.	Torave Ramayanam	Kumara Valmiki (a) Narahari	16 AD	Kannada	Hinduism
36.	Ezhuthachan Adhyatma Ramayanam	Thunchaththu Ezhuthachan	16 AD	Malayalam	Hinduism

No.	Title	Author	Date	Language	Religion
37.	Bhavartha Ramayana	Ekanath	16 AD	Marathi	Hinduism
38.	Ramcharitmanas*	Tulsidas	16 AD	Hindi	Hinduism
39.	Jagamohan Ramayana	Balaram Das	16 AD	Oriya	Hinduism
40.	Persian Ramayana	Abdul Qadir	16 AD	Persian	Hinduism
41.	Thakkai Ramayanam	Emperuman	17 AD	Tamil	Hinduism
42.	Hikayat Seri Rama	Unknown	13-17 AD	Malay	Hinduism
43.	Rama Vatthu (Burmese Ramayana)	Unknown	17-19 AD	Burmese	Hinduism, Buddhism*
44.	Maharadia Lawana (Filipino Ramayana)	Unknown	17-19 AD	Filipino	Hinduism, Buddhism*
45.	Ramakien (Ramakeerthi) (Thai Ramayana)	King Rama I	18 AD	Thai	Hinduism, Buddhism*
46.	Gvay Dvorabhi	Unknown	18 AD	Lao	Hinduism, Buddhism*
47.	Phra Lak Phra Lam	Unknown	19 AD	Lao	Hinduism, Buddhism*
48.	Prakash Ramayana	Prakash Bhatt	19 AD	Kashmiri	Hinduism

* Provided by Publishing Editor to facilitate reader understanding. Professor Manavalan had left these slots blank.

Map 1
The Indian Subcontinental Ramayanas*

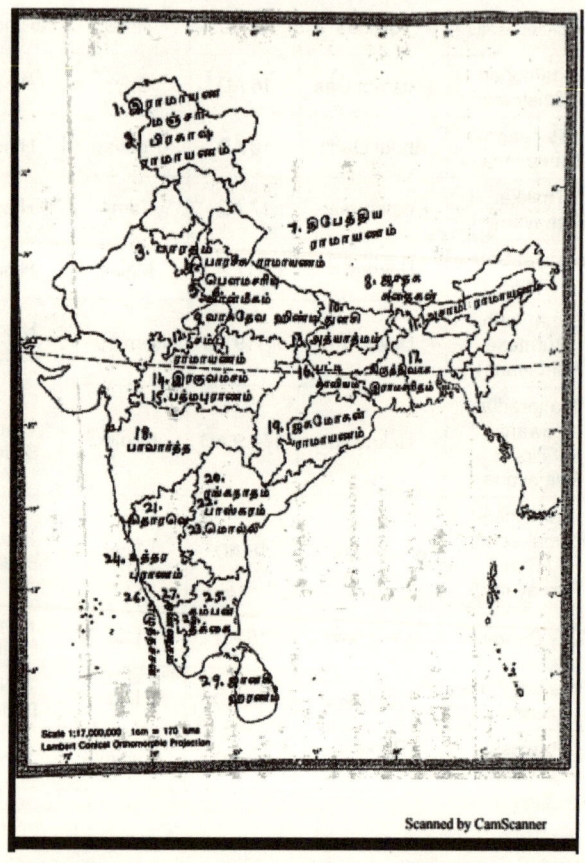

1. Ramayana Manjari 2. Prakash Ramayanam 3. Bharatam 4. Parasika (Persian) Ramyanam 5. Pauma Cariyu 6. Vanmikam 7. Tibetan Ramayanam 8. Jataka Tales 9. Vasudeva Hindi 10. Tulsi 11. Assamese Ramayanam 12. Champu Ramayanam 13. Adhyatmam 14. Raghuvamsam 15. Padma Puranam 16. Bhattikavyam 17. Krittibasi Ramacharitam 18. Bhavartha 19. Jagamohan Ramayanam 20. Ranganatham 21. Torave 22. Bhaskaram 23. Molla 24. Uttara Ramayanam 25. Kamban 26. Ezhuthachan 27. Kannassam 28. Thakkai 29. Janakiharan.

---

* This is a standard Outline Map issued by the Government of India for use in schools. It is not to scale and is just an indicator of geographic location. Professor Manavalan had himself indicated in Tamil the regional spread of the various Ramayanas in the Tamil original. The map is reproduced here from the original *Ramakaathaiyum Ramayanangalum*.

—Publisher's Note

Map 2
The Southeast Asian Ramayanas*

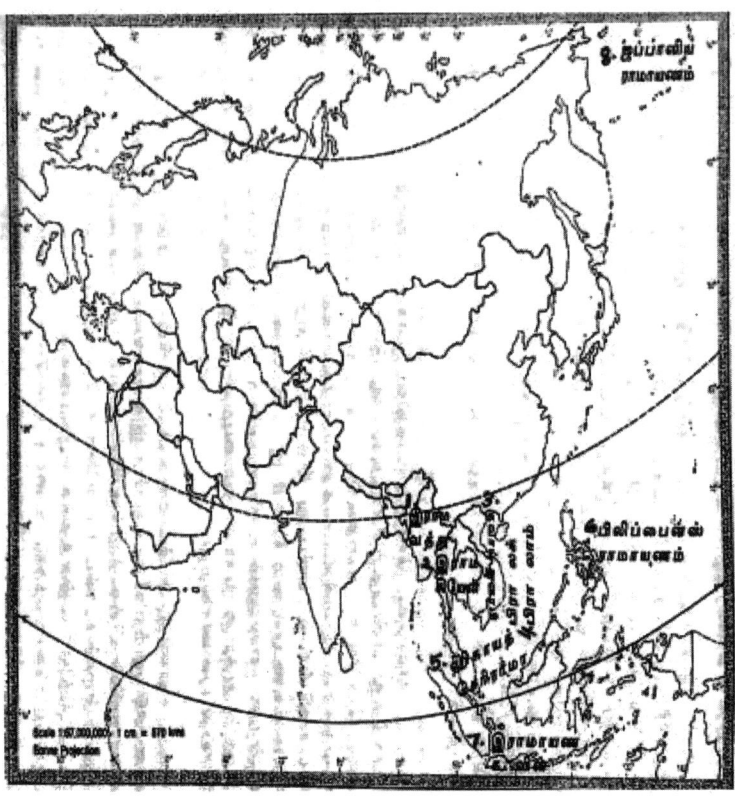

1. Rama Vatthu 2. Ramakien 3. Gvay Dvorabhi 4. Phra Lak Phra Lam
5. Hikayat Seri Rama 6. Filipino Ramayana 7. Ramayana Kakawin
8. Japanese Ramayana.

---

*   This is a standard Outline Map issued by the Government of India for use in schools. It is not to scale and is just an indicator of geographic location. Professor Manavalan had himself indicated in Tamil the South-Asian regional spread of the various Ramayanas in the Tamil original. The map is reproduced here from the original *Ramakaathaiyum Ramayanangalum*.

—Publisher's Note

Origin & Development Of Rama's Story

Rama's Story in the Vedas

THERE IS A prevalent opinion that the story of Rama had been in circulation even during the Vedic period, based on the fact that the names of Ikshvaku, Ram, Aswapati, Janaka, Sita and such *Ramayana* characters are found in the *Veda*s. However, there is no mention of stories related to characters bearing these names or any other stories related to the Ramayana in the Vedas. Although references to Janaka and Sita are found in many places, there is no reference to the father-daughter relationship.

It is therefore clear that there is no evidence in Vedic literature that the Ramayana had been composed during the Vedic period or that there were songs and tales relating to Rama's story. What becomes evident is that many ancient historical names match with those in the Ramayana, which goes to show that such names were in use during the Vedic period and even before.[1]

Even so, scholars like Hermann Jacobi think that the Ramayana Sita is a mature image of the Sita mentioned in the Vedas and that the source of the latter-day version of Rama's story is found in the Vedas. This view does not appear to be strong enough to be acceptable nor viable for research.[2]

Rama's Story and Buddhist Works

Valmiki Ramayana belongs to the fourth or third century BC. Buddhist Jataka tales like *Dasaratha Jataka* belong to the period between the fifth and first century BC. Hence some scholars have put forward the argument that Valmiki's Ramayana might have been composed based on the Jataka tales. There is also another view prevalent that since the conduct of Rama, Bharata, Sita and such major characters display values such as non-violence and peace which are incompatible with the code of *kshatriyas* (the royal/warrior caste), they might have been created under the influence of Buddhist doctrines.

Valmiki's epic is not the source of Rama's story. Centuries before Valmiki's time many features of the Ramayana lore were prevalent via various stories and folk narratives in various regions of India; based on them, the Buddhist Jataka tales, the Valmiki Ramayana, as well as a few short works containing Jain ideas, appeared. This information is presented in detail under the heading Valmiki Ramayana in this book.

---

1 Camille Bulcke, *Ramkatha* (Origin and Development). (Hindi). Allahabad: Allahabad University, (1950), 1971, pp.1-24.
2 Camille Bulcke, ibid. pp.103-106.

The Ramayana lore which is narrated in Buddhist Jataka tales is told in prose form with a view to explaining Buddhist doctrines. For example, we find that in Dasaratha Jataka, Lord Buddha said that 'In ancient times the Pouranic pundits did not grieve in the slightest over one's father's death' and added by way of illustration that Rama did not grieve over Dasaratha's death. Hence it is evident that much before such tales came into being, the Ramayana story was in existence in the country (Bulcke 57).

As far as the Jataka tales are concerned, the capital of Dasaratha is Varanasi; Rama and Sita are siblings; their sojourn in the forest is in the Himalayan region; the duration of the stay in the forest is twelve years. In the Aadi Ramayana of Valmiki, the capital is Ayodhya; Rama and Sita are, from the beginning, husband and wife; the forest region they move into is Dandakaranyam; the duration of their exile in the forest is fourteen years. A little before the period of the Guptas, the Valmiki lore expanded so as to make the exile in the forest go beyond Dandakaranyam and to include the destruction of Ravana in deep South Lanka.

Looking at these variations we can discern that – keeping those stories relating to Ramayana which were in vogue in the country for a long time as the core – Buddhist works, and poets like Valmiki, designed their characters and events in the story according to their respective codes or value systems. Since there are Valmiki's phrases and ideas found in some of the later Jataka tales, scholars consider that they might have come up after Vanmikam* or they might have been interpolations.

---

*   Vanmikam: body of renditions based on Valmiki's work.

Jataka Tales

The ancient works of literature belonging to Buddhist religion are known as the *Jataka Tales*. These Jataka tales narrate the story of how Lord Buddha in his previous human and animal incarnations showed the right way for mankind. Using the various stories prevailing among the people, these tales attempted to teach Buddhist doctrines. Within these ancient tales, many details of Rama's story are contained. Hence it becomes clear that long before the Jataka tales, Rama's story was prevalent among the people.

The Structure of Jataka Tales

Every Jataka tale has a prologue, an exemplar tale and an epilogue. In the prologue, the contemporary incidents which were instrumental in the telling of the tale are narrated. By way of a resolution or explanation of those incidents which are centred around a man-made complication, Lord Buddha tells a story that is found in the exemplar. The epilogue explains what role Buddha played in a previous birth in the tale narrated in the exemplar section.

It is in the narrative portions found interspersed in these three divisions that the details concerning Rama's story find a place. These tales are contained in three collections, *Dasaratha Jataka, Anamakam Jatakam* and *Dasaratha Kathaanam*. Among these, Dasaratha Jataka is hailed as the most ancient and most valuable.

Dasaratha Jataka

Dasaratha Jataka is included in the compilation **Jatakatta Description**. This Jatakatta Description is translated into New

Pali from a Sinhala text appearing in fifth century AD. These stories are in the form of a prose commentary on the songs composed in Old Pali.

That is, there were many stories narrated in the commentaries on ancient Pali poetical literature. They were transliterated into Sinhala language in fifth century AD. Later these stories were again transliterated into the New Pali language with the name Jatakatta Description. It is this form that is now extant.

Neither the poems in Old Pali nor the commentaries are now extant. Thus we come to know that stories which appeared before the Christian Era (BC) were transliterated in Sinhalese and again took shape in Pali in the Christian Era (CE). Hence some scholars hold that Dasaratha Jataka belongs to fifth century BC on account of its original form while other scholars contend that it belongs to fifth century AD, taking into consideration its later form.

Anamakam Jatakam

Around third century AD, Anamakam Jatakam was translated into Chinese. It has not been possible to find out which Indian text was its source, nor is it available. Scholars believe that this too belongs to the fifth century BC, based on the source text and also on its similarity to Dasaratha Jataka.

In this Jataka tale, none of the Ramayana characters have been mentioned. But incidents pertaining to Rama's story such as Rama and Sita's life in the forest, the abduction of Sita, the story of Jatayu's life, the battle between Baali (pronounced Vaali in Tamil) and Sugriva, the building of the Setu, the fire ordeal of Sita are narrated without mentioning the names of the characters. These are shown as happening in the life of Bodhisattva.

Dasaratha Kathaanam

The story called Dasaratha Kathaanam is found in a **Tipitaka collection** containing heroic stories, which is a Chinese translation (472 AD) of an Indian source text, now extinct, believed to belong to second century AD. Since in many of the stories found in the Chinese Tipitaka collection a Kanishka (Kushana dynasty) king appears as a protagonist, these stories are regarded as belonging to second century AD. However, there is also another view held among scholars that the source text might have appeared before the Christian era because it is the Pali source story which has been transliterated into Chinese and later translated again into Pali language.

The distinguishing feature of Dasaratha Kathaanam is that **in this there is no character called Sita, the Princess**. Hence this story stands as a Ramayana with none of the episodes such as Sita's birth, marriage, exile in forest, abduction by Ravana and battle of Rama and Ravana.

All the Jataka tales depict Rama as one of Lord Buddha's incarnations (Bulcke 56-62).

Valmiki Ramayana

The Indian literary tradition hails Valmiki as the primal poet and the Ramayana he composed as the primal Ramayana. This claim is certainly true of Sanskrit, also referred to as the Northern Language. There is no doubt that it was Valmiki who, for the first time, created a special pattern of prosody for the literary genre of the epic and brought it into vogue, and that it was Valmiki who, for the first time, forged the grand form *Itihasa* or the epic in the Sanskrit language.

Even leaving aside the Sanskrit literary-historical tradition, we can look at the following verses from Kamba Ramayanam:

> Though there are three poets who composed this tale
> In the divine language of Sanskrit
> According to the earliest of them...
>
> (Payiram 10)
>
> and
>
> Valmiki who forged the four-footed stanza none can replace.
>
> (Kamba Ramayanam I.2:1)

Kamban tells us in the above verses that it was Sage Valmiki who first created the sloka metre and the Tamil cultural tradition too has accepted, hailed and upheld the primacy of Valmiki in Itihasa.*

However, we know that it was not Sage Valmiki who created the Ramayana story and that, much before him there had been stories related to Rama's story in vogue in several parts of India. Keeping in mind the point that even before Valmiki, sketches of Ramayana story were in vogue in various parts of India in orature and in tales, many scholars have put forward different views on the origin of Rama's story. Important among them are Albrecht Weber, Hermann Jacobi and Dinesh Chandra Sen.[3]

It is Weber's contention that Buddhist Jataka tales such as Dasaratha Jataka and Homer's epic *The Iliad* are the basic sources for the origin of Rama's story. Jataka tales are mostly in line with Vanmikam. However, to relate Iliad to Rama's story on the basis of the issue of abduction of a woman and a great war ensuing, is indeed a weak position to take. For, such events are common features of human society present in different cultures. Hence many Western as well as Indian scholars long ago rejected Weber's view.

---

3   a. Albrecht Weber, *Uber das Ramayana*, Berlin 1870, pp. 1-88.
    b. Hermann Jacobi, *Das Ramayana*, Bonn 1893.
    c. Dinesh Chandra Sen, *The Bengali Ramayanas*, Calcutta, 1920.

*   See note at Chapter end.

As does Weber, Jacobi also cites two sources as the basis of Rama's story. In his opinion, Rama's story is a long narrative linked by two different parts. The first part is constructed based on the incidents taking place in Ayodhya. The second part is made of the incidents taking place in Dandakaranyam and the eventual killing of Ravana. Jacobi considers that among the two parts, the incidents in Ayodhya were based on history while the sources of the second are those found in the Vedas. Many of the contemporary scholars accept this view.

Jacobi does not deny the view that there was no Ramayana story nor stories connected to Rama prevalent during the Vedic period. Notwithstanding that, he is not inclined to give up his stand which links Ramayana characters with Vedic gods. Be that as it may, Camille Bulcke's opinion (103-106) that Jacobi's stand is not acceptable seems to be relevant.

Majority of the Ramayana scholars consider that Aadi Ramayana is the source of the Ramayana story composed by Valmiki and that Vanmikam is the form of the present-day Rama story; they also aver that the Aadi Ramayana was made up of five cantos, from Ayodhya Kaandam to Yuddha Kaandam, and that it might have emerged roughly around fourth to third century BC.

Most scholars also believe that the Valmiki Ramayana in existence today settled itself as containing seven cantos from Bala Kaandam to Uttara Kaandam, barring a few interpolations and later additions, around second century AD or third century AD (Bulcke 30-32). Various scholars, who have brought out critical editions of Valmiki Ramayana, have pointed out that after this, almost till the tenth century AD, a host of lateral stories, descriptions, and philosophical ideas were inserted as interpolations down the ages.

Editions

1951-1971	*Valmiki Ramayana*. Critical Edition (Northern Recension). Baroda University: Oriental Institute.
1995	*Valmiki Ramayana*. (Southern Recension) Gorakhpur: Gita Press. Fourth Edition.
1993	*Valmiki Ramayana*. (Southern Recension) Dharmalaya Reprint, Kovai-108: Arsha Vidya Ashram, Anaikatti, Tamil Nadu.

Various Versions of Valmiki Ramayana

Scholars are of the view that stories relating to Rama's story which were in vogue in the North, West, South and other regions in the form of orature, gradually took the written form, and many centuries later the Ramayana lore settled down after taking a literary shape and that it was at that stage that Rama's story got forged for the first time into the form of Itihasa in Sanskrit by Valmiki (see note at Chapter end).

Researchers have also found that Valmiki's epic too was first heard in various regions of India in oral form through bards and literary scholars and later got transliterated in the respective regional languages and came into circulation.

It was during this stage when Rama's story was heard, learnt and taught that several changes and new additions in the episodes, their locations, and the characters were effected. Textual variations and story variations proliferated to such an extent that if you mentioned any one episode, you might be asked which region's Valmiki said so.

Ramayana scholars began researching the Valmiki Ramayana palm-leaf manuscripts, categorising them as northern, north-eastern, eastern and southern recensions, based on such emendations, additions and deviations. Towards the end of the nineteenth century and in the early twentieth century, it became easily possible for scholars to identify such variations when the different regional versions took the printed form.

At a time when India's foremost epic Valmiki Ramayana was thus prevalent in many versions, the Oriental Institute in Baroda University, impelled by the efforts of many scholars who felt that a critical edition must be prepared for it, took up the task with GH Bhatt as its first editor in the year 1951. It approached the various libraries in the country as well as those abroad dealing with Indology, and collected around 2,500 Ramayana scripts, of which it selected eighty-six scripts. The task of preparing a critical edition was launched, keeping as its basis those transliterated scripts in Devnagari, Sarada, Telugu, Grantha, Malayalam and Nevari scripts as complete texts.

For the purpose of preparing this edition, thirty-seven texts for Bala Kaandam, twenty-nine each for Ayodhya, Aranya, Sundara Kaandams, thirty-two for Kishkindha Kaandam, thirty-four for the Yuddha Kaandam and forty-one for Uttara Kaandam were compared and examined.

The Valmiki text transliterated in the Nepali language of Nevari in 1020 AD is the oldest among those found so far. This text, which has been preserved in the Bir Library at Kathmandu, belongs to the Northern Recension of Vanmikam.

While the scholars were thus scanning several Valmiki scripts, they discovered many versions which deviated from the source Valmiki story in a few fundamentals. After sorting them and examining them, they noted how changes and additions very characteristic of the Northwestern, Northern, Eastern and Southern regions have made their way into the text. Based on them, they initially identified four recensions: Northern, Northwestern, Eastern and Southern recensions. The textual parts which are common to all recensions were taken as the

Northern Recension. Except for a few variations there was much similarity and based on that, the North-western was included under the Northern and the Eastern under the Southern and in the end they were classified as two kinds of texts, namely, Northern Recension and Southern Recension, and examined. Since the scholars noted that some of the Eastern Recensions appeared to conform to Northwestern and Northern Recensions, they have put them along with the Northern Recension and have studied them.

In this (Baroda University) critical edition, they have kept the Northern Recension as the text and explained in footnotes those versions which vary from it. Following is the list of scholars who examined and published this edition.

Table 2
Kaandams and Editors

Bala Kaandam	GH Bhatt	1962
Ayodhya Kaandam	PL Vaidya	1962
Aranya Kaandam	PC Divanji	1963
Kishkindha Kaandam	DR Mankad	1965
Sundara Kaandam	GC Jala	1966
Yuddha Kaandam	PL Vaidya	1971
Uttara Kaandam	UP Shah	1975

Some important details found only in the North-western, North-eastern (Eastern region) and Northern Recensions:

- Explanation of the character of Dasaratha's daughter Santa (Bala Kaandam).
- Explaining in detail in two *sarga*s about Bharata and Shatrughna going and staying in the royal palace (Eastern regional version – Bala Kaandam, North-eastern version –

Ayodhya Kaandam). In the Southern version there is just a mention that both of them left (Bala Kaandam).
- A Brahmin casting a curse on Kaikeyi (Ayodhya Kaandam).
- Sita being born to Janaka and Menaka (Aranya Kaandam).
- Tara cursing Rama (Kishkindha Kaandam).
- Kumbhakarna telling Ravana, 'Narada said to me that the Devas were planning to destroy Ravana through one of the incarnations of Vishnu' (Yuddha Kaandam).

Details found only in the North-western Recension
- Kaikeyi learns the art of warfare from a Brahmin. She saves her husband in the battlefield (Ayodhya Kaandam).
- When Lakshmana stands struck by the Nagastra (a potent arrow), Narada comes and reminds Rama that he is an incarnation of Narayana (Yuddha Kaandam).
- Having come to know through Vibhishana that Ravana was conducting a *homam* (fire sacrifice) and if that sacrifice were to be completed none could defeat him, the monkey army tries to disrupt it, but fails. In the end Angada drags Mandodari by her hair and brings her to Ravana. Enraged at this, Ravana attacks Angada. Thus, Ravana's *yagnam* or fire sacrifice is aborted (Yuddha Kaandam).

The following details found in the Southern Recension of Vanmikam alone were considered later additions:

Bala Kaandam
- The positions of the planets at the time of birth of the four, starting with Rama, are pointed out (SR 1 18:8-11).
- The many Purana stories found in Bala Kaandam:
  - Vishnu incarnating as Trivikrama, son of Sage Kashyapa, in response to the sage's wish (SR 1-28:10-17).
  - Sage Jahnu drinking up the Ganga (SR 1: 43: 34-41).
  - Vishnu taking the form of Mohini and snatching away the celestial nectar during the churning of the ocean of milk.

- Description of Vishnu's incarnation as a tortoise (Koormavataram) (SR 1.45:27-32).
- Birth of Sagara – the first of the Ikshvaku-Raghu dynasty (SR 1:70:28-37).

Ayodhya Kaandam

- The tale of Kaikeyi's mother deserted by her father (SR 2:35).
- Sita appealing to the river Yamuna to help her cross it (SR 2:55:13-21).
- Rama, Sita and Lakshmana together meeting Valmiki in Chitrakootam (SR 2:56:16-17).

Aranya Kaandam

- Agamban narrating to Ravana the incidents which took place in Janasthana and Ravana going to Maricha (SR 3:31).
- The story of Ayomukhi, a demoness (SR 3:69:11-18).

Kishkindha Kaandam

Sugriva sending Tara to pacify Lakshmana who was rushing down in great wrath (SR 4:33:25-61). Here Tara refers to herself as the wife of Sugriva (4:33:58) whereas in Yuddha Kaandam Sugriva calls Tara his lady-love (6:126:30).

Sundara Kaandam

Hanuman fighting Lanka's Guardian Deity (SR 5:3:20-50).

Yuddha Kaandam

Sugriva fighting Ravana (SR 6:40-41). Dharmalaya's fortieth sarga alone mentions this.
Agastya advising Rama to recite Aditya Hrudayam (SR 6:105) (In Dharmalaya 107th sarga).

Sita requesting Rama to invite Tara and the wives of the other monkeys to Ayodhya (SR 6: 123:23-38). (This detail is found in the 126th sarga of Dharmalaya; 25: Sloka 26).

The Mahabharata

The **Bharata** epic, regarded as Vyasa's creation, is considered to have been composed after Valmiki's Ramayana. The fact that details relating to Rama's story are found in the Bharata which is in vogue today, the absence of details concerning Mahabharata in Valmiki Ramayana and the point that sage Valmiki is hailed as the primal poet – all go to reinforce such a view.

Details pertaining to the Mahabharata story are mentioned in *sutras* or aphorisms such as *Sankhyanam* and *Paniniyam*; but there are no references to Ramayana. All those scholars who have researched on the Bharata epic hold the view that the story of Bharata had appeared much before the time of Valmiki, that in course of time various details were added as interpolations, swelling into *The Mahabharata* around the beginning of the Christian era and that Valmiki's Ramayana emerged in between these two periods. Scholars are also of the view that the Bharata and the Ramayana appeared independently and were in vogue in India's western and eastern regions respectively, and that in later times when they came into contact with each other, Bharata grew into The Mahabharata.

Vyasa's original text consisted of 24,000 slokas (Deshpande 7). The Bhandarkar Research Institute in Pune, after half a century of hard work, published a critical edition of The Mahabharata, engaging various scholars (European, American, Indian) from 1918 to 1966 (Deshpande 11). According to it, there are 73,900 slokas in the critical edition, 82,136 slokas in the Northern Recension, and 95,585 slokas in the Southern Recension

(Deshpande 3).These details reinforce the opinion of the scholars mentioned above that the Bharata developed in two or three stages and came to have the content and form that it has at present.

That is to say, we come to know that when the original Bharata blossomed forth as The Mahabharata, the Ramayana stories started finding a place in the epic of Bharata.

The Ramayana details are related in The Mahabharata in the following places (the details are given with reference to the Bhandarkar critical edition):

1. Aranya Parva (III.147: 28-38)
2. Drona Parva (VII. 59: 1-31)
3. Santi Parva (XII. 22: 51-62)
4. Aranya Parva (III. 252-275)

According to this critical edition, the Ramayana details (*Ramopakhyanam*) are related in 704 slokas and among those, 200 slokas are descriptions of the war. While narrating the Ramayana details, The Mahabharata differs from Valmiki in various places. By way of illustration, the following few may be pointed out:

- In The Mahabharata there is no reference to Dasaratha performing a yagna (fire sacrifice), praying for progeny and handing the payasam (a sweet milk pudding) obtained from the yagna to his wives.
- Nowhere is there found any suggestion that Sita was *ayonija* (divine born).
- It is mentioned that Kaikeyi secured just one boon.
- Manthara is mentioned as an incarnation of the Gandharva damsel Dundubhi.
- It is mentioned that only once did Vaali and Sugriva fight.

- Description of Ravana's court, the burning of Lanka, Hanuman fetching the hillock of medicinal herbs, Sita's fire ordeal and such episodes are not mentioned.
- In the battle, it is Lakshmana who kills Kumbhakarna.

On account of these differences, scholars such as EW Hopkins and Dahlmon Ludwig maintain that The Mahabharata relates the Ramayana details based on sources other than Valmiki. The scholar Jacobi considers that the Ramayana references in The Mahabharata are all derived from a version which had been in vogue a long time before Valmiki.

Camille Bulcke, who supports the view of Jacobi among these scholars, contends that it is not possible to understand some of the Ramayana episodes which appear in the Bharata without the help of Valmiki. Bulcke also claims that, since in about eighty-six places, words and phrases in The Mahabharata look identical with those in Valmiki Ramayana as demonstrated by the critical edition, and such words and phrases that are very similar to Valmiki appear in The Mahabharata too, it is not wrong to argue that the Ramopakhyanam in The Mahabharata is largely along the lines of Valmiki.[4]

Edition
1918-1966   *The Mahabharata*: Critical Edition, Bhandarkar Oriental Research Institute, Pune.

Raghuvamsa

Raghuvamsa of Kalidasa was composed during fourth or fifth century AD. In seven sargas of this epic (9-15) details

---

[4] a. (Bulcke, 46-55).
b. CR Deshpande, *Transmission of the Mahabharata Tradition*, Simla: IIAS, 1978, pp.3, 7, 11.

concerning Rama's story are found. It can't be claimed that Kalidasa composed his epic entirely following Vanmikam. He might have composed his epic, using those Ramayanas existing in his time but appearing much earlier and other sources such as folk songs. It seems possible to think that since many details pertaining to Uttara Kaandam are found in Raghuvamsa, Uttara Kaandam might have been in vogue even during Kalidasa's time.

Even though there is a hint that Sita is a superhuman being, it is not said here that she is an incarnation of Goddess Lakshmi. The episode of Ahalya being cursed to turn into stone is mentioned. There are thus only a few differences from Vanmikam (Bulcke 186).

Jain Ramayanas

Even as the Buddhists used Rama's story to expound their doctrines, the Jain scholars too composed their religious literary texts incorporating Rama's story. The sources of the Buddhist Ramayanas are written in the Pali language. The Jains, on the other hand, have composed texts connected to Rama's story in the three languages of Prakrit, Apabhramsha and Sanskrit.

The Jain religious doctrines are divided into two ways or *marga*s: the *Digambara* and the *Swetambara*. Similarly the Jain Ramayanas too are categorised into **Swetambara Ramayana** and **Digambara Ramayana**. Among the Swetambaramarga Ramayana, Vimalasuri's *Pauma Chariyu* composed in the Prakrit language is regarded as the most famous (third or fourth century AD). Following his lead, among the Rama stories which came up in the fifth century AD, Sankha Dasa's *Vasudeva Hindi* in Prakrit, Ravisena's *Padma Charita* in Sanskrit (985 AD), Swayambu Deva's *Pauma Chariyam* or *Ramayana*

Purana composed in Apabhramsha (eighth century AD) are considered excellent works. Among the Digambaramarga Ramayanas, Gunabhadra's *Uttara Purana* (ninth century AD) in Sanskrit is considered an excellent creation.

Both the margas present Rama as one of the *Trisashti Mahapurushas*[5] (Sixty-three Great Souls).

Pauma Chariyu

The word *pauma* means lotus. In Jain parlance *padmam* means Rama (one who has eyes like the lotus petal) and the word *cariyu* means oral recital or chronicle or Purana. It is also known as Pauma Chariyam.

Scholars divide the subject matter that Pauma Chariyu narrates into 6 parts and 118 parvas. Although closely following Valmiki for the most part, the changes found in Pauma Chariyu are many. It is possible to think that such alterations were effected because of religious doctrines.

Edition

1914　　　*Pauma Chariyam (cariyu),*
　　　　　Jacobi (publishing editor), Bhavanagar.

Vasudeva Hindi

The Jain narrative literature titled Vasudeva Hindi, meaning Vasudeva's journey as well as Vasudeva's life history was composed by Sankhadasa in Marathi Prakrit language in fifth century AD. In the fourteenth section of the first kaandam of this work, details of Ramakatha are narrated. We find that although it is a

---

5　The Jaina tradition has sixty-three Mahapurushas (Great Souls). This includes twenty-four Tirthankaras, twelve Emperors, nine Baladevas and nine Vasudevas, besides nine Prativasudevas. In the text *Tiloya Pannathi* that appeared in the fifth century AD this chronicle is told for the first time (Bulcke, 63).

Jain literary text, Vasudeva Hindi mostly follows Valmiki's story. However, details like the following are added for the first time to the Ramayana story by Sankhadasa: that Sita was born in Sri Lanka, that Bharata's army participated in the Rama-Ravana war on invitation from Sugriva, that Kaikeyi obtained her two boons on two different occasions. One can detect the influence of Vasudeva Hindi in many a later-day Ramayana, starting with Gunabhadra's Uttara Purana (Bulcke 214-215).

Narasimha Purana

Narasimha Purana, which is written in Sanskrit, has six chapters. This book condenses the content of the first six kaandams of Valmiki Ramayana.[6] In sargas forty-seven to fifty-two of this text, details of Ramakatha are narrated. In this text, which mostly conforms to Valmiki Ramayana, there are a few divergences from it. Some of them are:

- The purpose of the incarnation is reiterated. It is also claimed that Rama is the *Poornavatara* (complete incarnation) of Narayana and Lakshmana is the incarnation of *Adisesha*.
- Ahalya is cursed to become a stone (*Baashaanaboota*).
- Ravana carries away Sita without touching her (Bulcke 161).

Edition
2003   *Narasimha Purana,* ed. KL Shastri and Bindiya Trivedi. Delhi: Parimal Publications.

Ravanavaho (or) Setubandha

Written in Marathi regional Prakrit language, *Ravanavaho* or *Setubandha* is considered to belong to the sixth century

---

6   AN Jani, 'Different Versions of Valmiki Ramayana in Sanskrit', *Asian Variations in Ramayana*, New Delhi: Sahitya Akademi, 1983, pp. 29-56.

(550-600) AD. Some say it was composed in fifth century AD. It is said that this kavya was composed by Pravarasena, the Vaagaadaka king, or one of his court poets. Scholars think that later works such as *Bhattikavya, Janakiharan* and *Ramayana Kakawin* have drawn much upon the descriptions of the Yuddha Kaandam in this text.[7]

Bhagavata Purana

One of the great Puranas, *Bhagavata Purana* (*Srimad Bhagavatam*) is considered to have been written during sixth and seventh centuries AD. In the opinion of Professors RC Hazra, Krishnamurthy Sarma, Siddheswara Bhattacharya and Swami Tapasyananda, the Bhagavata Purana evolved in three stages. Some old features were extant even during the early Christian era. This was the first stage. Later, during the third and fourth centuries AD, when the puranas emerged and proliferated, more features being added, it evolved into a *Mahapurana*. This was the second stage. In the third and final stage, with the rise of the Bhakti movement in the Tamil region and the Vaishnavite movement fostered by the *Azhwar*s (i.e. between the sixth and eighth centuries AD), a great Vaishnavite scholar living in the South forged the new form of the **Bhagavata** combining the developments of the first two stages with the ancient Tamil tradition as well as the stories in vogue based on the hymns of the Azhwars relating to Krishna. The Bhagavata Purana extant now is the form that took shape in this third stage. It is thus that the Bhagavata Purana attained

---

7   (a) Bulcke, pp. 186-187.
    (b) V Raghavan, *The Ramayana Tradition in Asia*, p.10.

its final form during the Tamil Azhwars' time and this seems to be the general opinion prevailing among scholars.

As it exists today, the Bhagavata Purana consists of 12 skandas (parts) and 335 adhyayas (chapters). There is as yet no critical edition of the Bhagavatam, as there is of Valmiki Ramayana, as well as of the *Vyasa Bharata*. Hence it has not been possible to ascertain which features were added during the aforesaid three stages of evolution of the Bhagavatam.

Ramakatha events are presented in the ninth skanda, tenth adhyaya of this book. That Sita is the incarnation of Goddess Lakshmi is a point mentioned for the first time in the Bhagavatam. Other details such as Rama slicing off Surpanakha's ears and nose and disfiguring her, Rama renouncing Sita when he hears a washerman's comment (Adh.II) are also mentioned in this book.

Edition
1996   (1990) *Srimad Bhagavatam* (with English translation), Swami Tapasyananda (translator). Chennai: Ramakrishna Mutt.

Bhattikavyam or Ravanavadham

This book was composed in the sixth or seventh century AD by a poet called Bhatti. Camille Bulcke affirms that Valmiki's Rama story has been expounded to demonstrate the grammatical rules of Panini (187). V Raghavan[8] says that while narrating Rama's story the poet also provides examples for Panini's grammar. Matter relating to Valmiki's six kaandams is narrated here, except for a few changes. Ramayana Kakawin (roughly

---

8   'The Ramayana in Sankrit Literature', *The Ramayana Tradition in Asia*, p.8.

about eleventh century AD), which is a very old epic from Java, is regarded more or less as a translation of Bhattikavyam.

Janakiharan

The epic Janakiharan was written in Sanskrit by Kumaradasa who belonged to the Sinhala country. However, for long, that source text was not in circulation. Its Sinhala translation was extant in Sri Lanka. By the method of 'word-for-word' translation called *sanna*, the Sinhala Janakiharan was again translated into Sanskrit and became known to the rest of the world. It is in South India, rather than in the North that most of the Sanskrit literary texts have been preserved. This perhaps explains how the source Sanskrit text of Janakiharan again got a Sanskrit form (through Sinhala translation) and was in circulation in the South. Later, slowly, it started to spread in the North too and came to be learnt.

In this text, the impact of Kalidasa can be discerned in every *padalam* (subsection). When comparing padalam XII of Raghuvamsa with the Janakiharan section which deals with that subject, one can easily realise to what extent Kumaradasa has followed Kalidasa. Although it is not considered a great literary creation, we find that Janakiharan is indeed very useful in examining the history of the evolution of Ramakatha. Various details present in the Southern Recension of Valmiki are found in Janakiharan too. We can say that this text displays, besides Kalidasa's influence, the influence of the Southern literary traditions, and also of the Valmiki of the North-eastern regions. Since the Sanskrit dramatic poet Rajasekhara writes extolling Kumaradasa, Kumaradasa is presumed to have lived before his time, i.e. ninth century AD.

Rajasekhara makes a thought-provoking observation on

Kumaradasa as follows:

> Nobody else but Kumaradasa would have the audacity to sing about the abduction of Sita even while Kalidasa's Raghuvamsa was very popular with the people; even as none except Ravana would have dared to abduct Sita while the princes of Raghuvamsa were still living on the earth (cited: AB Keith, p. 119).

From this statement of Rajasekhara it can be inferred that Kalidasa's Raghuvamsa was considered the very best work of Ramakatha and that Kumaradasa too, who hailed from Lanka that was ruled by Ravana, boldly sang about the abduction of Sita.

Edition

1967 *Janakiharan* (with Hindi translation),
       Allahabad: Mitra Prakashan.

Uttara Purana

Gunabhadra is the author of this work, composed in the ninth century AD. A student of Jinasena, Gunabhadra lived in the Karnataka region. Uttara Purana is regarded as the second part of *Trisashtilakshana Mahapuranam*. In this, the Ramakatha events are told in 1,117 slokas in the 67th and 68th parvas. The subject matter vastly differs from that of Valmiki and Vimalasuri.

It is not possible to find out on what basis many of the details of Gunabhadra's Ramakatha were told. However, scholars think that Vimalasuri's and Sankhadasa's influence as well as that of Parameswara is discernible in Uttara Purana (Bulcke 63-71).

Edition

1954 *Uttara Purana*, Kasi: Bharatiya Jnanapith.

Tibetan Ramayana – I

Tun-Huang – I

The Ramayana which got written in the Tibetan language when the Tibetans captured the north-west region of China called Tun-Huang (787–848 AD) is known as **Tun-Huang.** This Ramayana text, which runs to around 500 lines, begins like other South Asian Ramayanas, with Dasagriva's history; it ends with Uttara Kaandam.

The name of the author of the oldest Tibetan Tun-Huang Ramayana is not known. The characters who appear in this work are as follows:

Dasagrivan (Ravana), Ramanan (Rama), Lakshana (Lakshmana), Sita, Purpala (Surpanakha), Maruche (Maricha), Sugrivan, Vaali, Hanumanta, Ambakarna (Vibhishana), Kumbhakarna.[9]

Edition

'The Tun-Huang manuscripts of the Tibetan Ramayana Story'. *Indo-Iranian Journal,* 19 (1977), pp. 37-88.

Kamba Ramayanam

Among the literary works that appeared after the advent of Tamil Bhakti literature, it is the *Kamba Ramayanam* which is the most famous text. Although Kamban, who lived in the tenth century AD, titled his work as *Ramavataram,* Tamil society continues to call it by the name Kamba Ramayanam.

Kamban says that he sings the story of Rama in Tamil only along the lines of Valmiki's epic; except for a few changes, he does, to a large extent, follow it fairly closely. Since it is an

---

9   JW De Jong, *A Critical Inventory of Ramayana Stories in the World,* Vol. II, pp.xxxviii-vii (sic).

epic that appeared after the advent of Tamil Bhakti literature, Kamban's Rama has been cast in the incarnation mould. This becomes clear when we notice that Kamban has added the story of Hiranyakashipu, which is not found in the source.

Kamba Ramayanam consists of six kaandams, from Bala Kaandam to Yuddha Kaandam. Kamban did not include Uttara Kaandam. The internal divisions of a kaandam are named padalam. In all there are 118 *padalangal* (sub-sections) and around 10,500 *viruthapaadalgal* (a variety of Asiriyappa in Tamil prosody written in stanzas of four lines each consisting of six to eight feet) in the text. Apart from this, the Chennai Kamban Kazhagam's critical edition has identified around 1,300 verses as *migaipaadalgal* (superadded stanzas) and published them separately. The Annamalai University Variorum edition shows the text as containing around 10,500 verses.

The Annamalai University Variorum edition cites a total of approximately 100,000 textual variations, at an average of ten for each of the Kamba Ramayanam verses.

In the history of Tamil literature, no other work seems to have had upwards of 1,000 additional verses and more than 100,000 textual variations. These figures go to indicate the magnitude of the number of people who taught Kamba Ramayanam in the last one thousand years and of those who made copies, not to mention the number of those who learnt it. From this we can perceive the influence Kamba Ramayanam had gained in the Tamil country.

Apart from the greatness of the subject matter, which has a nationwide reach, its fertile imagination, pleasing poetic finesse, a verse style appropriate to the emotions, the way the characters are cast as ideal heroes, the dramatic mode, flawless epic structure and other such features of excellence are what make the epic an incomparable one. Even though there were a few Ramayana texts that appeared before and after Kamban's, when we remember that they are not extant today, the greatness of Kamba Ramayanam will become obvious.

Some consider Kamban's period to be ninth century AD, while some others think it is twelfth century AD. The opinion of TP Meenakshisundaram, M Arunachalam, AS Gnanasambandan and such others, that the time Kamban lived could be taken as mid-tenth century when viewed on the basis of the circumstances, literary ethos and the stylistic feature of refraining from the use of the 'royal we' for an individual and such aspects, seems to be convincing.

Kamba Ramayanam consists of six kaandams, namely Bala Kaandam, Ayodhya Kaandam, Aranya Kaandam, Kishkindha Kaandam, Sundara Kaandam and Yuddha Kaandam which comprise 118 padalams and 10,368 verses in all.

Editions
1952-70   Annamalai University – Variorum edition.
1976   Chennai Kamban Kazhagam,
           Chennai – Critical edition.

Ramacharita

Abhinanda, the son of Sadananda, hailing from Bengal, composed a work called *Ramacharita* towards the end of the ninth century AD or early tenth century AD. We learn that this work, well-known not only during its period of origin, and not only in the region of its origin, was composed with the patronage of Dharmapala and his son Devapala (815-854 AD).

Like Pravarasena's *Setubandha*, Abhinanda's Ramacharita too begins with Kishkindha Kaandam, containing thirty-six divisions, and ends with the killing of Kumbha-Nikumbha in the Rama-Ravana battle. Scholars think that this work might have been originally composed or planned with 100 divisions. However, as it stands edited today, there are only thirty-six divisions in the work (Winternitz III – 82 n.1; V Raghavan, p.79).

Edition
The Ramacharita of Abhinanda, edited in the GOS (XLVI 1930).

Ramayana Kakawin (Indonesian Ramayana)

Indonesia's famous Ramakatha is known as Ramayana Kakawin (kavya/epic). This Ramayana is written in the Old Javanese language *kawi*. There are two varying opinions prevalent, one holding that this Ramayana was written by Yogeswara and the other claiming that Yogeswara is not its author.

Its Dutch translation states that the Ramayana Kakawin was composed following Bhattikavya which is believed to have appeared in sixth century or seventh century AD.[10] The Ramakatha details which are found in the Bhattikavya in the eleventh chapter appear without any change in Ramayana Kakawin too. On this basis, scholars like V Raghavan think that Ramayana Kakawin is in many places a direct translation and in some places a transcreation of Bhattikavya.[11]

Edition
1980   *Indonesia Ramayana* (ed. trans) Soewito Santosa, New Delhi.

---

10 Camille Bulcke, p. 259.
11 Dr V Raghavan, 'The Ramayana in Sanskrit Literature,' *The Ramayana Tradition in Asia*, New Delhi: Sahitya Akademi, (1980), 1989 p. 9.

Sambo-ekotoba (Japanese Ramayana)

In the tenth century AD, a work related to the Ramayana was created by one Minamotono Tamenori. It is titled *Sambo-ekotoba*. This work, which was made up of three scrolls containing in pictorial form Ramakatha details, is not extant now. But the story elements drawn from those paintings are in vogue. They are about the son of an ascetic who was unwittingly killed by Dasaratha, which is a part of Ayodhya Kaandam in Valmiki Ramayana. Sambo-ekotoba is the first among the Japanese works dealing with Ramakatha. The whole of Ramakatha does not find a place in it.[12]

Champu Ramayana

Champu kavya is a literary genre in Sanskrit, which appeared in the medieval period. The definition of *Champu* as a writing mode, which is a mixture of verse and prose, is found for the first time in *Kavyadarsa* (1:31) of Dandin who lived in seventh century AD. Champu kavyas were first written by Jains; later they were written by Hindus too. Scores of Champu kavyas were written in Sanskrit, from the eighth to the eleventh century, narrating stories from puranas and legends.

Champu Ramayana is considered to have been composed by Bhojaraja, who ruled the Vidharbha region during 1019-1060. Scholars, however, are of the view that Bhojaraja composed the first five kaandams of the Ramayana while Lakshmana Suri (Bhatta) composed Yuddha Kaandam. They also think that Champu Ramayana is based on the Southern Recension of

---

12 Minoru Hara, 'Rama Stories in China and Japan: A Comparison', *Asian Variations in Ramayana*, (New Delhi: Sahitya Adademi, 1983), pp. 348-356.

Vanmikam and that the influence of Kalidasa's Raghuvamsa is also discernible in this text (Bulcke 215-216).

Editions
1956 (1970)   Chowkamba Vidyabhavan, Varanasi.
1998   Krishnadas Academy, Varanasi.

Ramayana Manjari

Abhinava Gupta's disciple Kshemendra, belonging to the Kashmir region, was a poet and critic of high repute. He has the distinction of having written *Ramayana Manjari* following Valmiki Ramayana, *Bharata Manjari* using the incidents in the Vanaparva of the Mahabharata (1037 AD), a small poetical work called *Dasavatara Charitam* and a collection of stories called *Brihatkatha Manjari*. Among these, Ramayana Manjari (1037 AD) and Dasavatara Charitam (1066 AD) invite special attention in the context of Ramakatha.

Ramayana Manjari, following the north-western version of Valmiki Ramayana, tells the Ramayana story in 5,386 verses; however, it deviates from Vanmikam in a few places. As far as Vanmikam is concerned, in several places, this text seems to be constructed following north-western, eastern and southern versions. We can cite instances such as Sita's birth and the curse on Ahalya.

After Ramayana Manjari, Kshemendra's Dasavatara Charitam delineates the incarnation of Rama in 294 verses. In keeping with the epic tradition, instead of beginning the narrative from Bala Kaandam, it starts from Lanka. All the epic incidents are created from the perspective of Ravana. In consonance with that perspective, the epic story-weave commences with Lanka and moves backwards to Panchavati in retrospective narration and then the happenings between

Bala Kaandam and Panchavati are narrated to Ravana. Such a technique of *in medias res* is a device employed in Western tragedies as well as epics.

Indian epics, in general, follow the tradition of the chronological narrative. Even so Dandin, in his Kavyadarsa, extols the epic mode of beginning with the antagonist's history and going back once again to the protagonist's story right from the beginning (I.22). We can take it that Kshemendra's Dasavatara Charitam followed this, beginning with the antagonist, as done by Dandin.

Dasavatara Charitam differs from Vanmikam also in dealing with various details such as Sita's birth and Ahalya's curse. Since Kshemendra's Ramayana works are all collections, they tell the same matter in various ways, following different texts. Hence these texts are not very helpful for systematic historical research as well as for development of ideas (V Raghavan, pp. 144-150).

Edition:
1903   Kshemendra's *Ramayana Manjari* (Bala Kaandam-Uttara Kaandam), Bombay: Kavyamala Publications (Sanskrit).

Bhusundi Ramayana

This is a lengthy medieval Ramayana containing 36,000 slokas by an unknown author. It is marked by the spirit of devotion. It has served as the basis for writers like Tulsidas.

Besides Valmiki, the influence of Bhagavata Purana is quite prominent in this. For the preponderance of *sringara rasa* (erotic element) here, the *Hanumat Samhita* and *Gita Govinda*, and for the touch of devotion to Krishna, the Bhagavata, form the basis. This work is also called *Rama Gita*.

Its larger divisions are known by the names of the four directions, East, West, South and North. Such divisions suggest that the text has been constructed according to Tantric doctrines. *Bhusundi Ramayana* says that Rama, Sita and Lakshmana consumed meat while in exile in the forest for fourteen years (pp.484).

It was Ramanuja's philosophy that was responsible for the spread of the Rama cult and the Ramayana Katha. It is, therefore, believed that this work appeared in the twelfth century AD, when Ramanuja's Vaishnavite doctrines were beginning to be disseminated in North India.

Valmiki Ramayana presents Rama as an ideal human being. Bhusundi Ramayana projects Rama as an incarnation, but also as an erotically or amorously inclined person, subscribing to Tantric doctrine.[13] On account of this, the deep impact of Bhusundi Ramayana is discernible in various latter-day works such as *Adhyatma Ramayana, Bengali Ramayana, Ananda Ramayana, Tulsi Ramayana, Jagamohan's Oriya Ramayana, Satyopakyanam, Brihad Goshal Kaandam* and *Ramalingamrutam*.

Bhusundi Ramayana embeds Gnanayoga within the doctrine of surrender or *Saranagati* which forms the core of *Visishtadvaita*. On the other hand, the Adhyatma Ramayana is marked by the Advaita doctrine.

Edition

1975　　　　　Bhagawat Prasad Singh (Publishing editor)
　　　　　　　Bhusundi Ramayana (Purab Kaandam),
　　　　　　　Varanasi. Viswa Vidyalaya Prakashan.

13　*The Ramayana Tradition*, p. 475ff.

Padma Purana

Pataala Kaandam, Srushti Kaandam and Uttara Kaandam, which constitute the three parts of this Sanskrit text, seem to have been composed in three different periods. Pataala Kaandam is considered to have been composed in twelfth century AD and the Uttara Kaandam in fifteenth century AD. In both these divisions, details relating to Ramakatha are narrated. Many ideas from Raghuvamsa of Kalidasa are found here. This work appears to be a mixture of the doctrine of incarnation and the emotion of bhakti.

It is not possible to know the author who composed this text. Some regard it as having been composed by Ravisena. The Uttara Kaandam of this text says that it was Rama himself who mutilated Surpanakha (Bulcke 159-160).

Udara Raghava

Although it is claimed that this epic, composed by Sakalya Malla in fourteenth century AD, contained eighteen sargas, only nine sargas were found available and were published. It largely follows Vanmikam. The notion of incarnation is widely present in it. This work says, Rama is the complete incarnation and the three brothers are incarnations of his aspects. In contrast to the ancient epics, this work is characterised by artificiality, an ornate style and excessive erotic descriptions.

At one place in the text, insisting that she too would go to the forest in exile with Rama, Sita says, 'I have listened to many Ramayanas and in none of them is it said that Rama went to the forest without Sita'. This part of the work appears to be a stroke of innovation (Sarga 5:149) (Bulcke 190).

Hobutsushu (Japanese Ramayanam)

In the twelfth century AD appeared a Ramayana text based on the folk tales presenting Ramayana details prevalent in Japan. It is titled *Hobutsushu*, meaning a string of ornaments. Tairano Yasuyori is the author of this text. The influence of Buddhist doctrines is discernible in this Ramayana.[14]

Tibetan Ramayana – 2 (prose commentary)

Saskiya Pandita (1182–1251) composed the work *Subhashita Ratna Nidhi* in the Tibetan language, consisting of 457 verses. Ramakatha is told in the course of the commentary on this work written by his student Dmar-Ston Chos-rgyal. This text defines rhetoric and style and in the commentary on the 321st verse (sutra) it says, 'Wise men must be able to control the five senses; Ravana (Dasagiri), the Lankan king was killed, because he was immersed in sensual gratification, goes the ancient saying'. And it is at this point that the Ramayana story is narrated in detail. Since it is an exemplar, it can be construed that the portion on the harmful consequences of lust alone are dwelt upon here, for in this Ramayana, many parts of Bala Kaandam and the entire Uttara Kaandam have been omitted.[15]

Tibetan Ramayana – 3 (prose commentary)

Dandin's Kavyadarsa was one of the famous Indian works prevalent in Tibet. Among the many commentaries which appeared on the Tibetan translation of this text (thirteenth century AD), two commentaries deserve to be

---

14 Minoru Hara, 'Rama Stories in China and Japan: A Comparison', *Asian Variations in Ramayana*, (New Delhi: Sahitya Akademi, 1983), p. 340-348.
15 JW De Jong, p. xlii.

specially mentioned. In both of them Ramakatha is narrated in detail.

The first commentary on this text was written in 1429 AD by Sangasri. In the commentary which was printed in the Timpu town of Bhutan in 1976 AD, in pages 107-128, the Ramayana story is narrated. In the concluding part are presented the affluence of the *rakshasa*s (demons) and Rama's nobility. The story of Rama is used in this commentary to illustrate excessive opulence and pride of clan, two aspects of supremacy.[16]

Ranganatha Ramayanam

The first Ramakatha to appear in the Telugu language is known as *Ranganatha Ramayanam*. Majority of the scholars think that this Ramayana was composed by one Gona Budda Reddy in 1240 AD. It is said that Gona Budda Reddy gave his work the name of his patron ruler or his own father (Panduranga Vittalanatha).

Composed in the euphonious metre, known in Telugu prosody as *dwipad,* this Ramayana contains six kaandams consisting of 17,290 couplets. Uttara Kaandam is not found. The kaanda division does not, however, conform to that in the source. Some incidents and lateral stories not found in Vanmikam are present here. Scholars think that such incidents may have been derived from Telugu folklore. Ranganatha Ramayanam depicts Ravana as possessing several noble qualities.

Editions
1941	Chennai: Vavilla Ramaswamy Sastrulu (cited).
1942	Waltair: Andhra University.
1958	Cuddappa: Rayalu & Company.

---

16 JW De Jong, xlviii-lii.

Bhaskara Ramayanam

Bhaskara Ramayanam, which appeared in thirteenth century AD after Ranganatha Ramayanam, is regarded as a famous Telugu Ramayana. This work, which is made up of six kaandams containing 6,081 verses and prose portions, is composed in epic metre in the form of songs and verses interspersed with commentary. Although this Ramayana has been jointly composed by four people, Bhaskara, his son Mallikarjuna Bhattu, his disciple Kumara Rudra Deva and his friend Ayyalarya, it still goes in the name of Bhaskara. It is said that Bhaskara composed only Aranya Kaandam and one portion of Yuddha Kaandam while the other three composed the remaining kaandams. This is perhaps the reason why the text lacks evenness of style. As in Ranganatha Ramayanam, here too many new episodes and stories which are not found in Vanmikam have been added.

The total number of verses is 6,081.

Edition:
1941 Chennapuri: Vavilla Ramaswamy Sastrulu & sons (cited).

Assamese Ramayana

The Ramayana composed by Madhava Kandali, who lived in the mid-fourteenth century, is regarded as the first Ramayana composed in the Assamese language.

It is said that Kandali composed this work in accordance with the wish of King Maha Manikya belonging to the Varaha clan (*Kachaari*). Maha Manikya honoured Kandali, who was his court poet, with the title 'Kaviraja Kandali'. Sankara Deva, who was the uncrowned monarch of the Assamese literary world, also showered encomiums on Madhava Kandali and his Ramayana.

In Madhava Kandali's Ramayana, Bala (Aadi) Kaandam and Uttara Kaandam are not found. Madhava Kandali probably did not compose these two kaandams either because he followed the Eastern Recension in circulation in the Northeastern regions or because he considered the two Kaandams as not composed by Valmiki. Sankara Deva, the Vaishnava intellectual who came about 100 to 150 years after Madhava Kandali, composed the Uttara Kaandam and his student Madhava Deva composed the first kaandam, Bala Kaandam, and added them to Madhava Kandali's Ramayana. There are also those who think that these two parts were not composed by the two preceptors, but by a later poet, with the blessings of Sankara Deva. The opinion held by Madhava Kandali on Vanmikam deserves to be pondered upon. In his prefatory portion Madhava Kandali addresses his audience thus:

> Valmiki composed his Ramayana in prose as well as in euphonious metrical form. I have composed it in Assamese metre as a form of transcreation after learning it with much effort. I was able to intuit the core thought of the source in concise form. Poets compose their verses following the tradition of their times and the way of the world. Hence some aspects of the subject of the poem would be true and some imagined. This (Ramakatha) is not narrated by God; it is only a story told by people (*daiva vaani nahi, loka kahee katha* – दैववाणि नहि, लोक कहे कथा). Therefore you should not find fault with my poetical effort at trying to omit some and include some.[17]

---

17 'Ramayana in Assamese Literature' – Biswanarayan Shastri, *The Ramayana Tradition in Asia*, New Delhi: Sahitya Akademi, 1989 (1980), p. 583-592.

In consonance with such a poetical principle, Madhava Kandali has added a few stories and incidents and descriptions. Even though he lived at the time of the spread of the Vaishnavite cult, he has not inserted too much of religious doctrines or for that matter moral codes in his epic. He has not altered the basic features of the source text even while rendering his Ramayana as an epic story filled with enjoyable literary flavour.

Kannassa Ramayanam

A scholar called Rama Panikkar composed towards the end of the fourteenth century a Ramayana in Malayalam in the metre called *paatu* closely following Valmiki Ramayana. Using the name of his clan 'Kannassa' as an epithet, this work is most often referred to as *Kannassa Ramayanam*. Employing the Sanskrit language but keeping it to a minimum, and combining ancient Tamil sounds as well as prosody, this work contains seven kaandams and 3,059 verses. He has composed his epic, introducing in some places a few new details and compacting in many places the source text. It is said that Kannassa Ramayanam's fame declined with the rising popularity of the latter-day work *Ezhuthachan Ramayanam*, on account of the spirit of devotion as well as other poetical excellences found in the latter. Notwithstanding this, Kannassa Ramayanam is held highly by scholars even today as an epic cherished by the world for its literary finesse, mellifluousness and excellence of characterisation. The kaandams are of unequal length, totalling 3,059 verses.

Edition
1993   *(Kannassa) Ramayanam* (editor) RS Varmaji.
                Trivandrum: Prakkati Publishers.

Adhyatma Ramayana

Among the Ramayana texts which were based on the Vaishnavite tradition, the famous Sanskrit work *Adhyatma Ramayana* is the foremost. However, it has not been possible to definitively establish either its authorship or the period of composition. It has been said that a great poet belonging to the Ramananda tradition composed it. Since it is mentioned in the Marathi work Bhavartha Ramayana (sixteenth century) that Adhyatma Ramayanam was composed 'in recent times', it is thought that the latter might have been written during the fourteenth or fifteenth century. The influence of Adhyatma Ramayana is quite pervasive in *Ananda Ramayana*, Eknath's *Bhavartha Ramayana* and Tulsidas's *Ramcharitmanas*.

This work is praised highly for its various excellences such as style, mellifluousness of prosody, crystal clear Vedantic thoughts, and melodious rhythms charged with the spirit of devotion. The influence of the Tantric mode of worship is widely present in this work. Vanmikam presents Rama as an exemplary man among human beings. Adhyatma depicts Rama as one who acts with the self-awareness that he is an incarnation. We find Adhyatma Ramayana varying from Vanmikam because of this fundamental difference, and also on account of the social and religious doctrinal differences ushered in by the passage of time.

As in Valmiki Ramayana, there are seven kaandams in this work, with the internal divisions of 65 sargas and 4,399 slokas. Some editions have published it as having only six kaandams in 56 sargas with 3,634 slokas, omitting Uttara Kaandam.

Edition
1985   *Adhyatma Ramayana*, ed. Swami Tapasyananda (with English translation), Madras: Sri Ramakrishna Mutt.

Krittibasi Ramayana

This Ramayana was composed in the fifteenth century in Bengali by Krittibas Ojha along the lines of Vanmikam. Since its appearance, till date, this remains the best known Ramayana in Bengali. *Krittibasi Ramayana* has contributed much to the making of Bengal's literary and social culture. Hence it is justly called Bengali Ramayana. Although it follows Vanmikam in its basic outline of the story, very many stories, incidents and descriptions and practices belonging to Bengal have been so cast that the Bengalis regard it verily as their cultural repository. Hence this work is considered Bengal's national epic.

Since it was a text very much liked and read by pundits and laymen alike, many a song was interpolated and interspersed by scribes down the ages. This situation was put to an end only in 1802 when for the first time the work got printed.

Krittibas Ojha, who was born in the village of Phulia in West Bengal in the fifteenth century, was a Kulin Brahmin. He makes three important points relating to his Ramayana:

- Valmiki is the best among seers.
- He (Krittibas) had composed this sapta-kaandam Ramayanam in accordance with the king's order.
- The reason for writing this Ramayana in Bengali is the desire to see that this divine work is read and enjoyed by laymen.

Krittibas does not mention the name of the king who gave him patronage and encouraged him to write the Sanskrit epic in Bengali. Sukhomoy Mukhopadhyaya says that the king was a Muslim and his name was Rukkannuddin Barbak Shah.[18]

---

18 WL Smith, *Ramayana Traditions in Eastern India*.
New Delhi: Munshiram Manoharlal Pvt. Ltd., p. 38.

Editions

1802	Krittibasi (Valmiki) Ramayanam; Serampur Mission Press, (editor) Jayagopal Tarkaalankara.
1955	(14th edition) (editor) Dinesh Chandra Sen, Calcutta: Bhattacharya & Sons.
1981	(2nd edition) (editor) Sukhomoy Mukhopadhyaya, Calcutta.

Molla Ramayanam

Aatukuri Molla, a female poet, in the early fifteenth century composed a Ramayana consisting of six kaandams and 631 verses. Molla states the purpose of her epic thus: 'I am writing this epic in very simple, fluent Telugu style for the lay people who cannot read and enjoy Valmiki's Sanskrit epic.' Her Ramayana characters bring home to us the devotion to Rama and the humanism of this lady who was born in the potter's clan in a tiny village near Nellore. Rama and Guha's meeting in Ayodhya Kaandam can be cited as a good example. *Molla Ramayanam* has held the distinction of being loved and read virtually by everyone, pundits and ordinary people alike till today.

Edition

1917	*(Molla) Ramayanamu*: Chennapuri: Ramaswami Sastrulu (cited).

Ananda Ramayana

It is believed that Ananda Ramayana in Sanskrit was composed during the interim period before Eknath's Bhavartha Ramayana and after Adhyatma Ramayana. Hence it may be taken as belonging to the fifteenth century AD. The name of its author is not known. But it goes in the name of Valmiki.[19] Containing

---

19 *Asian Variations in Ramayana*, p.45.

nine kaandams and 109 sargas, Ananda Ramayana is composed in 12,252 slokas. The details told in the eighth and ninth kaandams have no correlation with Ramakatha at all. Very many stories from a far later period have been added to it. The impact of Bhusundi Ramayana, Adhyatma Ramayana, Bhavartha Ramayana, the Bhagavata stories, as well as that of Tantric doctrines, can be found in this work (Bulcke 168-170).

Nine kaandams titled *Sara Kaandam, Yatra Kaandam, Yaga Kaandam, Vilasa Kaandam, Janma Kaandam, Vivaha Kaandam, Rajya Kaandam, Manohara Kaandam, Poorna Kaandam* are found in this Ramayana. Among these, not a single division or name is to be found in any of the texts from Vanmikam to other Ramayanas.

It is only in the first kaandam, i.e. Sara Kaandam, that the Ramayana story is narrated with some semblance of order along the lines of Vanmikam. The rest of the eight kaandams, using Ramayana characters, sing of various imaginary stories. Hence Sara Kaandam details alone are used in the present research study, in relevant places.

Edition

2003 (rpt.) *Ananda Ramayana* (with Hindi Commentary). Ed. Ramteja Pandeya. Delhi: Chaukhamba Sanskrit Pratishthan.

Torave Ramayanam

The Kannada Ramayana by one Kumara Valmiki alias Narahari appeared in the sixteenth century AD. Structured as 112 subsections, this Ramayana is composed following Valmiki. We understand that as far as the Kannada region is concerned, Narahari's *Torave Ramayana* is not as much cherished as Naga Chandra's *Jain Ramayana*.

Jainism and Saivism are two very influential religions in the state of Karnataka. Hence this neglect, perhaps.

Editions
1810 (Ed.) Ramaswami Sastri, Dakshinamurthy Sastri, Venkatarama Sastri. Bangalore: Krishnaraja Vilasa Press.
1956, 1959 (Ed.) Basavaradya (vol.1), Channaiya (vol.2). Mysore: Mysore University.
1977 Bangalore: Kannada Sahitya Parishad.

Ezhuthachan's Adhyatma Ramayanam

In the sixteenth century AD, a very great poet called Thunchaththu Ezhuthachan translated into Malayalam the Sanskrit work *Adhyatma Ramayana*. Although scholars hold this view (*Ramayana Tradition*, p. 208), nowhere in his work does Ezhuthachan record such a detail. Not only in the epic genre but in the entire Malayalam literature Ezhuthachan remains a supreme poet, especially in the genre of devotional verse. Ezhuthachan's Ramayanam stands as a peerless epic of devotion to Rama in the Vaishnavite bhakti tradition. Composed in six kaandams and 15,841 lines, Ezhuthachan's Ramayanam is esteemed by the Hindus as deserving a daily recital and by the rest as a profound literary creation. It is the contention of Malayalam scholars that Ezhuthachan stands comparison with such great epic poets as Valmiki, Kamban and Milton.

Edition
1977 (Reprint) Hari Sarma (Editor), Kottayam: Sahitya Pravartaka Cooperative Society.

Bhavartha Ramayana

Among the Ramayana works which appeared in Marathi, the oldest is Bhavartha Ramayana. Composed towards the close of the sixteenth century AD by a saintly man called Eknath, this Ramayana contains seven kaandams. Of these, the first six kaandams, it is believed, were composed by Eknath, while the last, the Uttara Kaandam, was composed by one of his disciples. The three works Vanmikam, Adhyatma Ramayana and Ananda Ramayana form the basis of Bhavartha Ramayana. Among these, for the story line or plot Vanmikam and for details related to the bhakti movement, Adhyatma Ramayana, have formed the basis. In some places, while narrating details and events not found in Valmiki Ramayana we find Eknath following Ananda Ramayana.

As far as Vanmikam is concerned, more than the northern version, the influence of the north-western version appears more dominant in Bhavartha Ramayana. On account of this, many details found only in north-western and eastern versions, and not in northern or southern versions, find a place in Bhavartha Ramayana. As examples, the following might be cited:

> The story of Dasaratha's daughter Santa; the episode of Tara cursing Rama; the dialogue between Narada and Kumbhakarna; the story of Kalanemi and so on.

Certain incidents not found in Vanmikam and Adhyatma are narrated in Ananda Ramayana. All of them are repeated without any modification in Bhavartha Ramayana. Here are some, testifying to the deep impact of Ananda Ramayana:

> The marriage of Dasaratha and Kausalya; Bharata and Shatrughna as siblings; Ahalya cursed to turn into a stone;[20]

---

20 Camille Bulcke mentions that the detail of Ahalya being cursed to turn into a stone is not to be found in either Vanmikam or Adhyatma Ramayana (p. 251).

Rama undertaking a pilgrimage as a little boy; Ravana also taking part in Sita's *swayamvaram*; Sita as being born of fire (agni); Bharata punishing Manthara by beating her up; Lakshmana drawing a line around the hermitage as a ring of defence; marriage of Ravana and Mandodari; Hanuman born out of the payasam which Dasaratha received from the yagna and such details.

Some Ramakatha incidents and details are found only in Bhavartha Ramayana. To be noted here is that in the Vanmikam, Adhyatma Ramayana and Ananda Ramayana, cited as the basis for Eknath's Ramayana, these incidents are not mentioned. A few examples will suffice:

> Bharata and Shatrughna as Kaikeyi's children; a battle breaking out between Bharata and Lakshmana in Chitrakootam; Sage Valmiki reciting the entire Ramayana story and explaining it in order to make things clear to Bharata; the story of Kaikeyi receiving the boon from Dasaratha for assisting him in the battle with Indra; the argument between Sita and Mandodari; the strategy to prevent Rama's feet from treading on the boulders while building the bridge across the sea.

Even so, such details cannot be construed as Eknath's own inventions. It is likely that Eknath might have drawn them from earlier Ramayana texts such as Pauma Chariyu, *Yoga Vasishta Ramayana, Narasimha Purana* and so on (Bulcke 250-252).

It is true that the Northern Recension of Vanmikam as well as the Bombay and Gorakhpur editions of the Southern Recension do not talk of Ahalya being cursed to turn into a stone. However, the Dharmalaya edition of the Southern Recension of Vanmikam does state that Ahalya was cursed to turn into a stone (*sila bhutva*) (1:48:34).

Further, as far as Adhyatma Ramayana is concerned, in the Ramakrishna Mutt edition, it is stated that Ahalya was cursed to become a stone (*sila*) (1:5:27).

From this it is known that in the recensions used by the scholar Bulcke as well as in the other editions of Adhyatma Ramayana, this detail is not mentioned. When looking at all these, a mind-boggling truth comes to light – that it is virtually impossible to arrive at definitive, indisputable conclusions on Pan-Indian themes without closely examining all the editions or the regional versions.

Edition

1981-1982   *Bhavartha Ramayana* (Critical Edition)
ed. BG Ghate, NS Pohnikar, SV Dandekar, SR Kulkarni and VP Deulgaokar. Bombay: Government of Maharashtra.

Ramcharitmanas (Tulsi Ramayan)

Among the acclaimed poets during the period when the Bhakti movement took deep roots in North India and flourished, Goswami Tulsidas is a significant name. He gave the title *Ramcharitmanas* to his Ramayana. However, his Ramayana is commonly called *Tulsi Ramayan*. He completed his Ramayana in 1574 AD, composing it in the literary dialect of the Hindi language *Avadi*.

The Bala Kaandam of Tulsi Ramayan consists of 361 couplets (*doha*) with a four-line stanza (*chaupayi*-quatrains) at the end of each couplet. In some places, under one number more than one couplet (29 – a, b, c), more than four quatrains (327) and some rhyming quatrains in *iyaipu-t-totai* (concatenated sound patterns) between the quatrain and the couplet (326) are widely present. Save for the kaandam division, Tulsi's epic is not constructed with any internal divisions such as padalam and sargam.

In Tulsi's Bala Kaandam, the first forty-three couplets contain invocations, professions of humility on his part and other such prefatory material. Couplets 44 to 187 narrate a wide variety of events and episodes such as Siva-Sakti exchange, the disruption of Daksha's *yagna* (sacrificial ceremony), the marriage of Siva and Sakti, the destruction of Manmatha, the reasons for Rama's incarnation, the arrival of Narada, the penance of Manu and Shatrupan and the boons thereof, the story of Pratapa Bhanu, the birth of Ravana, his tapas, boon and atrocities, the complaint of Bhooma Devi (the Earth Goddess, Bhoomi), Lord Vishnu agreeing to take on an incarnation and so on. In the remaining couplets, which are less than half, from 188 to 361, matters such as Rama's birth and details related to Bala Kaandam are narrated.

Except for the Bala Kaandam and the Uttara Kaandam, Tulsidas has sung the intervening Kaandams mostly following Vanmikam. We find that keeping close to the doctrines of bhakti prevalent in his contemporary times, Tulsidas has presented the events in the Bala Kaandam and Uttara Kaandam drawing from Adhyatma Ramayana, *Mahanataka, Prasanna Raghava,* Bhagavata Purana and the *Bhagavad Gita.*

Ideas pertaining to incarnation, spread far and wide as a result of the path of bhakti, are pervasive in Tulsi Ramayan. Besides, we can find Tulsidas extolling the devotion of the devotee more than even the matters pertaining to the Lord.

All over India Valmiki Ramayana was popular among pundits and scholars. But it is Tulsi Ramayan which has attained great fame in North India, to the extent of spreading among the learned, the pundits, the laymen, the researchers and people hailing from multifarious social strata and has been deemed worthy of being recited every day. We may say that

Tulsi Ramayan can boast of such eternal fame, thanks to the spirit of devotion that attracts and draws at once those who read it or hear it because of its simple metrical rendering of events and thoughts closely mirroring people's beliefs, the gradually rising prestige of the Hindi language and the cumulative influence of all these factors.

Edition
Ramcharitmanas, Gorakhpur: Gita Press.

Jagamohan Ramayana

In the sixteenth century AD, one Balram Das composed a Ramayana in the Oriya language called *Jagamohan Ramayana*, taking as its basis the Valmiki Ramayana prevalent in Bengal. Although Sarla Das before him and Viswanath Gundia after him had composed Ramayana works, it is Balram Das's Ramayana that is regarded as the best Oriya Ramayana. There is no village in Orissa that does not have a copy of his Ramayana. Hence Jagamohan Ramayana is regarded as the national epic of Orissa (Odisha).

Even though he took the Bengal regional version of Vanmikam as his basis, Balram Das also drew from other Ramayana versions such as the Southern Recension as well as folktales circulating among the people of Orissa for his epic. Hence several incidents and stories not found in the source Vanmikam are present in his Ramayana. As an example, we may cite the Oriya Ramayana saying that Rama, Lakshmana and Sita stayed in places such as Chandrabhaga, Konark, Ramachandi, Bhubaneswar, Puri, Beleswar, Rishikulyam and several other places.[21]

---

21 Nilamani Mishra, 'Ramayana in Oriya Literature', *The Ramayana Tradition in Asia,* p. 625.

Persian Ramayana

In compliance with the imperial dictates of the Mughal Emperor Akbar, one Abdul Qadir Badayuni translated Valmiki Ramayana into Persian couplets in the year 1588 AD. Badayuni had earlier been part of a group of translators who rendered the Mahabharata in the Persian language. Badayuni says that it took four years for him to carry out this translation.

Written in 365 folios, this translation was presented to Akbar along with 176 paintings executed by a renowned group of painters, as a scroll gilded in gold. Badayuni, who, in the beginning, mentions that the Valmiki Ramayana is a far superior literary work than even the Mahabharata, however, considered this task of translation 'an unholy duty' because of his religious conviction.

On the back of the jacket of this scroll, which was completed in the month of November 1588 AD, there is a hand-written note by Emperor Jehangir that reads as follows:

> As per the orders of Badshah Akbar's son Emperor Jehangir, this book is entered in the register of the palace library in the Hijra year 1013 (1605 AD). This Ramayana is one of the renowned creations of the Hindus; my father ordered that it be rendered in Persian. The stories which are found here, particularly those in third and fifth chapters, are not believable (AK Das, p. 146).

From this note we come to know that the Mughal emperors maintained a library; that every work that was added to it was signed by the monarch and registered; and that the succeeding rulers too took care to continue this practice. We also come to know that Jehangir, before registering the work obeying his father's command, read through it carefully and that, much like the opinion of Badayuni who translated it, he too did not regard the Ramayana as a holy text and he ordered that the work be registered and kept in the library in deference to Badshah Akbar's command.

Emperor Akbar's friend and advisor Abul Fasal mentions the context in which the translations of the Mahabharata and Ramayana cited above were undertaken as follows:

> Realising the fierce animosity prevailing among the Hindus and the Muslims, the emperor (Akbar) felt that the reason for this was the ignorance of one another's culture and achievements and hence it pleased him to remove that darkness of ignorance by arranging to have the sacred texts of the Hindus translated into the Persian language to enable the Muslims to read them. Accordingly, he first chose the Mahabharata which was exhaustive and the very foundation of Hindu culture, and ordered a team of impartially-minded scholars, totally free from religious prejudice, both Hindu and Muslim, to translate it (p. 147).

When four fine scholars, toiling hard for eighteen months, completed the task of translating the Mahabharata in 1584 AD, it was further refined by the court poet Sheik Faisi and submitted to Emperor Akbar along with a long preface by Abul Fasal and embellished with various pictures. Absolutely taken in by it, the Badshah ordered that every nobleman in his court should obtain a copy of it and keep reading it. He orderd Badayuni to translate the Ramayana in the same way. Badayuni too completed the task of the Ramayana translation, with the assistance of Sanskrit and Persian poets (p. 148). This incident brings home to us Emperor Akbar's political wisdom. It is no wonder then that historians hail him as 'Akbar the Great'.[22]

---

22 AK Das, *Asian Variations in Ramayana*, p. 144-153.

Preserved in the form of palm leaf manuscripts, this Persian Ramayana is kept in the Maharaja Sawai Man Singh II Museum in Jaipur. For this reason, this Ramayana is also called the *Jaipur Ramayana*. Although the epic story and the characters belong to ancient Indian culture, the characters appearing in this Persian Ramayana are described as attired in Mughal fashion, and living like those in Mughal kings' courts and palaces (p. 152).

Thakkai Ramayanam

Thakkai Ramayanam is an epic written in Tamil by a poet named Emperuman who lived in Sankagiri of the Kongu region. History says that Emperuman Kavirayar, hailing from the Yadava clan, which worshipped the deity of Varadharaja in Sankagiri Durgam, had lived both in Sankagiri and in Madurai as an official involved in discharging the royal responsibilities of the Nayaka rulers. Launched in the Varadharaja Perumal temple in Sankagiri, Thakkai Ramayanam may be regarded as composed towards the close of sixteenth century AD or the beginning of seventeenth century AD.

Thakkai is a leather percussion instrument like the small drum *udukkai*. Thakkai, an instrument mentioned by Adiyaarkku Nallar as a drum belonging to *Agam* and *Puram* literature (Tamil Classical Literature on the themes of love and war), is in use even now. It is played in the Srirangam 'Big Temple' in the annual festivals during the *Araiyar Sevai* (minstrels singing and dancing with a peculiar distinctive rhythm and music in front of the deity). Since this work was so composed as to be sung in harmony with the thakkai musical instrument, it was titled Thakkai Ramayanam. Hence this work is also known as 'Musical Ramayana' and 'Musical Tamil Epic'.

Right from Kamban's time, many scholarly poets had studied his epic intensively and delivered discourses on it. In the Malabar, Karnataka and Telugu regions such readings and lectures were presented interspersed with music and rendered through singing and dancing performances. Emperuman Kavirayar, who was adept at this mode of musical performance, condensed the approximately 10,000 *viruthangal* (verses) of Kamba Ramayanam into 3,250 musical verses. He has done so without in the least damaging the structural integrity of the Kamba Ramayanam, its tempo, imaginative finesse and dramatic vigour, leading one to think that Thakkai is verily Kamban condensed. Kamban titles the fifth kaandam as *Sundara Kaandam* following his source author. Emperuman calls it *Saundarya Kaandam*.

Thakkai Ramayanam follows Kamba Ramayanam very closely. Hence there is no doubt that it is highly useful in finding out how the Kamba Ramayana verses had existed about four hundred years earlier and also to distinguish the superadded verses of Kamban from textual variations, interpolations, superadded verses and such features which often befuddle scholars.

Edition

1983 *Thakkai Ramayanam* (Parts 1, 2) (Bala, Ayodhya, Aranya, Kishkindha, Saundarya Kaandams). (Editor) K Arunachala Gounder, Chennai: Tamil Nadu State Archaeological Department.

Hikayat Seri Rama (Malaysian Ramayana)
The Story of Sri Rama

Composed in Malay language in prose form, there is a very long and exhaustive Ramayana called *Hikayat Seri Rama* (HSR). It is not possible to figure out who the author of this work is; nor is one able to say anything definite about its period. It is believed that it could have been composed in its present form between the thirteenth and seventeenth centuries AD.

Some scholars think that its source is Valmiki's Ramayana while some others think that ancient narratives which were in vogue in Indonesian countries as well as the oral tales of folks like the merchants who migrated from various parts of India, are the basis of this work. There are also those who consider that stories, puranas and orature which were in circulation in the western and eastern coastal regions of India, are the basis of the Malay Ramayana.[23]

Edition

1964   *Hikayat Seri Rama.* (ed.) Rev WG Shellabear. Singapore: Malaysia Publishing House Ltd (p. 298).

Rama Vatthu (Burmese Ramayana)

Among the texts of Ramayana stories which came up in Burma, *Rama Vatthu* is regarded as the oldest. In 1973, for the first time, two palm leaf manuscripts were discovered in two Buddhist monasteries near Rangoon. Considered as belonging to the seventeenth century AD, the text that is contained in these two manuscripts is Rama Vatthu. Written in prose form, running to forty pages, this work contains six chapters or sections. Beginning with Ravana's birth, this book ends with Sita's return to Ayodhya in Uttara Kaandam.

Following this, other Ramayana texts in Burmese appeared in later times, such as *Rama Thagyin* composed in poetic form in

---

23   S Singaravelu, *A Critical Inventory of Ramayana Studies in the World.* Vol.II.p. lxxiv-lxxv.

1755 AD and *Rama Yagan* composed in verse form in 1784 AD.

Many Burmese Ramayanas refer to Rama as the incarnation of the Buddha. Some of the Ramayana texts begin with Ravana's birth. Yet others begin with Sita's birth and Rama's birth. Some end with Yuddha Kaandam and some others with Uttara Kaandam. Thus the Burmese Ramayanas appear to have different structures.[24]

Ramakien (Thai Ramayana)

The Ramayana in vogue in Thailand called *Ramakien,* meaning 'The Story of Rama', is a very long epic. This Ramayana was composed in 1798 AD by King Rama I hailing from the Chakkiri dynasty, who ruled Thailand along with his assistants, keeping Bangkok as the capital. We come to know that this work was composed based on the Ramayana-related stories in vogue in that country from ancient times as well as plays and paintings executed in lacquer and over palm leaves.

Although resembling Valmiki Ramayana in its basic story line, Ramakien differs from it in many places. It is a mixture of various details found in Tamil, Hindi, Bengali and Malaysian Ramayanas.

Composed as it is, keeping as its centre the ancient story, within this story we find, alternately and in combination, religious ideas, reflections on everyday life, the mingling of gods, men and monkeys. In characterisation there are huge changes. Specially, Hanuman is so created as to make us believe that he is the protagonist of this epic.

---

[24] U Thein Han and U Khin Zaw, 'Ramayana in Burmese Literature and Arts,' *The Ramayana Tradition in Asia,* (Sahitya Akademi, 1980, 1989), pp. 301-314.

Moreover, all the Ramayana story incidents are presented as having taken place in Thailand. In tune with this, the places, rivers, mountains, forests and their names are presented as related to the Thai language. (*Ramakien*, Preface, pp.5-12.)

Edition

1993   *Ramakien* (The Thai Ramayana), published by Patamini Ltd., Chorakaebua, Bangkok, Thailand-10230.

Gvay Dvorabhi (Laotian Ramayana)

Gvay Dvorabhi is one among the many little Laotian Ramayanas which are not based on Valmiki's epic. This Ramayana is written in Yuvan script in a dialect in vogue in the northern part of Laos. This work has been composed having as its basis the life history of three regional chieftains who ruled over Laos during the period between 1711 and 1731 AD. The story has been woven linking these three chieftains to the Ramayana characters, Ravana, Rama and Vaali. The title of the work has been derived from the substory of the buffalo called Dundubhi in Vanmikam. Most of the episodes have Kishkindha as their centre. Vaali, Sugriva and Hanuman are the characters who are accorded primacy.

The name of its author, his period and such details cannot be clearly ascertained. Scholars believe that it could have been composed during the eighteenth century.[25]

Edition

1976   *Gvay Dvorabhi (*ed.) Sachchidananda Sahai (with an English translation).

---

25   Kamala Ratnam, 'Socio-Cultural and Anthropological background of the Ramayana in Laos', *Asian Variations in Ramayana*, (New Delhi: Sahitya Akademi, 1983), pp. 230-251.

Phra Lak Phra Lam (Laotian Ramayana)

Meaning 'Beloved Lakshmana, Beloved Rama', this Laotian Ramayana was written in the early nineteenth century AD, about a century after the Laotian Ramayana called *Buddha Goshacharya*. It has gained fame on account of its literary merit and creative versatility.

Drawing just the bare story from Vanmikam, this epic is entirely rooted in Laos's geographical formation, contemporary politics, social backgrounds, and the habits and customs of the people. Therefore, the characters are cast not as embodying some ideal but in tune with contemporary culture.

It is true that the names of the Ramayana characters are not drastically altered; but prominence has been given to the primate characters. Hanuman's heroics have been so eulogised as to make us think that he is the protagonist (Kamala Ratnam 234-235).[26]

Edition
1973   *Phra Lak Phra Lam* (in Laotian language) (ed.) Sachchidananda Sahai, Laos: ICCR (Vientiane).

Prakash Ramayana

Among the Kashmiri Ramayanas, *Prakash Ramayana,* written by one Prakash Bhatt in 1846 AD is very well-known. *Sankar Ramayana,* which is chronologically older, is yet to be published. Prakash Ramayana has the distinction of having

---

26 Sun Wukong, also known as the Monkey King, is a mythological figure who features in a body of legends that can be traced back to the Song dynasty (960 AD–1279 AD) in China. He appears as a main character in the 16th century Chinese classical novel *Journey to the West* and is found in many later stories and adaptations.
All far eastern cultures are influenced by stories of the Monkey King and tend to give prominence to primate characters in folk literature.— Publishing Ed.

been printed in all the four scripts, Roman, Persian, Devanagiri and Kashmiri; in Persian script three times (1910, 1936, 1965), in Devanagiri twice (1935, 1975).

Regarding the basics of the story, Prakash Ramayana toes the line of Vanmikam. There are seven kaandams in it. The influence of various puranas, Sanskrit epics, and the Vaishnava Bhakti movement is present in this work. Prakash Ramayana reflects Kashmiri culture in presenting behaviour, dress, attitudes as well as food and shelter and habits and customs related to them.

The word 'Ramayana' in the Kashmiri language is employed in the sense of 'a very long narrative, telling of sufferings "never to be experienced"'. A Kashmiri proverb 'You listened to the Ramayana from dawn to dusk and yet you ask "Who is Sita to Rama?" God help us!' suggests in a satirical vein the inordinate length of the Ramayana and the sheer fatigue one feels after listening to it.[27]

Editions

1910	*Ramayan* (Persian script) Srinagar: Pratap Steam Press.
1975	*Kashmiri Ramayan* (Devanagiri) (with Hindi trans.) Dr Shiban Krishnan Raina.

Filipino Ramayan (Maharadia Lawana)

Maharadia Lawana, which is a Rama story prevailing among the tribe of Maranao living in the Philippine Islands, is a highly condensed work. *The Fairy Tale*, then in vogue in that country, is regarded as having appeared in sixteenth century AD. The Philippine Ramayana, which is thought to combine that and

---

[27] PN Pushp, 'Ramayana in Kashmiri Literature and Folk lore', *The Ramayana Tradition in Asia*, pp. 534-546.

the Malaysian Hikayat Seri Rama, is considered to have been composed between seventeenth and nineteenth centuries AD. Islamic influence is predominant in the Filipino Ramayana more than even in the Malaysian Ramayana.[28]

Summing up

Among the forty-eight works chosen as relevant for this research project, nearly half are full Ramayana texts, having Ramakatha i.e. Rama's story as the subject. The rest present Ramakatha details in the course of each text narrating its own subject. Buddhist Jataka tales, The Mahabharata, Jain Ramayanas, Raghuvamsa, Bhagavata Purana, Narasimha Purana, Padma Purana are texts belonging to the latter category. Even among these, in the Ramakatha works which came up in the South-Asian languages such as Japanese, Laotian and Thai there are no internal divisions of kaandam. Only in about twenty or more Indian Ramayanas do we find kaandam divisions.

Among these, we find that several works starting with Valmiki Ramayana contain seven kaandams, from Bala Kaandam to Uttara Kaandam, whereas works like Kamba Ramayanam contain only six kaandams, excluding Uttara Kaandam.

In some Ramayana texts, the names of a few kaandams appear to be different from Vanmikam. For example, in the Assamese Ramayana, and in Krittibas's Bengali Ramayana the first kaandam, namely Bala Kaandam, goes in the name of **Aadi Kaandam**. In the Bengali Ramayana and Tulsi Ramayan the Yuddha Kaandam goes in the name of **Lanka**

---

28 Jaun R Francisco, *A Critical Inventory of Ramayana Studies in the World*, vol.II-pp. cxix-cxxxvii.

Kaandam. Thakkai Ramayanam in Tamil gives the title **Soundarya Kaandam** to Sundara Kaandam. The work Ananda Ramayana is composed as consisting of nine kaandams, all of them named differently from Vanmikam and other Ramayanas.

Similarly, in Bhusundi Ramayana all the four larger divisions are called kandam; they take the names of the four directions, East, West, South and North. In no other Ramayana text do we find such names.

There are variations also in the way the narrative is begun. Starting with Valmiki Ramayana and extending to many widely known Ramayana texts, most begin chronologically with Bala Kaandam and end in Yuddha Kaandam; some also sing of the Uttara Kaandam events.

Some texts like the Jataka tales begin with the subject matter of Ayodhya Kaandam. Pravarasena's Setubandha and Abhinanda's Ramacharita begin with Kishkindha Kaandam and end with Yuddha Kaandam. Kshemendra's Dasavatara Charitam starts with the story from Lanka and through the flashback technique narrates the Aranya Kaandam and then the Bala and Ayodhya Kaandam events. We find that some of the Southeast Asian Ramayanas too begin their tale from Lanka and follow the tradition of going back to the beginning. Thus we find that the works narrating Ramakatha contain among themselves varying structures with regard to the number of kaandams, the names of kaandams, the beginning of the epic and so on.

The claim of Bhusundi Ramayana that 'Ramayanas are countless' (*Ramayanam anantakam*) stands borne out by the fact that the story takes hundreds of avatars i.e. there are hundreds of versions in multifarious languages differing in several aspects among themselves in terms of subject matter, character, character traits, story events and plot structures.

Although the Ramayanas are countless, among them only a few are regarded as foundational texts, presenting the indispensable base pitch of Ramakatha. There are two different points of view prevalent in this regard. The very source of Ramakatha is Valmiki Ramayana alone; the rest of the Ramayanas are all its progeny – this is one viewpoint. The source of the Ramakatha is the oral tale charged with mythical quality and widely spread all over India. Starting with Vanmikam and up to the twentieth century and those yet to come – all such Ramayanas are incarnations of that source; they appear in very many forms depending upon the factors of time, place and cultural practices of their genesis. This is the second viewpoint.

The first viewpoint operates on the basis of traditional faith; it is not based on any historical sense. The second perspective operates on the basis of social science, not however ignoring philosophical tradition. Among the various incarnations that Vishnu took, some are regarded as *poornavatarangal* (complete incarnations), whereas the rest are *amsavatarangal* (incarnations of some aspects). Accordingly, more than the incarnations of the aspects, the complete incarnation of Rama and Krishna are hailed as supreme. The incarnations of aspects are those which appeared to explain a few features of human life; whereas the complete incarnations are those which expound many of the fundamental aspects of life and explicate common human existence. That the rest of the incarnations derive their value from the complete incarnations is the implication of the Bhagavata Purana.

The incarnations of Ramayanas too, more or less, function in the same way. We may say that those which narrate the

Ramakatha simply as a story are *Amsavatara Ramayana*s (incarnations of aspects of Ramayana) while those which contain several special features such as an elaborate Rama story and characterisation, sociologically and psychologically oriented incidents and a universal outlook embracing entire humanity, literary niceties, and so on, may be regarded as *Poornavatara Ramayana*s (complete incarnations of aspects of Ramayanas). We may find that Poornavatara Ramayanas such as Vanmikam, Kamba Ramayanam and Tulsi Ramayan are not only famous by themselves but have given a sense of direction to other Ramayanas too.

We can also explain this on the basis of linguistic phenomena saying that, although several Ramayanas appeared, only a few have become influential in accordance with their respective time, place and cultural practices. That is to say, a language, based on the spoken and written modes, can traditionally exist in different dialects. These dialects exist variously at the social and regional levels. Although a language may thus have several dialects, only one among them would gain the status of 'standard language', depending upon its contemporary social, political and literary prestige. In course of time that dialect would attain the standard form of that language and establish itself.

Everyone knows that in the Tamil language there were two dialects – *Chenthamizh* and *Kodunthamizh*. Between the two of them the dialect that was in vogue in a particular area of the Pandiya region got established as *Chenthamizh*. Similarly, we may compare how the dialect *Khari Boli* (pure language), that was in vogue in Meerut and other areas adjoining Delhi, became established as the prime form of the Hindi language; and how among the various dialects in England, the East Midland dialect spoken in and around London city became the official form of the English language and emerged as Standard English. History shows that these dialects attained such a status because of political influence.

History shows us that although several Ramayanas appeared in Pali, Prakrit and Sanskrit, Valmiki Ramayana alone remains immensely influential; so too Kamba Ramayanam, Ranganatha Ramayanam, Ezhuthachan Ramayanam, Krittibasi Ramayana, Tulsi Ramayan and all such works remain excellent Ramayanas, famous each in their culture because of social and political factors, besides literary standards and such reasons.

In identifying the works necessary for this research project, a text considered the most excellent in each language alone has been selected based on the principle mentioned above. Leaving aside the variable literary standards, the preoccupation with how the Ramakatha events and morals drew a whole society, or guided its way of life, functioned decisively in identifying and selecting these texts.

Note 1 Page 16: There is considerable debate as to whether Ramayaana is Itihasa. In pages 17 and 19, Valmiki's rendition is considered as the first Itihasa form. However, many scholars contest this as Valmiki is supposed to have said, he is describing an Ideal Man who he saw 'in his mind's eye'. So Valmiki *Ramayana* is considered a Kavya by many, Valmiki as Aadi Kavi and it is *not* Itihasa. Whereas, *Mahabharata* is considered Itihasa. An example of differing viewpoint would be the sociologist Iravati Karve's *Yuganta: End of an Epoch*.

Ref. https://archive.org/stream/Yuganta-TheEndOfAnEpoch-IrawatiKarve/yuganta_djvu.txt

Note 2 *Padalgal, paadalgal* means verse or stanza *padalam, padalangal* means subsection.

Note 3 The two critical editions are referred to also as Baroda University edition and Bhandarkar edition, for clarity.

—Publishing Editor

BALA KAANDAM

Preliminary Remarks on the chapter Bala Kaandam
- Purpose of the Epic
- Invocation
- Subject Matter
- Scholarly Modesty
- Preface to Bala Kaandams

Descriptions of the Country and the Capital
The Birth of Rama and his Brothers
- Birth and Incarnation
- Planetary Positions

The Slaying of Tataka
The Tale of Ahalya
- Texts that narrate Ahalya's story and those that do not
- Ahalya recognising/not recognising Indra
- Curse-Redemption Variations
    - The story of Indra's curse
    - Redemption from the curse
    - The disguises assumed by Indra
    - The curse incurred by Ahalya
    - The redemption from the curse

Sita's Birth
- Daughter of Janaka
- Girl found in the furrows/Ravana's daughter
- Janaka's foster daughter
- Incarnational birth
- Dasaratha's daughter
- The Ramayana culture

Sita's Wedding
- The victor's reward
- Ravana in the bow festival
- Sita in the Swayamvara Hall
- Scene of clandestine meeting of Rama and Sita

The Challenge of Parasurama

Sloka Variations in Bala Kaandams

Bala Kaandam

Preliminary Remarks on Bala Kaandam

THE OBJECTIVE OF **Valmiki Ramayana** is to conceptualise and present an ideal man among human beings.

Dasaratha Jataka, Anamakam Jatakam, Dasaratha Kathaanam and **Buddhist texts** and the **Jain texts** such as Vimalasuri's Pauma Chariyu, Gunabhadra's Uttara Purana depict Rama as an exemplar of the verities of their respective religions. In the subject matter, these works vastly differ from Valmiki's source tale and the Sanskrit Ramayana stories like Bhagavatam.

Purpose of the Epic

Kamba Ramayanam states that the purpose of rendering Valmiki's story of Rama in Tamil is to spread Valmiki's fame as well as Rama's glory among the Tamil people.

Works such as Narasimha Purana, Bhagavata Purana, Bhusundi Ramayana, Padma Purana, Adhyatma Ramayana and Ananda Ramayana hold as their goal the inculcation of spiritual awareness in people by projecting Rama as the incarnation of Vishnu and by elucidating the tasks he undertook in this incarnation to contain the wicked and protect the good. These works are composed in the vein of purana or mythological narrative, deviating from the line of a human epic.

The author of **Ramayana Kakawin** says that the Ramayana epic was composed to impel not only the learned but also the illiterate to realise the value of righteousness, obtain wisdom and attain liberation.

The **Telugu Ranganatha Ramayanam** claims that it was composed for the reason that the Ramayana story alone has the potential to bestow worldly gains such as fame and wealth, as well as other-worldly gains such as blessings earned through meritorious deeds (*punyam*), deliverance and so on. 'How can anyone who listens to the story of Rama not attain liberation?' asks the author of **Bhaskara Ramayanam** and says, he therefore composed his Ramayana.

The first woman epic poet in the Telugu language, Aatukuri Molla, says that she created **Molla Ramayanam** with the aim of attaining the other-worldly reward of liberation. She adds,

> It is Ramachandrudu who asked me to tell his story.
> I have not done it on my own.
> This sacred tale will help attain everything here in this life
> and in the life after.

Then, Molla goes on to explain the purpose of her writing a Ramayana in Telugu when there is Valmiki's Ramayana:

> Since the epic text of Valmiki was in Sanskrit, lay people were not able to read it, comprehend its meaning and

relish its contents. Reading the Sanskrit Ramayana would be like blowing a conch in a deaf man's ear, and like the deaf and the dumb conversing with each other. Hence, I have composed this Ramayana in simple words in Telugu to enable the ordinary Telugu people to read and enjoy (Peetika, i.e. Preamble 15-18).

The monarch among Assamese poets **Madhava Kandali** says that he has rendered the best slokas from Valmiki Ramayana in Assamese language, complying with the request of King Maha Manikya of the Varahi Dynasty as well as for the benefit of the public; and that 'Just as you churn the milk and gather only the ghee, I have picked up the best of Valmiki's epic, dropping those not worthy of inclusion, and have included anew a few portions for the sake of epic flavour as desired by Maha Manikya'.

The author of the Bengali Ramayana, **Krittibas** says that the aim of his epic is to enable the ordinary people too to read and enjoy the divine creation of Valmiki, the supreme among the sages.

The authors of **Kannassa Ramayanam** and the **Malayala Adhyatma Ramayanam** say that they composed their respective Ramayanas for the benefit of the lay people who are not scholarly enough to study and appreciate the source text of Vanmikam, meaning for those who know only the Malayalam language, to read and benefit.

Tulsidas makes clear his objective thus: 'I sing of this story for the satisfaction of my soul, emulating the avowal of the primal poet Valmiki and my predecessors, following the line of the Vedas, Puranas and *Agamas*' (1:7).

Summary

We find that Valmiki Ramayana, the Buddhist Jataka Tales and the Jain Ramayanas have been composed with the aim of creating the character of Rama as a supreme guide for human existence.

In the Upanishadic period as well as later in the medieval period when religious philosophies evolved, works such as the Bhagavatam and Bhusundi Ramayana came up in Sanskrit. They all superimposed the doctrine of incarnation on the characters in the Ramayana and suitably altered the incidents. Therefore, the objective of these works is elucidation of the doctrine of incarnation with a slant of Vedantic and Tantric beliefs.

Kamba Ramayanam says that it cast the fabled Rama's unblemished heroic tale in the form of a Tamil epic in order to establish the greatness of the divine poet Valmiki. Thus, the objectives of Kamban appear to be proclaiming Valmiki's greatness and singing of Rama's untarnished victory, thereby enabling the Tamil people to know and enjoy them.

None of the other authors of the books taken up for this research mentions that he/she wrote it in order to spread the fame of Valmiki. It is not clear why Kamban alone makes such a claim.

We come to know that the Ramayanas which were produced in the Telugu, Assamese, Bengali, Kannada, Malayalam and Javanese languages were composed out of the compassionate aim of facilitating the lay people, speaking their respective languages, to attain the state of enlightenment by reading, listening to and appreciating the Ramayana story which in the Sanskrit language is comprehensible to the pundits alone. On the one hand, all these writers seem to be endowed with a noble heart and the desire of conveying to their own people the cultural greatness embodied in another language; on the other hand, we may say that these are large-hearted persons who resuscitated a profound poet called Valmiki, each in their own language, bestowing on his creation several incarnations.

Goswami Tulsidas alone says that he renders the Ramakatha in Hindi for the satisfaction of his own soul. Even so, Tulsidas appears to be equally large-hearted in desiring that all the people must seek after the nectar of Rama's fame and redeem themselves. We find in this epic the fervour of devotion, surging and inundating as the great river Ganga. The aim of spreading that feeling among the people lies subtly concealed all over Tulsi Ramayan as the fruit lies hidden among the leaves.

Invocation

In the primal epic Vanmikam, there is no invocation. Valmiki, who was the author of the primal Ramayana, undoubtedly set upon himself the task of narrating the story of Rama, but he did not pay obeisance to any deity by way of an invocation. As generations changed, those who recited Valmiki's Ramayana scripted invocatory verses in praise of myriad gods, each according to their tradition, and included them in the beginning of the epic. This tendency can be found in both the Northern and the Southern Recensions.

In the opening verse of Kamban's work, the prayer to the transcendent entity is offered in general terms. During the period of proliferation of minor religious literature as well as later, there were countless men who learnt Kamban, those who used him for religious discourses and those who made copies from manuscripts. It is possible to construe that such men, impelled by their own experience, fervour as well as leanings, composed and added an invocatory verse for each kaandam. Not stopping with it, they might have been the ones who composed invocatory verses for Nammazhwar, Goddess of learning Saraswati, Brahma, Vishnu, Vinayaka and such deities, Ramayana characters like Rama, Sita and Hanuman, and crafted them so deftly that such verses could easily pass for Kamban's own creation and got them included in the prologue. The 'Kamban Kazhagam' edition has marked them as super-added verses and published them separately.

During the period when the Telugu Ramayanas appeared, schools of Bhakti traditions of Saivism and Vaishnavism as well as Purana or mythological narrative traditions had spread widely in the delta regions of Andhra. Therefore, the Ramayana poets themselves, depending upon their religious traditions, composed invocatory verses in their epics praying to multitudes of deities.

The Kannada text Torave Ramayanam came up at a point of time when the Bhakti or Devotional literary culture, not confining itself to the elite upper class, spread among the common public who did not have the opportunity to complete their education, through the agency of religious discourses and bhajans (collective singing and worship). Hence, we find in the invocatory part of this work the tendency to worship the (Hindu) trinity, the marshals of the celestials, Vinayaka, Saraswati and such deities, besides poet-predecessors starting with Valmiki, men of nobility, religious preceptors and a wide variety of leaders.

Since the Malayala Ramayanams too belong to the same period, there are, as in Torave Ramayanam, multifaceted invocations found in them.

The Bhakti movement in the Tamil region started as a highly confident, pragmatic, people's movement which embraced social revolution. However, soon after, it began to get diluted gradually into a literary movement and later became the philosophical movement of established religions. Such a decline of the Bhakti movement prevailed in North-Indian regions too.

In the beginning of the Mughal reign, the Bhakti movement was revived among the public as a movement with a social orientation. However, soon its vigour diminished when it transformed itself into religious propaganda, a movement of collective devotional-singing. Its self-confidence lost its fervour and it became diluted as a devotional movement in the line of Puranas. Poets like Tulsidas appeared as representatives of such a devotional movement. That is the reason why we find that Tulsidas's invocatory section runs very long, containing forty-three couplets.

Tulsidas, in his lengthy invocation section, pays obeisance to myriad gods and goddesses, demons, snakes, birds, *gandharvas* (semi-celestial singers or choristers in Indra's court), *kinnaras* (celestial musicians) and ghostly henchmen. Tulsidas says that he raises both arms to pay his respects to those who take pleasure in other people's misery or suffering, those wicked people who can't bear to see other people prosper and hence find pleasure in witnessing misfortune befall others. **Tulsidas must be the only one in the entire world of epics to invoke not only the good people but also the wicked.**

Kamban prays to the transcendent entity; he does not state openly the reason for the prayer. The Telugu, Kannada, Malayalam and Hindi poets pray that their epic should happily come to a fruition. Going beyond all this, Tulsidas prays that the fame of Rama, the noble qualities of Bharata and others, the supreme fame of Valmiki and others should spread all over the world.

Subject Matter

In the Bala Kaandam of the Vanmikam in vogue today, the first four sargas are so constructed as to set forth the theme of the epic. In this part Sage Valmiki states the noble qualities that the protagonist he wishes to create should possess. He then goes on to ask Narada whether such a personage exists in the world, to which Narada gives a reply. The dialogue between the two goes on thus:

Valmiki:
Who among those living today upon this world embodies virtuous qualities? Who is the one who is virile, righteous, grateful, ever speaking the truth, steadfast and firm in his vow? (Dharmalaya I.1:2)
Who is the one who has good conduct, loves all living beings, possesses wide knowledge of various arts, is versatile, and forever sporting a kind and smiling face? (I.1:3)
Who is the one who is brave, who has kept anger in check, who possesses an effulgent physique, who is utterly devoid of jealousy, feared even by the celestials when rising with martial valour in the battlefield? (I.1:4)
The desire to know such a person surges up within me. I know that you are the only one worthy of knowing such a human being (I.1:5).

Narada:
'O Sage! Indeed it is rare to come across in one single person all the good qualities which you have mentioned. On reflection, the one person who embodied in himself all these qualities was Sri Rama as he was called by the people, hailing from the Ikshvaku dynasty', so saying Narada narrated in brief the story of Rama (I.1:8 - 20).

The prologue verses cited state that Valmiki composed this epic on learning that such a human being embodying the good qualities and morals he had imagined, did exist. Valmiki composed his epic after listening to Narada narrating the story of this person named Rama who was a king. Valmiki Ramayana states that the story narrated by Narada blossomed as the subject matter of the Ramayana.

Kamban says about his subject matter that he attempts to recreate in Tamil poetry the story of the impeccable Rama, as Valmiki has told it. We find the twin motifs – of the ideal values which Valmiki wished to see and his deep desire to know the human being who embodied them – continuously running through the texture of Kamban's epic.

As far as the Buddhist Jataka Tales are concerned, the Ramayana details are employed as exemplars or illustrative stories. In some places it is stated that the Buddha himself incarnated as Rama. The Jain Ramayanas such as Pauma Chariyu, Vasudeva Hindi and Ravisena's Padma Purana have altered the Ramayana details, changing the names and incidents in keeping with their own religious doctrines. In these works too, the story of Rama is not treated as the direct theme or subject matter; it is used only as illustrative stories. It must also be mentioned that Rama has been depicted only as a human being in the tellings in these two religions.

The Telugu Ramayana composers, the Kannada Ramayana composer Kumara Valmiki and Rama Panikkar, who wrote the Malayala Ramayana, declare that they sing the story of Rama as narrated by Valmiki. Even so, the subject matter of their creation is not a human being; it is the incarnational personage of Rama. We can infer this from Kumara Valmiki's avowed statement that he sings of the deity Narahari who is consecrated in Torave, referring to Vishnu. Since Ezhuthachan affirms that the story of an incarnational person is conducive to people's spiritual well-being, the notion of incarnation forms his theme.

It is also obvious that the protagonists of Krittibas's Bengali Ramayana, Balaram Das's Jagamohan Ramayana, Bhusundi Ramayana and Adhyatma Ramayana are also the incarnational

Ramas. Since the source author of the Assamese Ramayana, Madhava Kandali, follows the primal Ramayana text, his subject matter is presented as the story of Rama, an ideal human being. However, the Bala Kaandam of today's Assamese Ramayana was composed by one Madhava Deva a few centuries later and added to the text, and its subject matter appears to be the incarnational Rama.

Tulsidas says that he narrates the story of Rama as the manifestation of Brahma (the Absolute), and Sita as the manifestation of the power of Brahma, who together established dharma. His epic shows Rama as the incarnation of Vishnu; it presents him as an ordinary human being too. Tulsidas's Ramayana is an excellent example to demonstrate how the ideal human being that Rama was, in the original Valmiki, has been created and recreated in the subsequent epochs from as many perspectives as there were social, societal, religious and philosophical transformations.

The Tibetan, Laotian, Burmese, Thai and the Malaysian Ramayanas too depict Rama as an incarnational being.

Scholarly Modesty

In Valmiki's epic there is no verse expressing humility or modesty.

In those Buddhist and Jain Ramayanas which appeared before the sixth century AD, there is no modest disclaimer.

The objective of the poet writing such verses constituting an avowal of humility appears to be to draw the attention of those who are fit to read his work and motivate them to read it. It can be construed that the portion on 'Scholarly Modesty' employed as a device by the poets in the early years, might have got established in the course of time as an indispensable part in some literary traditions.

It seems that Sage Valmiki in the opening of his epic, did not profess modesty probably because he was himself the primal poet, or at that juncture his epic theme was not known to others, or perhaps, he did not regard any specific community as the reader or listener of his epic, or the tradition of professing modesty was not in vogue in his time.

Since the Buddhist texts do not belong to the tradition of professing modesty and since in the Jain texts, paying obeisance to *Aruga* (Jain God) is itself regarded as an avowal of modesty, in these works, perhaps, sections on modesty did not find a place.

All those epics which contain sections on modesty, more or less, appear to have the same quality. We find that in all of them the strategy of reiterating simultaneously their own worthlessness and the worthiness of the reading public, in fact, serves in some ways to ultimately bring out the greatness of those poets. We see the section functioning as a means of getting to know the imaginative richness of the poet.

Kamban's profession of modesty is structured as three divisions. The declaration 'Not out of ability, but out of desire did this song emerge', is directed at the general readers; it reveals the deep love he developed towards the incarnational figure of righteousness. Of the next five verses which follow, two are directed towards scholars of the Sanskrit language who are well-grounded in matters of spirituality while the remaining verses are directed towards the Tamil poets. Through the first two verses Kamban hopes to win the support of Sanskrit scholars by praising Valmiki and belittling himself. Since his epic is to become part of Tamil Literature, in three verses he professes his modesty and simplicity in order to win the support of Tamil scholars who are adept in the triad (Verse, Prose and Drama) of

Tamil. We find that Kamban's profession of modesty functions with the twin aims of preemptng adverse scholarly criticism and thereby drawing the scholars and the general readers towards him by his utter humility.

Both the Kannassa Ramayanam in Malayalam and the Molla Ramayanam in Telugu structure their sections on modesty more or less in the vein of the strategy of Kamba Ramayanam, but are somewhat brief. The modesty portion of Tulsidas is extremely expansive and very, very elaborate, with the poet projecting himself as an utterly lowly and simple person in the manner of a devotee appearing humble before the Lord in an attitude of total supplication. Tulsidas' modesty, which is a parallel or an equal to the Tamil expression *adiyen* (my humble self), serves to explain how the Bhakti movement had turned into a movement of worship through devotional songs during his time.

The Torave Ramayanam in Kannada has a section on modesty which appears to be entirely different from the tradition cited above. This change is of two kinds. Of the four verses on modesty, two are set in the beginning of Bala Kaandam, in the first chapter, and the remaining two towards the end of Yuddha Kaandam in the fifty-second chapter. This change in the tradition concerns the placement of the songs in the work. Secondly, the poet says that he alone is qualified to compose the Ramayana, that there is none else who can accomplish it, that there is none who does not accept what he has composed, that he holds the distinction of creating by himself without emulating anybody else, that barring him, the rest of them are poetasters. Such a vein of self-praise, or call it an affirmation of excessive self-confidence due to an exaggerated sense of self-worth, is a novelty to be found nowhere in the epics of the world. This second change of the tradition is concerned with the poet's scholarly arrogance.

Preface to Bala Kaandams

The opening portion of most Ramayanas is called Bala Kaandam and that of a few Ramayanas is called *Aadi Kaandam*. Scholars like Weber hold the view that 'Aadi Ramayana', regarded as the source story, began with Ayodhya Kaandam and later, after a few centuries passed, around the first or second century AD, the portion of Bala Kaandam was 'interpolated'. At that stage the title 'Bala' Kaandam was given to it to refer to the narration of events concerned with the time of the birth and youth of the epic hero; and following the Mahabharata, the first part got named Aadi Kaandam, according to scholars. Mostly, it is only in the Ramayanas which came up in the Eastern region where the Eastern Recension of Vanmikam (ER) prevailed (Assam and Bengal) that the name Aadi Kaandam is found. The reason for this difference cannot be found.

The birth of the epic characters Rama, Bharata, Lakshmana, Shatrughna and Sita, Rama's slaying of Taraka (Tataka) acting on the wish of Viswamitra, the story of Ahalya, the wedding of Rama and Sita, and the challenge of Parasurama are the indispensable thematic features of Bala Kaandam. In the motifs of the killing of Taraka, the story of Ahalya and Sita's wedding, there are not too many differences among the various Bala Kaandams.

Two different views are found only in the way the details of the birth of Rama and the others are related. In the Buddhist and Jain Ramayanas, the royal folks, including Rama and Sita, are presented as human beings. Many scholars think that in the beginning Valmiki Ramayana too contained a similar line of thinking. Majority of the scholars believe that the notion of the four brothers including Rama as incarnations of Vishnu, and of Sita as a supernatural person as well as an incarnation of Lakshmi, prevailed or was constructed in the early years of the Gupta reign. Based on such views, this idea was interpolated as a later addition in the Ramayana works such as Vanmikam.

So far as the epic hero is concerned, we find the Bala Kaandam functioning as the narrative site wherein the personality traits of Rama grow, getting enriched by means of his incarnational birth, education, knowledge obtained through listening, successful martial arts training, obeying the five great mentors beginning with the father, carrying out their command without a demur, even if they be unrighteous, and understanding the perilous nature of the world from the story of Ahalya. When viewed from a comparatist perspective, we find that a kind of literary exchange which may be called counter influence, has taken place in Bala Kaandams. That is to say: Source text → Derivative text → Adapted text as the line of literary genealogy stands; we notice some ideas and incidents found in a few derivative texts countering the source text and finding a place in them as interpolations and emendations. Comparatists describe such literary cross-currents or movements as 'Counter Influence'.

For examples of such an influence with regard to Bala Kaandams, as noted by recent researches, we may note how in the early Valmiki scripts there was no mention of the details of the planetary conjunctions at the time of birth of the four, namely Rama, Bharata, Lakshmana and Shatrughna, and also of the detail that Ahalya was cursed to turn into a stone. All these go to suggest that they were added to Vanmikam as interpolations after being translated, due to the influence of a few later derivative texts.

Two renowned comparatists Henry HH Remak and Ulrich Weisstein have expressed the opinion to this researcher that to the best of their knowledge, they could not find occurrences of such literary counter influences in Western literary histories. It has not been possible from the available data at this point of time to account for the subtle reason for the presence of this new tradition in Indian literary culture which cannot be perceived in the European literary culture.

The Western literary epics became records of a particular time and geographical space. Hence, in the derivative works appearing down the ages there was no opportunity for their contemporary influence to make a mark on them.

Therefore, in the derivative texts no big changes appeared either; although a few changes were made by the authors of derivative works, they did not counter their original texts or alter them. On the contrary, with regard to the Indian Ramakatha, despite receiving its epic form in a particular locale at a particular period, its source story having become a living legend on account of it being an oral tale linked to ordinary people in the entire Indian subcontinent, derivative texts which appeared in every region down the ages, introduced and inserted innumerable new features, depending upon their regional oral practices.

In due course, such new details, on account of their literary and contemporary social influence, were added to the very source text of Vanmikam as interpolations. We can thus venture to explain the reason pertaining to the Indian context by stating that they were all new features connected to the sociological changes taking place down the ages in India and that they found a place in the source text as emendations and interpolations because of the influence of the derivative texts.

Descriptions of Country and Capital

In the Western literary history, there is no convention to be found of depicting the country and the city at the beginning of the epics. Critics like Aristotle think that epics started to emerge after the emergence of plays, particularly tragedies. Hence it appears that in them, descriptions of the country and city do not find a place, modelled as they are after dramas which begin *in medias res*, that is, starting the work in the middle of the story. This point gets confirmed when we look at the Western epics such as Homer's *Iliad* and *Odyssey*, Virgil's *Aeneid*, Tasso's *Gerusalemme Liberata*, and Milton's *Paradise Lost*.

Valmiki describes the city of Ayodhya in forty-seven slokas. In the fifth sarga, he dwells on its natural formation, its defence arsenal, its streets, its palatial dwellings and the general characteristics of its people. In the sixth sarga, he expatiates upon the splendid qualities of the people. He depicts their bounteous wealth, maturity of thinking, education, discipline, compassion and such noble qualities. The city of Ayodhya is a noble dwelling place; the thought that the people living there were endowed with multifarious blessings such as wealth, good physique, mental strength and strength of conduct, is derived from Vanmikam.

Creating a new section called *Aatruppadalam*, Kamban presents the descriptions of the four regions according to the Tamil tradition. **This innovation is Kamban's contribution to the epic tradition.** Both the *Naatuppadalam* describing the country life and the *Nagarappadalam* describing life in the city, narrate with poetical finesse the impressive wealth of the city of Ayodhya, its military prowess, the richness of the mental faculty of the subjects and their impeccable conduct. While Valmiki's depiction is modestly imaginative with the use of acceptable exaggeration, we find Kamban's depiction bordering on the fanciful and encomiastic. Both the epics contain an ideal perspective of the world. However, we find Kamban's depiction scaling the heights of maturity of the civilisation of the world as well as that of poetical excellence. He creates a pleasing society which is marked by individual self-discipline and economic equality; a society where none is poor, none is illiterate, none a thief. Though the core thought is found in Vanmikam, the imagination and poetical strategies are unmistakably Kamban's as borne out by a few verses which follow:

> No fear of death; for none commits any crime.
> No anger; for the mind is pure.
> Hence none who is sunk low,
> where everyone's thought is high and noble.
>
> (Naattuppadalam, 39)

> No penury; hence charity reveals not itself
> No enmity; hence valour boasts not itself
> No falsehood; hence truth sets not itself apart
> No pedantry; hence true knowledge flourishes.
>
> (Naattuppadalam, 53)

> No fear of thief; hence none cares to guard one's wealth.
> None going about begging; hence none to give alms either.
>
> (Nagarappadalam, 73)

Kamban's picture of the city also holds another novelty. In the picture of the city in Vanmikam, there is no reference to Rama. Valmiki says, Dasaratha ruled Ayodhya with glory whereas Kamban makes the fact of Rama being born in Ayodhya and ruling there, the reason for the glory of Ayodhya by way of reversing the praise.

Telugu, Kannada and Malayala Ramayanas, following the line of Vanmikam, offer, but in brief, descriptions of the country and the city. In the Bengali Ramayana of Krittibas, description of the city of Ayodhya does not find a place. Tulsidas too in his Ramayana does not make such a presentation.

The Birth of Rama and his Brothers

Birth and Incarnation

Buddhist Ramayana texts such as Dasaratha Jataka, Jain Ramayana texts like Vimalasuri's Pauma Chariyu, Gunabhadra's Uttara Purana and *Pampa Ramayanam* maintain that Dasaratha's children were born in the natural way. They don't regard Rama and the other brothers as incarnations.

Valmiki's epic, Vyasa Bharatam, Adhyatma Ramayanam, Kamba Ramayanam, the Telugu Ramayanam texts, Swayambu Deva's Padma Purana, the Malayala Ramayana texts, Bengali Ramayana, Balaram Das' Oriya Ramayana, Tulsi Ramayan, Eknath's Bhavartha Ramayana, all of them depict Rama and the others as incarnations.

This variation appears to have been caused by religious and philosophical perspectives. Buddhism and Jainism do not accept the doctrine of theism and hence they have not depicted Rama and the others as incarnations. Be that as it may, since many of the incidents embedded in Rama's story illustrate the way of the world, and are helpful in explaining doctrines, in particular the doctrine of karma, besides being widely known to people, it is possible to construe that each of these religions used this story to expound their respective religious principles.

Those texts which proclaim the principle of incarnation differ among themselves while talking about the nature of incarnation. That is, Vanmikam, Mahabharatam, *Harivamsam, Vishnu Puranam*, Tulsi Ramayan and such texts aver that Lord Vishnu himself incarnated as the four brothers. But

Kamba Ramayanam, Bhaskara Ramayanam and Adhyatma Ramayanam, all of which profess to follow Valmiki, say that the Lord was born as Rama and the conch, discus and the serpent Adisesha were born, respectively, as Bharata, Shatrughna and Lakshmana. The Tibetan Ramayana, for its part, says, Lord Vishnu incarnated as Ramana (Rama) while His son was born as Laksena (Lakshmana). One does not know whom Tun Huang refers to as Lord Vishnu's son.

Bhojpuri Folktale

A maid servant of the palace, who went to wake up Dasaratha at dawn, expressed her worry in a somewhat loud voice: 'This morning, I happened to run into an impotent man. I wonder how the day will go.' Dasaratha who heard this while waking up, became quite despondent.[1] Dasaratha brings over a medicine for his queens to conceive. Kausalya and Sumitra grind it and pour it in a bowl and drink it. Kaikeyi rinses the remnant in the bowl with a little water and drinks it. The three queens conceive and deliver babies. To celebrate the birth of the babies, Dasaratha gifts away gold and presents. Kaikeyi, who has been watching, warns him, 'Be careful before you squander away the riches. Because there must be something left for Bharata. For Rama may have to go to the forest at the age of twelve.'

A Folktale in Braj Bhasha

A gardener in the city of Ayodhya gave Dasaratha a potion for his wives to conceive. The three queens who consumed it conceived through Dasaratha.

---

1 Krishnadeva Upadhyaya, *Bhojpuri Gram Geet*, pp.10-11,qtd in Omkar Kaul, p.12. (Hindi footnote).

One day, as Dasaratha was sitting on the cot, Kausalya, who was sitting near him on the floor, said 'Oh King, to you are born lovely children. You please generously offer gifts and charities.' The King too, mightily pleased, was doing the same. At that time, Kaikeyi, who was inside the room, warned, 'Oh King! The child for the sake of whom you are throwing away your wealth and charity is going to be exiled to the forest in a few days'.

According to Reverend Camille Bulcke, one of the foremost scholars who have researched on the epics, puranas and editions stemming from the Ramayana story, it is only around the fourteenth century that, for the first time, the idea of incarnation of aspects is found in the text **Udara Raghava** composed by Sakalya Malla.[2] The works which came up later, such as Adhyatma Ramayana and Padma Purana, follow this idea and say that while Lord Narayana was born as Rama, his aspects were born as the other sons.[3] The Tibetan Ramayana says that Lord Narayana and his son incarnated as Rama and Lakshmana. Now, one cannot understand why Tulsi Ramayan, which follows Adhyatma Ramayana to a large extent, does not accept the idea of incarnation of the conch and the discus but depicts the four brothers as the incarnations of Lord Narayana Himself.

While noting Camille Bulcke's claim that before the thirteenth century AD, neither in Sanskrit nor in any of the languages of North India is found the idea of incarnation

---

[2] There are some who hold that Udara Raghavam was composed in the twelfth century. (AN Jain, *Asian Variations in Ramayana*, p. 52). In this Lakshmana, Bharata and Shatrughna are said to be incarnations of Aadhisesha, the discus, and the conch respectively.

[3] *Ramkatha*, p. 190.

of the conch and the discus, the question arises as to how it happens that this idea is found in Kamba Ramayanam (I,5:22) composed in tenth century AD.

Although the Chennai Kamban Kazhagam edition includes in the text, the verse containing this idea for the reason of its wide provenance, it demarcates it by an asterisk mark in view of its inappropriateness. In Udara Raghava and the Adhyatma Ramayana, the impact of Udaiyavar's, i.e. Ramanuja's, doctrine of *Vishishtadvaita* is clearly discernible.[4] When Ramanuja's philosophy spread among scholars via Sanskrit, these works too might have got extolled. As a consequence, the later generations of southerners might have incorporated the notion of Adhyatma Ramayana in their literatures. Ezhuthachan's Malayala Adhyatma Ramayanam is an excellent example for it. Therefore, the view that Chennai Kamban Kazhagam's editorial policy may be acceptable gets strengthened.

Incarnation in Kamban's Literary Tradition

Apart from the information cited above on divine incarnation, in two places in the Yuddha Kaandam in Kamba Ramayanam, the matter pertaining to Rama's incarnation is mentioned.

> He who stands tall, with none to excel him,
> That Vishnu incarnated Himself in human form.
> (VI, 2: 111)

Kamban says that Ravana, left utterly helpless in the battlefield, recalled the intimation of Vibhishana.

> He is neither Siva nor Brahma, nor even Vishnu.
> Could he be an ascetic? No, he cannot be,
> For such a one is incapable of carrying out such a task.

---

4 Amba Prasad Suman, *Tulsi Kaavya Chintan*. Aligarh: Granthayan, 1982. pp. 112-113. (Hindi Footnote)

> This one accomplishes rare feats with ease.
> Isn't he the Primal Cause which the Vedas speak of?
> (VI. 36:133,134)

As Kamban presents it, Ravana realised that Rama was an incarnation. In both these places, there is no mention of the idea of incarnation of the aspects.

Kamban's literary lineage is constituted by the Sangam anthologies, the Eighteen Super Anthologies, *Silappathikaram*, and *Manimekalai*, the first two epics to appear in Tamil, the Tamil Bhakti Literature of *Thevaram* and the hymns of the Azhwars.

Among these, in only two of the **Sangam Anthologies**, namely *Ahananuru* (70:13-16) and *Purananuru* (378.18-21), there are references to Rama. While citing some of the events in Ramayana, Ahananuru describes him as '*velpor Raman*', i.e. 'victorious, triumphant Rama' while the Purananuru hails him as '*kadumtheral Raman*' i.e. the 'unconquerable Rama', thus furnishing appellations highlighting Rama's valour. The idea that Rama is an incarnation is not explicitly stated.

Among the 'Eighteen Super Anthologies' known as *Pathinen Keezhkanakku* in the ninety-second verse of *Pazhamozhi Nanuru* (Proverbs Four Hundred), there is a mention of how Vibhishana ascended the Lankan throne with the help of '*polandaar Raman*' i.e. 'one who is decked with a garland of gold'. Here too, there is no reference to incarnation.

It is only the twin epics of Silappathikaram and Manimekalai which, for the first time in Tamil literary history, clearly state that Rama was Lord Vishnu incarnate, as follows:

> Don't you know that he who obeyed the command
> of his Sire
> And left for the forest with his wife,

where he lost her and endured untold suffering,
That one was Lord Vishnu who brought forth
Brahma, the custodian of the Vedas?
Is it not an ancient saying?
(Silappathikaram – Oor Kaann Kaathai – 46-49)

He who strode across the universe
And measured with His two feet the three worlds,
Whose reddened feet turned redder
when He walked the forest along with His younger brother,
He who broke down all the defences of Lanka
and blew to smithereens the high walls of its mighty fort
destroying its inhabitants,
Of what use is the ear which has not heard of the fame of such a hero?
Of what use is the ear which has not heard of the glory of that Vishnu?
(Silappathikaram, Aaychiyar Kuravai – Padarkkaip Paraval-1)

The cosmic Lord Vishnu, out of his intense desire
descended on earth and was born human.
He reached the unconquerable ocean and
strove to build a bridge across the waters
aided by the monkeys.
The big boulders the monkeys brought and cast
over the strait
All sunk into the depths of the infinite sea.
(Manimekalai, Ulaga Aravi Pukka Kaathai, 9-12)

Of the above two references found in Silappathikaram, the first says that it is Lord Vishnu who created Brahma, that He Himself incarnated as Rama and that this chronicle is a very ancient one. The second states that Trivikrama, who took the incarnation of Vamana, himself came down as Rama and that both these are incarnations of Lord Narayana. The reference found in Manimekalai states that the cosmic Narayana came down to the earth as Rama.

Although in the 'Eighteen Super Anthologies' as well as in Silappathikaram, Lord Vishnu is depicted as being armed with five lofty weapons, *Chanku* (Conch), *Chakram* (Discus), *Tandu* (Mace), *Vil* (Bow) and *Val* (Sword), there is no mention of the three brothers of Rama being born as incarnations of those aspects.

As far as Rama's story is concerned, we find Kamban mostly following the notion of the Azhwars. On Rama being an incarnation Poigai Azhwar (321-8), Periyazhwar (328,420), and Kulasekhara Azhwar (722,732,740,751) refer to him as Lord Vishnu incarnate. Thirumangai Azhwar (1684, 1727) and Periyazhwar (329) depict Rama as one of the ten incarnations. Hence we gather that the notion that Rama was an incarnational being was widely prevalent in the Tamil region of Azhwars' times. Therefore, that Kamban should present Vibhishana's claim that Rama was an avatar – intended to bring to an end Ravana's life – is a notion that is in accord with what has come down in tradition.

However, there are no evidences in the Tamil literary tradition prior to Kamban for him to claim that Lord Vishnu declared out of grace that 'We shall be born in Ayodhya followed by the conch, discus and Adisesha as the younger siblings'. It is true that from the days of *Paripadal*, the idea that Lord Vishnu is armed with five lofty weapons is present; but nowhere is it said that they incarnated as persons. Periyazhwar in a hymn talks of:

> The glorious Rama who holds
> the sword, the conch, the mace, the bow
> and the sacred discus (329).

Thus, in describing Rama as armed with five lofty weapons, he refers to Lord Vishnu himself as Rama, as we gather. But he does not say that among the weapons, the conch and the discus and the serpent Adisesha who was the bed of the Lord, were born as the younger brothers.

From the reasons cited above, the view that the verse found in Kamba Ramayanam (1, 5:22) relating to incarnation of aspects might have been added in later times gets reinforced.

Planetary Positions

Twelve months had gone by after the completion of the sacrificial ritual praying for issue; four sons, starting with Rama, were born to Dasaratha. In Vanmikam, there are two different versions to be found regarding the birth of the four. In the Northern Recension of Vanmikam there is just the mention of the four sons being born.

In the Southern Recension (Gorakhpur, Dharmalaya) the planetary positions as they were at the time of birth of the four sons are stated.

Professor GH Bhatt, who edited the Baroda University's critical edition of Bala Kaandam, states in a footnote pertaining to this section that slokas relating to the planetary positions at the time of birth of Rama and the others are to be found only in the copies of the Southern Recension (G1,G2,G3,M1,M2) and that they are not found in the Northern and North Western Recensions.[5]

Professor UP Sha, who has edited the Uttara Kaandam in the same series, considers that the details of the planetary positions at the time of birth of Rama and the others are found

---

5 *The Valmiki Ramayana: Critical Edition*, Vol 1, Bala Kaanda ed GH Bhatt,1959 (I: 17.5).

in the Valmiki scripts of the Southern Recension alone and not in the Valmiki scripts of Northern Recension and that these were inserted later as interpolations in the scripts of the Southern Recension by the Southerners.[6]

After mentioning this matter and explaining it, Camille Bulcke says, 'Such details are present in many Ramayana texts in Indian languages', citing Adhyatma Ramayana, Ananda Ramayana, Padma Puranam, Krittibasi Ramayanam, Balaram Das Ramayana, Ramcharitmanas and Bhavartha Ramayanam (*Ramkatha* 332). However, it is not clear why Bulcke left out Kamba Ramayanam, Telugu Ranganatha Ramayanam and Bhaskara Ramayanam as well as Ezhuthachan's Adhyatma Ramayanam.

Barring Sanskrit, among the rest of the Indian languages, it is Kamba Ramayanam which is the first to render the story of Rama (tenth century AD).

Camille Bulcke, who researched into the various recensions of Valmiki, avers that the details regarding planetary positions which are found only in the southern Vanmikam could have been inserted as interpolations mostly after fifth or sixth century AD (*Ramkatha* 282).

From the research notings of Professor UP Sha and Reverend Bulcke, we come to know that these details were added as interpolations in the Southern Recension of Valmiki, particularly in the Grantha manuscripts as well as the Malayalam manuscripts. If such is the case, one needs to look for the basis for these conclusions. When viewed on the

---

6 'Thus the date of birth and the references to signs of zodiacs at the time of birth of Rama found only in Southern versions is a Southern insertion.' 'Ramayana Manuscripts of Different Versions', *The Ramayana Tradition in Asia*, p. 102.

basis of currently available documentary evidence, it is Kamba Ramayanam that provides this information for the first time. We learn that the Grantha script came to be used widely because of the emergence of the Manipravala mode after around ninth century AD during the reign of the later Cholas. Hence it may be surmised that after Kamban's time, these could have been added in the Southern Recension of Vanmikam which were being transliterated.

This surmise deserves to be studied in the context of the rise of the Vaishnava faith and the *Ubhayavedanta* (fusion of Tamil and Sanskrit) discourses of *acharya*s (preceptors) such as Ramanuja and others. Now, if we take it that these details of nativity might have found a place in Vanmikam following Kamba Ramayanam, it is but natural to ask, what the basis for Kamban's claim is. However, given the state of currently available evidences, one is not able to find an answer to this question. The Azhwars did assign *Thiruvonam* as the star of Krishna's birth, but they never said anything about the planetary positions with regard to Rama. Some clue may become available if the Telugu, Kannada, Malayalam and Tamil folklore were to be collected and studied. Until such time, this question will continue to remain unanswered.

It is indeed astonishing that while in the Vanmiki scripts leaning on northern culture wherein appeared Aryabhatta, the famous astronomer and Varahamihira, the renowned astrological expert, the planetary positions at the time of Rama's birth were not indicated, they have been interpolated in the southern Vanmiki scripts. It may be recalled that the southern culture dared to sing a *padikam* (a form of Tamil verse) rejecting belief in auspicious days and the influence of planets as superstitions. Hence this idea turns out to be one which must be more deeply pondered with the assistance of sociologists and archaeologists.

The Slaying of Taraka (Tataka)

In Valmiki Ramayana, on the way to the Tataka* Forest, Viswamitra narrates to Rama and Lakshmana the story of Tarakarakshasi's curse i.e. the story of how she became a demoness on being cursed by Agastya. (There is no reference to Ravana in it.)

After explaining to Rama Taraka's atrocities, her destruction of the sacrificial rituals conducted by the ascetics, Viswamitra asks him to slay Taraka in spite of her being a woman, and thereby uphold righteousness. Rama replies, 'When I was leaving Ayodhya with you, I was ordered by father not to act against your words. Hence, in accordance with your command, I shall slay Taraka' (1.26:4). However, when Taraka appears right in front of him and challenges him, Rama tells Lakshmana, 'I don't have the heart to kill her, she being a woman. I am thinking of destroying her powers alone'. When Taraka comes in war-like form, raining stones in all the four directions, opposing Rama, Viswamitra again orders him: 'Rama! You change your notion that it is revolting to kill a woman. Her demonic power is increasing as dusk draws near. Therefore, kill her fast.' Rama at once shoots an arrow felling her (1,26:12, 24, 27).

The Buddhist and Jain Ramayana texts do not talk about the killing of Taraka.

Kamba Ramayanam narrates it thus: Rama and

---

* Taraka is pronounced Tataka in the southern languages.
This story is of Tarakarakshashi in Northern Recensions.

Lakshmana, placed under the tutelage of Viswamitra, arrive at Tatakavanam (forest of Tataka) along with him. Looking at its desolate condition Rama wants to know its history. Even while Viswamitra is narrating how, cursed by Sage Agastya, Tataka was transformed into a demoness and how, because of the activities of her sons, Maricha and Subahu, this forest had come to such a state and also how, instigated by the Lankan King Ravana, she continues to cause hindrance to their penance, an infuriated Tataka appears before them and starts raining stones and hurling spears. When Rama, having regard to her as a woman, refrains from reaching for the arrow, Viswamitra, spelling out all her atrocities, says, 'Don't regard her as a woman; I don't hate her out of animosity; it is good that she is destroyed for the sake of righteousness; therefore you will kill her'. On hearing this, Rama says, 'Sire! Even if you command me to do what is unrighteous, I must deem it as the word of the scripture and complete the task; that is my dharma'. So saying, he despatches a fiery arrow.

The Telugu Ranganatha Ramayanam and the Bhaskara Ramayanam conform to Valmiki in narrating Tataka's destruction. Noticing Rama's hesitation on account of her being a woman, Viswamitra explains to him, 'Even though she is a woman, because of her ruthless atrocities she deserves to be killed; by killing her only merit will accrue and not sin' and recalls to him, in detail, incidents in which such evil creatures, even if they were women, were killed by the celestials in earlier times. In the beginning, Rama considered only chopping off her ears and nose and weakening her; but as dusk approaches he begins to see her demonic power increasing. He then sends a powerful arrow and kills her. Molla Ramayanam, too, provides the same matter; it leaves out only the incident of chopping off the ears and nose.

The Kannada Pampa Ramayanam avoids narrating the slaying of Tataka. Torave Ramayana relates it as follows:

> Viswamitra said, 'This is the first stage of the purpose of your incarnation, which is meant to relieve the earth of its burden. Kill her without any hesitation' (1, 10:8).
> 'Does it become a Kshatriya (a man of the ruling class) to kill a woman? If I do so, my ancestors who are in swarga (heaven) will laugh at me along with Devendra. It is enough if we humiliate her. Therefore, please don't order me to kill her', said Rama. (1,10-10)
> 'Indra himself has killed Mahabali's younger sister. Therefore, political justice calls for destroying those who cause harm to good people, whoever they may be, even if they are women and thereby protect the good people. I swear this is truth; I have no doubt about it. Therefore you may go ahead and kill her', said Viswamitra. (1,10-11)

On hearing this, Rama shot an arrow and killed Tataka.

In Ezhuthachan's Adhyatma Ramayanam there is no debate on Tataka's slaying. Pointing to Tataka, Viswamitra says 'Kill her'; at once Rama sends an arrow and kills her, thereby carrying out his orders.

In Tulsi Ramayan, it is said that, although Rama consented to kill Taraka upon the dictates of the Sage, he bestowed redemptive status upon her out of pity for her as a woman. Adhyatma Ramayana (1-4:30-32), Padma Purana (Uttara Kaandam Chapter 269:121) also present this matter.

In Folk Literature, the Tamil Bow-Song *Sita Kalyanam*, which tends to follow Kamban, states that Rama bestowed his grace upon Tataka by granting her 'a stellar status'. It narrates that when the great Sage Viswamitra conducted a fire sacrifice for the celestials in the Mountain of Tataka, Tataka, who was Ravana's grandmother, arrived there and desecrated the fire sacrifice by urinating on it. Viswamitra then sought Rama, saying,

> Please send Rama with me
> To kill the demoness.

Lakshmana too is sent along with Rama. The three of them reach the Mount of Tataka. Keeping Rama and Lakshmana as sentinels, Viswamitra conducts the fire sacrifice. Seeing that, Tataka, in fury, hurls trees and stones. The thought runs like this in the Lord's mind: one should not just think of her as a woman any longer. That is to say, going by the utterance of the Vedas even if that which comes to kill you is a cow, you may kill it. Therefore, we should not let her go without being killed, so thinking,

> Rama hurriedly strung the arrow of fire to the bow
> And pulled it firmly right upto his ear.
> The goodly arrow darted and
> pierced Tataka's chest.

'Lord, not knowing that you are the divine trickster, I, a heinous sinner, have gone astray. What penance must I have done to get killed at your hands! You must grant me a boon which will proclaim my name to the world forever', thus pleading she bowed to him.

> Then the compassionate Rama gave her a boon saying,
> 'You shall rise unerringly on the southeast corner of the sky.
> The world will call you the star "Tataka"'

In this manner with the Lord bestowing on her a stellar status, Tataka's life breath departed.

In the Chennai Kamban Kazhagam edition there is no mention of this. However, in the super-added verses, the tale of Tataka's curse is described in an elaborate manner. Moreover, in Vai Mu Gopalakrishnamacharyar's (Vai Mu Go) edition, they are shown in the text itself.

Therefore, there is difficulty even in getting to know about Kamban's view in this regard. Besides, Kamban speaks of Tataka being related to Ravana as a grandmother (VI.13:32).

Viswamitra says that it was because of Ravana's instigation that Tataka causes hindrance to the sacrificial ritual. The poet too makes the fall of Tataka an analogy for the fall of Ravana's flag. Sita Kalyanam, which follows this work, also mentions Tataka as Ravana's grandmother. This point, made keeping in mind the motif of incarnation, is not to be found in the Northern Recensions of Ramayana starting with Valmiki.

The Ahalya Story
Texts with Ahalya's Story and those Without It
Vanmikam (Southern Recension)
Viswamitra relates to Rama and Lakshmana the tale of Ahalya's curse as follows:

> One day, when Sage Gowtama had gone a long distance from the *ashrama* (ascetic abode), Indra, who came to know of this, arrived there. Looking at Ahalya, he said, 'You slender-waisted beauty! Those who are seized by lust won't wait for the appropriate hour for having physical union with women; I wish to have you'. That evil-minded woman, despite knowing full well that the man who had come in the disguise of Gowtama was none other than Indra, felt proud that the king of the celestials himself had come desiring to have her, and yielded to his wish. After that, much pleased, she pleaded with him, 'Lord of the celestials! I am much blessed; Oh! Saviour of honour, please protect yourself and me from being caught; please leave the premises fast'. Indra too, laughingly, said, 'You who possess beautiful thighs, fear not. I shall leave as I came, much satisfied'.

Coming out, when he saw Sage Gowtama approaching the ashrama after his bath, he trembled and lowered his head. Gowtama realised who it was who had come in the disguise of a rishi (sage). The enraged sage cursed him saying, 'You evil-minded one, you who took my form and indulged in an act that is forbidden, you shall become one who has lost his genitals' (1,48:18.30). Then turning to Ahalya, he cursed her saying, 'You shall remain petrified here for thousand years, living on air, restless at heart, covered by dust, not visible to any living thing. The time when Dasaratha Rama arrives in this forest, then will you get purified; on offering him the worship due to a guest you will renounce unrighteous desire, be rid of delusion, regain your original form and return to me'. Thus Gowtama pronounced his curse. After narrating the chronicle of Indra's dejection at being cursed and subsequently his redemption in detail, Viswamitra looked at Rama and said, 'Rama! You will enter such a sage's ashrama and redeem Ahalya from the cruelty of her curse'. As soon as they entered the ashrama, Ahalya, who until then was not visible to anybody, became visible to them. Then Rama and Lakshmana prostrated at her feet and offered their respects to her. Recalling Gowtama's utterance, she offered worship to the guests and pleased them. The three of them left for Mithila after receiving the blessings with due honour from Sage Gowtama who arrived just then (I.49: 13, 14, 18, 19, 20, 24).

The Buddhist and Jain Ramayana texts completely set aside Ahalya's story. Texts like Dasaratha Jataka, Vimalasuri's Pauma Chariyam, Vasudeva Hindi, Gunabhadra's Uttara Puranam and the Kannada Pampa Ramayanam also completely set aside Ahalya's story. The Buddhist and Jain religions' disinclination to present the story of a woman's fall into dishonour and the incident of Rama, whom they have chosen to depict as an ideal hero, bestowing his grace upon such a woman, may be the reason for this omission. Moreover, in their religious epics, although we do come across men who have strayed from the moral path and then mended their ways, they do not come forward to depict such women. We may say that the philosophical perspective of these religions may be the reason for this. In Bhattikavya too Ahalya's story is not to be found (V Raghavan p. 64).

According to Kamban's epic, when the three of them were on their journey towards Mithila, they entered an ashrama. At that very moment, with the touch of dust from Rama's sacred feet, a stone turned into the form of a woman who stood on one side of the pathway. Looking at this, Rama was greatly astonished. Viswamitra turned to Rama and said, 'She is Ahalya, wife of Sage Gowtama'. On hearing this, Rama exclaimed, 'Oh! How strange is the nature of this world!' and wanted to know, 'Did this sorrow befall someone who is like a mother, out of fate or because of the sins committed in this birth?' In reply, Viswamitra narrated in detail the story of her being defiled by Indra and how as a consequence both of them were cursed by Gowtama. On listening to this, Rama, who came to realise the ways of the world, addressed Ahalya thus: 'Mother! Do not grieve over what has happened, please conduct yourself in such a way as to earn the kindness of the great sage; you may leave.' Thus did he bestow his grace upon Ahalya after which Ahalya paid obeisance to him and left for Gowtama's place (1,9:14-25).

In all the three Telugu Ramayana texts, the story of Ahalya is told in the same manner as is found in the Southern Recension of Vanmikam. In all the three, Indra assumes the shape of a cock and falsely heralds the dawn and makes Gowtama go out for morning ablutions.

In all the three Telugu Ramayana texts, Ahalya was well aware that it was Indra, yet she welcomed him into the hermitage and entertained him, and was later cursed to turn into a stone by Gowtama. **Ranganatha Ramayanam says,**

> Knowing Indra and his sexual intentions
> You invited him into this hermitage;
> With base thoughts you entertained him and
> enjoyed all pleasures...
> Gowtama returned and cursed...
> O, fallen woman! Lie here like a stone.
> (Bala Kaandam pp.44-45)

Bhaskara Ramayanam too expounds Ahalya's culpability more or less as follows (Bal:verse 521):

> On that day Ahalya, realising that 'Indra himself, desiring me has come in the guise of Gowtama', invited him in, saying 'Please come here quickly'. Entertaining him and also drawing pleasure for herself, she said, 'You please save yourself as well as me'.
> (Bala Kaandam, verse 521)

After fulfilling his intention while stepping out in trepidation, Indra runs into Sage Gowtama and is cursed to lose his manliness, while Ahalya is cursed to become (turn into) a stone.

Molla Ramayanam briefly narrates Ahalya's story thus: On the way to Mithila, when Rama stepped on a stone, a beautiful woman emerged from the stone. Viewing it, Viswamitra said, 'By the touch of the dust of your foot this stone has taken the form of a woman' and narrates that beautiful woman's story while moving towards Mithila (Bala: 61-64).

The Kannada Pampa Ramayanam has not narrated the story of Ahalya. **Torave Ramayanam** recounts it as follows:

> Noticing the lack-lustre appearance of the Gowtama Forest, Rama enquired the reason for it. Viswamitra

explained, 'Infatuated by Ahalya, Indra entered Gowtama's ashrama and enjoyed union with her. Gowtama, who had gone out, returned to witness that spectacle, and feeling outraged, cursed Indra saying that his whole body be marked by vaginas. Upon this, Indra lost his manliness. Ahalya was cursed to turn into stone. This is the location where that incident happened'. At this juncture, as soon as the dust of Rama's feet touches a stone, Ahalya emerges from its midst. On seeing Rama, she pays him her respects and praises him. When Rama is surprised by this turn of events, Viswamitra explains, 'This is the Ahalya about whom I spoke to you earlier. By your graceful glance she has regained her form'. Gowtama who arrives there at this point, looks at Rama and, realising that he is an incarnation, offers obeisance to him. Blessing him and Ahalya, the three of them start wending their way to Mithila (I,12:17-23).

Tulsi Ramayan speaks only of the redemption from the curse. It does not tell the history of how the curse came to be cast.

> Gowtama's wife who has been cursed to turn into a stone is waiting for the touch of the dust of your feet. You redeem her by your graciousness (Doha 210).

Ahalya, who regains her old form, folds her hands together in respect. Tongue-tied by ecstasy, she sheds tears holding Rama's feet. Then, recovering to some extent, she exclaims, 'Raghu Nandana! Even I, the woman who has been defiled, have been blessed to see you, who can be seen only by those who have attained spiritual realisation. I offer obeisance to my husband who was instrumental in my receiving this blessing. Please grant me the boon of never losing the grace of your sacred feet'. Thus she pleaded with him and was granted the boon. Again, offering worship at his feet, she went to her husband's ashrama with great joy (chandam 1-4).

Tamil Bow-song

> When the three of them arrive at Ahalika woods,
> the sacred foot of the dark-hued one will touch
> the granite stone.
> That stone will change into a woman
> and worship the dark-hued.
> This, the Lord comes to know of.

'Oh sage! The world over when a human foot hits a stone, blood oozes out. Here, as soon as my foot touched this stone, this stone became a woman and offered obeisance to me, what is the reason for it?' the Lord asked. Viswamitra explained, 'Rama! All this is nothing but your glory. That is, this lady is Gowtama's wife. Her name is Ahalya. For her sin of infidelity to Gowtama, Gowtama cursed this lady to turn into a stone'.

> When will I be redeemed from this curse of mine?
> asked Ahalya in plaintive melancholy.
> When the three arrive here and
> when the sacred foot of Achuta (Rama)
> touches the inert stone,
> the stone will turn into a woman.

He added, 'Rama! According to the word of Sage Gowtama, even the stone turned into a woman, the moment your foot touched it'. At this, Rama suggested, 'Sire! If that is so, we must leave only after taking this woman Ahalya to the great Sage and handing her over to him'[7]; they accordingly left Ahalya in the care of Sage Gowtama and continued on their way.

Among those works which do narrate Ahalya's tale, Tulsi Ramayan and the Tamil folk song only mention that Ahalya

---

7 TC Gomati Nayagam, pp.220-222.

became accursed. They leave out the reason for it. These works, perhaps, did not feel inclined to depict the incident which was the cause of the curse.

Again, there are differences seen even in narrating the story of Ahalya, either fully or in parts. Texts like Vanmikam, Raghuvamsam, Ranganatham and Bhaskaram among the Telugu Ramayanas, the Kannada Torave and Tulsi Ramayan narrate the tale of Ahalya even before the redemption from the curse. Kamba Ramayanam, Molla Ramayanam and the Tamil Bow-song present the history of Ahalya to Rama who stood astonished after the removal of the curse. It appears that it was Kamban who, for the first time, effected this change.

Scholars would regard this as a technique which enhances the dramatic effect.

Ahalya Recognising/Not Recognising Indra's Identity

Reference to Ahalya's misconduct is found for the first time in the *Udyoga Parva* of Mahabharata (5-12:6).The account states that Sage Gowtama, concluding that he who came disguised as Gowtama and by deceit deprived Ahalya of her chastity was none other than Indra, cursed him. However, in many a place in the Bharatam, Ahalya is referred to as unblemished. That is why the Mahabharata does not talk of any curse being cast on Ahalya.

In the Uttara Kaandam of Valmiki Ramayana (Sarga 30), Ahalya is stated to be unblemished. On the other hand, the Bala Kaandam of Valmiki Ramayana (in both the recensions) states that Ahalya was aware that the one who entered Sage Gowtama's hermitage infatuated by her beauty was none other than Indra himself. She welcomed him gleefully and fulfilled his desire while making herself happy in the process (1.48.16). The three Telugu Ramayana texts, the Telugu poet Errana's

Mahabharata (Aranya Parva) as well as the Kannada Torave Ramayanam, the Malayala Ezhuthachan Ramayanam, also talk of Ahalya as culpable. The Bengali Ramayana of Krittibas says that Indra came in his own form and deluded Ahalya's mind and enjoyed her. Therefore, the Bengali Ramayana says that Ahalya is innocent.

The Ahalya of Kamba Ramayanam at the first instance did not know that he who came in the disguise of Gowtama was Indra. Kamban does not say that she welcomed him. Hence it is probable that she must have yielded to the advances of the man who came in, taking him to be Gowtama. Later, during the act of physical union, although she realised that he was not Gowtama, she did not deem the act as unbecoming of her; on the contrary, she too sought it and consented to him, says the poet.

Some scholars hold that the Ahalya, as presented by Valmiki and the others, willingly lost her chastity whereas the Ahalya depicted by Kamban, consented to the act thinking that the one who came in was her husband and hence Ahalya's loss of chastity was an accident; she was indeed guileless and pure, a paragon of virtue. They hold up the phrase of Kamban, 'At heart unblemished' as the evidence of such a perspective.[8]

Should we take chastity as a matter of bodily purity, both of them possess the same quality; should we even take it that chastity is a matter of mental or inner purity, then chastity is that quality which would not allow bodily purity to be defiled knowingly; and there does not seem to be any inevitable difference between the two.

---

8   T Gnanasundaram, *Kamban Malar* 1991 (Coimbatore: Kamban Kazhagam), pp 21-22.

The phrase 'ஒக்க உண்டிருத்தலோடும்' [*okka undiruthalodum* (enjoying with him)] shows her deep attraction leading to 'ஈடு பாட்டையும்' [*eedupaadu* (involvement)]; the word 'உணர்ந்தனள்' [*unarnthanal* (realised)] shows that she became well aware that he was not her husband; the phrase தக்கதன்று என்ன ஓராள் [*thakkathanru enna oral* (inappropriate)], reveals that she did not deem union with a man other than her husband as forbidden and the phrase 'தாழ்ந்தனள் இருப்ப' [*thaazhnthanal iruppa* (existing at base level)] clearly shows that despite that, she willingly had intercourse with him. However, of the two Ahalyas, the Ahalya that Vanmikam depicts, knowing that it was Indra and feeling proud and egotistic that she was desired by Indra himself, welcoming and entertaining him with elan, thus shows herself up as a person of base character. Kamban's Ahalya has been created as a woman subject to temptation who, even after realising that the man she admitted in, taking him to be her husband, was really not so but a rogue, yet does not feel outraged, does not rise in shock, nor oppose or spurn him, nor think of the act as improper but willingly stays with him and goes through with the act.

The modification made by Kamban serves to mitigate the severity of the sinful lapse as well as to remove the mental perversion fundamental to the sin. Notwithstanding that, the phrase 'at heart unblemished' does not seem to suit Ahalya nor does it strike one as Kamban's view either. In this regard it is worth reflecting upon the following: Kamban has presented Viswamitra as describing Ahalya as 'Gowtama's wife, who destroyed the ideals of a wife and embraced infamy' and as saying, 'she has earned eternal shameful stigma which will last as long as the world lasts'. He has also recorded as Gowtama's outburst, 'You too, like a prostitute'. Having stated all this, would the poet now present the following as Viswamitra's words: 'at heart unblemished'? Moreover, Kamban Kazhagam has published this verse with an asterisk mark. Vai Mu Go also says this verse is not found in some copies.

Parimelazhagar, in his commentary on the lines (19:50-52) from Paripadal which tell the story of Ahalya's transformation into stone, states, 'They say that this is the one who became a stone as a punishment for gross lapse of conduct'. From this we understand that he agrees that Ahalya received the punishment for having committed a sin.[9] Vatsyayana cites the view of Konikaputra as an example which holds that 'It is natural for women to feel sexually aroused when they see totally strange men who have physical charm as well as the effulgence of the celestials'. It is worth noting here that he mentions Ahalya as one such woman who had a clandestine lover.[10]

Therefore, a doubt arises about the authenticity of this verse being penned by Kamban. Nowhere else in his epic does Kamban make moralising statements with regard to chastity such as 'she was very chaste, she was a little chaste', treating chastity as a gradable virtue nor hails anyone saying 'she is more chaste' in a spirit of comparative morality. Kamban may have completed this section with the verse 'அன்னை நீ போதுகென்னப் பொன்னடி வணங்கிப் போனாள்' (Mother you may now go) 'so saying, Rama left after she paid her respects at his golden feet'. Mostly Kamban refrains from offering any comment in such contexts where his characters stand charged with some wrongdoing. We find that he stops with description

---

9 *Paripadal: Original with Parimelazhagar's Commentary*. U Ve Swaminatha Aiyar, Madras: 1935, p.141 (Tamil).
10 Biswanarayan Shastri, 'Ramayana in Assamese Literature', *The Ramayana Tradition in Asia*, p.588.n.4.

of the background of the wrongdoing. Rama maintaining silence during the killing of Vaali is worth recalling here.

As far as Rama is concerned, when we reflect on how in the beginning of this story, he who wonders saying, 'Oh who can understand the nature of this world!', ends up giving her the following advice as soon as Viswamitra finishes telling her story: 'You may conduct yourself in a befitting manner so as to receive the grace of the sage. You may leave', the view of Rama as well as that of the poet on Ahalya's sin will become very clear.

Curse-redemption Variations

There are innumerable variations in the story of the cursing of both Indra and Ahalya as well as in their redemption from it.

The Story of Indra's Curse

Bala Kaandam of Valmiki's Ramayana states that Indra was cursed by Gowtama to be deprived of his genitals. Both the Northern and Southern Recensions of Vanmikam state this matter in an identical manner.[11]

As a result, they also say his genitals fell on the ground severed. In the next sarga, it is said that upon the supplication of the celestials, the genitals of a goat were affixed to Indra.

But in the Uttara Kaandam of Valmiki's Ramayana, it is stated that Gowtama cursed Indra saying he would be defeated

---

11 Northern Recension: *The Valmiki Ramayana Critical Edition* (Baroda: MS University, 1959) Bala Kaanda 47: 26, 27.
Southern Recension:
1) *Srimad Valmiki Ramayanam*, Bala Kaanda (Gorakhpur: Gita Press. 1969), 48:27:28.
2) *Srimad Valmiki Ramayanam*, Dharmalaya Edition (Palghat: Kalpathi Subrahmanya. Vadhyar & Sons, 1940) 48:30:31.

in all future wars. Further, he also cursed him saying that half the share of such sins committed by humans would attach to Indra and that Indra's status or position thereafter would never remain permanent (Sargas: 60:32-35).[12]

The Mahabharata states that on account of Gowtama's curse, Indra's beard turned grey (Santi Parva 329-14 (1) (Gita Press).

Kamba Ramayanam says that Indra was cursed as follows: 'May the vaginas of a thousand women appear on your body (I.9:21).' In the explanation for this verse, Vai Mu Gopalakrishnamacharyar says, 'Such a proclamation of a curse is a citation from another text (Bala 9:78)'. But it has not been possible to find the other text mentioned by him. However, it becomes clear that Vai Mu Go was aware that this detail was not found in Vanmikam.

But what is stated in the majority of the Indian Ramayanas is that because of Gowtama's curse vaginas of a thousand women appeared all over Indra's body. Among those the following are most significant:

Brahma Purana (59, 87), Skanda Purana (Nagara Kaandam Ch. 207), Katha Charit Sagar (3,17), Padma Purana (5:51,28), Adhyatma Ramayana (I-5:26), Ranganatha Ramayanam (1:29), Ananda Ramayana (1,3:19), Assamese Ramayana, Krittibasi Ramayana (1:59), Torave Ramayanam (1:12), Balaram Das Ramayana and Tatva Sangraha Ramayana (1:25).

Among these, the Brahma Purana appeared approximately in the tenth century AD or a little later.

This is not a source text. It is a compilation. It tells of

---

[12] Camille Bulcke, *Ramkatha* p.299.

Ramakatha matters based on Harivamsa as well as leaning on *Gowtami Mahatmiyam*.

The Skanda Purana appeared after eighth century AD. It is a book of interpolations, endlessly adding to itself various kinds of tales which cannot be assigned to any specific period. Katha Charit Sagar is also a compiled work whose basic source appeared around eleventh century AD. The rest of the works are all dated after twelfth century AD (vide list of works). Tatva Sangraha Ramayana is regarded as belonging to seventeenth century AD.[13] The point is that among the works mentioned above, those which are complete Ramayanas, created by a particular poet in a specific period, are all works which appeared after Kamba Ramayanam.

When looking at it chronologically, according to the data available till date, one is led to hold that it is Kamba Ramayanam which, for the first time, tells of Indra being afflicted with a thousand vaginas. Vai Mu Gopalakrishnamacharyar's note might have been made on the basis of the later puranas in Sanskrit which are anthologies. We may also take it to refer to a text which is about such a curse in Kamban's Tamil tradition. When we examine the history of the redemption of Indra's curse, we may get some clues.

---

13   (a) Camille Bulcke, pp.170.
     (b) It is also said that this work belongs to late 18th century. This work holds the view that to learn the Ramayana in languages other than Sanskrit is like the desire of a man to scoop and drink water from a mirage.
     Samskritam Ramacharitam parityajya naraadhamaha
     Padan bhashandra kritam mruga trishna jalam pibet.
     Velcheru Narayana Rao, 'The Politics of Telugu Ramayanas'. *Questioning Ramayanas*. Oxford University Press, New Delhi: 2000, p.172.

In the **Ramayana Manjari**, Indra is cursed by Gowtama in the following manner:

> He will be defeated in battle and will be imprisoned.
> Half of the sins of men who commit such a sin following Indra's example will attach to him.
> The assumption that the status of 'Indra' belongs to only one person will change and henceforth any deserving person may be titled 'Indra' (645-646).

Redemption from the Curse

The detail of Indra being affixed with the genitals of a goat upon the request of the celestials is found in the forty-ninth sarga of Bala Kaandam of the Southern Recension (6-12) and in the forty-eighth sarga of the Bala Kaandam of the Northern Recension (6-8).

This detail is not mentioned in either the Mahabharata or the Uttara Kaandam of Valmiki Ramayana.

The Kamba Ramayanam says on the redemption of Indra's curse:

> The celestials who saw Indra in that state,
> came along with Brahma
> and pleaded with Gowtama.
> He too, his anger abated, changed them into a thousand eyes.
> All left for their respective worlds.
> Left alone, she lay as stone.

Pitying Indra's plight the celestials came to Sage Gowtama and pleaded with him for the redemption from the curse. The celestials were led by Lord Brahma himself. Kamban narrates the history of this redemption through a verse which tells us how the Sage Gowtama too, with his rage abated, bestowed his grace upon Indra.

He changed the thousand vaginas all over Indra's body into a thousand eyes.[14]

The texts cited above from Brahma Purana onwards, which say that Indra was cursed to have a thousand vaginas all over the body, state that Indra became the thousand-eyed one. Following what Kamban says, the Telugu Ramayana texts, Ezhuthachan's Ramayanam as well as Balaram Das's Ramayana, all narrate Indra's redemption. By taking bath in the Gowtami river he underwent this change, says Brahma Purana, while Krittibasi Ramayana says that, as a result of Indra performing the *Ashvamedha Yagnam*, the vaginas turned into eyes (1-60) whereas Padma Purana says that because of the boon bestowed upon him by Goddess Durga, Indra became the thousand-eyed one – thus they all tell the history in various ways.[15]

The Bala Kaandam of Ramayana Manjari says that Indra was cursed to lose his manliness and later regained it after a goat's genitals were fixed (308).

When Gowtama is away from his hermitage, Indra in his guise appears before Ahalya and gratifies himself (Uttara. 650-652). When he is mating with Ahalya, Gowtama returns and knocks at the door. Fearing Gowtama's curse Indra takes the shape of a beetle and hides himself inside Ahalya's vagina (Uttara. 657). Gowtama curses Indra saying, 'Let a thousand vaginas like the one in which you are hiding appear all over your body' (Uttara. 661).

---

14 Chennai Kamban Kazhagam edition has printed this verse as a superadded verse. In the Vai Mu Go edition, this verse is kept as a part of the text. Some other editions too have kept it within the text. When examined in the light of the Tamil literary tradition, this appears to be Kamban's own verse.

15 Camille Bulcke, p.300.

The redemption from the curse was: if he bathes in the river 'Kawaksha' where the two rivers Vitasta and Sindhu meet, those one thousand vaginas will turn into as many eyes (Uttara. 662).

That is how the story of Ahalya as well as Indra's curse and his redemption from it are narrated in the Uttara Kaandam of Ramayana Manjari.

Indra coming in the guise of Gowtama and being cursed to lose his manliness as well as Ahalya being cursed to turn into a stone is to be found in other texts too. The version of Indra being cursed into one with a thousand vaginas and later getting changed into one with a thousand eyes is found in folklore. The version of Indra assuming the form of a beetle and concealing himself inside Ahalya's vagina and later bathing in the river Kawaksha and obtaining redemption from the curse, is to be found only in a Kashmiri dialectal version (V Raghavan 142).

Be that as it may, the moment it is said that he was cursed to have a thousand vaginas, there is a compulsion for poets to state the means of redemption. One is led to think that each poet narrates the story of redemption in consonance with his social and literary culture.

When we examine the basis on which Kamban must have narrated the curse and the redemption, we find some data in Tamil literary history. Chronologically speaking, the earliest reference to this is found in Manimekalai. Chitrapathi smiling said,

> 'Oh Prince! The celestials too have indulged in lecherous acts.
> Did not Indra the Lord of the celestials
> fall a prey lusting after Sage Gowtama's beautiful
> wife Ahalya?
> Was he not subject to unspeakable sufferings,
> did he not pay for his lapse and acquire a thousand eyes?'
>   (18.88-91)

From this reference in Manimekalai one comes to know of the curse which Indra incurred on account of Ahalya and his redemption from the curse.

Next, there is a hymn in Sambandar's *Thevaram* pertaining to Indra's redemption from the curse.

> The sage's curse incurred by Indra once upon a time
> was absolved when the celestials pleaded with Lord Siva.
> He too condescended, and gave him a thousand eyes.
> That Lord dwells consecrated in the temple of Kannaar Koil
> where virgin girls go to worship daily.
> (First Thirumurai. Thirukannaar Koil 7)

In the glossary on sacred places and the special features associated with them compiled by Balasubramanya Mudaliar and placed as an Appendix in the portable Thevaram edited and published by Professor AS Gnanasambandan, there is the following note on the temple of Kannaar (*Kannaar koil* – temple of the God of Eyes):

> Because he had union with Ahalya
> Lord Indra's whole body came to be
> marked by a thousand vaginas.
> The celestials prayed to the consecrated
> Deity in this holy place that
> the unfortunate curse be removed; and worshipped Him.
> He too out of compassion turned
> The thousand vaginas into a thousand eyes.
> Hence the place became known as Kannaar Koil.[16]

In this hymn, there is mention of the curse that Indra received and the reason for it as well as those who sought his redemption (the Devas).

---

16 *Thevaara Thirupathigangal* Chennai: Gangai Puththaga Nilayam,1998, p.1325.

However, Lord Shiva, and not Gowtama, is mentioned as the one who granted the redemption from the curse. As we saw above, the Brahma Purana, the Bengali Ramayana and the Padma Purana narrate the story of the redemption from the curse, each according to their tradition.

When we view the Tamil tradition cited here chronologically, we come to know that Manimekalai was composed during the interim period between second century AD and fourth or fifth century AD while the period of Thirugnana Sambandar was the later part of seventh century AD.

Hence we can venture to say that Kamban could have come to know of Indra's curse and his redemption from it from the two Tamil literary traditions existing prior to seventh century AD. None of the studies which have come up so far say that these references were found in any of the other Indian literatures which appeared or were in vogue during the above-mentioned times (fourth/fifth century AD and the seventh century AD).

Therefore, it must be taken that it is Kamba Ramayanam which for the first time differs from Vanmikam in narrating the story of the curse which Indra incurred and his redemption.

The question then arises, on what basis the Tamil works narrated the story of a curse and redemption from it, which Aadi Ramayana and the source text of Valmiki Ramayana do not narrate. In the present state of knowledge, no other answer is found. Some oral tale or some mythical dimensions so far not known, or perhaps some ancient tales of the tribal people, may have been the basis for this rendition. This is just a conjecture.

Alternatively, one wonders if a few references in the Mahabharata and even a few phrases which occur in Vanmikam could have been the imaginative reason for this change. That is, in the Aadi Parva of the Mahabharata (21:12) Indra is said to be the thousand-eyed one. It is also said in Aadi Parva (203:26) that because of his desire to watch and enjoy the sight of Tilottama (a celestial damsel), Devendra (Lord of the celestials) made himself the thousand-eyed one. We saw above how the Santi Parva of Mahabharata says that Indra's beard turned grey on account of Gowtama's curse. Therefore, it becomes clear that the appellation 'the thousand-eyed one', mentioned in the Mahabharata, was held by Indra even before he was subject to the curse.

Moreover, the Northern Recension (1.49:8) and the Southern Recension of Vanmikam (1.49:8), in the sargas of Bala Kaandam preceding the story of Ahalya as well as in the slokas which talk of Indra's redemption from the curse, refer to him only as the thousand-eyed one. It becomes altogether clear that the appellation 'the thousand-eyed one' has been widely attributed to Indra in Vanmikam and that there is no connection whatsoever between this appellation and the redemption from the curse.

The folklore stories, by way of explaining how Indra got the appellation 'the thousand-eyed one', might have fancifully connected the curse cast on him and the form of redemption appropriate to it. Later, considering their plausible appropriateness, it is possible to think they might have found a place in written literature.

The world of scholars knows that many small episodes which have found a place in Itihasa are indeed a contribution of oral literatures in this manner. We may cite as example 'the squirrel story' which was in vogue in Gujarat and which found a place in the Azhwars' hymns of the Tamil region and later in the southern Ramayanas. Except for such a surmise, the real reason for the change relating to Indra's curse and his redemption as told by the Tamil works is not clear from the evidence available at present.

The Disguises assumed by Indra

The Udyoga Parva of the Mahabharata (5.12:16) says that Indra first came as a Brahmana and received Ahalya's hospitality, then had sexual union with her by assuming the guise of Gowtama.

The Bala Kaandam of Vanmikam says, only by assuming the guise of Gowtama did he approach Ahalya. Kamba Ramayanam as well as the Telugu Ramayana texts and the Malayala and Kannada Ramayana texts too narrate it in the same way. Krittibas's Bengali Ramayana[17] says that Indra arrived in his own form and deluded Ahalya's mind and seduced her. The Telugu Ranganatha Ramayanam (1-29), Bhaskara Ramayanam and Tatva Sangraha Ramayana say that in order to engineer the exit of Gowtama from the hermitage, Indra took **the form of a cock,** crowed at an unearthly hour, and woke him up. After fulfilling his intention, Indra came out of the hermitage in **the shape of a cat,** say Kamba Ramayanam (1.6:76), Brahma Purana (ch. 87:44-50), Padma Purana (Srishti Kaandam, 51,57), the Katha Charit Sagar (3-17) and Balaram Das' Ramayana.

Kamban refers to the cat form of Indra following Paripadal, which belongs to Tamil Sangam literature. The other works which mention this matter are all chronologically later than Kamban.

The Curse Incurred by Ahalya

Vanmikam

According to the Northern Recension of Vanmikam, Ahalya is cursed thus: 'Living on nothing but air thou shalt lie down on

---

17 Dinesh Chandra Sen edition; Bulcke, 297.

a bed of ashes, contrite with mental agony.' As was mentioned in the beginning of this section, the Southern Recension of Vanmikam says, Ahalya was cursed as follows: 'Living on just air, petrified, thou shalt lie down recumbent in dust, with intense mental agony.'

Uttara Kaandam, which goes in the name of Valmiki, says that Gowtama, turning to Ahalya, curses her saying: 'This calamity happened because of your beauty. Therefore, from now on, you alone will not be a beautiful damsel; everyone will share your beauty (Sarga 30:37,38).' Meaning, 'many will become beautiful like you'.

In the Mahabharata the matter of Ahalya being cursed is not spoken of at all. Bhojaraja's Champu Ramayana, following the Northern Recension of Valmiki, says that Ahalya was cursed to remain recumbent, not visible to anyone (1:90).

Thus, we learn that while the Northern Recension of Vanmikam says, 'Thou shalt remain living on nothing but air', the Southern Recension says, 'Thou shalt live on nothing but air and remain petrified'.

The slokas of Valmiki which admit different views are found as follows:

> Vayubhaksaa **niraahaaraa** tapyanti bhasma shaayini
> Adrshyaa sarvabhutaanaam aasramesmin bhavishyasi
> (I.47:29)

Thus reads the Baroda University critical edition. This is the Northern Recension of Vanmikam.

> Vadhabhaksaa niraahaaraa tapyanti bhasma shaayini
> (I.48:30)

Thus reads the Southern Recension of Vanmikam published by Gorakhpur Gita Press, altering the first line slightly.

Vayubhaksaa **shilabhutva** tapyanti bhasma shaayini
(I.48:34)

Thus reads the Dharmalaya edition. This too is the Southern Recension of Vanmikam.

In all the three verse quotes cited above, the first two feet appear different while the last two feet don't. The third foot would mean 'mentally agitated' while the fourth would mean 'recumbent on a bed of ashes'. As far as the first foot is concerned all the three verses give the same meaning, namely 'living just on air'. The Gorakhpur Press edition alone uses the word *vadha* in place of *vayu*. This version, which does not alter the meaning, is found only in the scripts of the Eastern Devnagari (D6, D8).

It is the textual variation in the second foot which has made the meaning of the verse problematic. The Northern Recension of the Baroda edition uses the word 'niraahaaraa' while the Southern Recension of the Dharmalaya edition uses 'shilabhutva'. But the Southern Recension of the Gorakhpur edition contains only the version of the Northern Recension.

Among the Southern Recensions, all the Telugu scripts and a few Grantha scripts (G4) contain the word 'niraahaaraa' of the northern version. The Baroda edition, providing the textual variation 'shilabhutva', adds a note that in the G1, G2 and G3 Grantha scripts and also in the M1, M2 Malayalam scripts this version is found.

Of these, the G1 Grantha script was written in the Kollam year 993 (1818 AD); the G2 Grantha script was written three hundred years before that. The G3 Grantha script in the Madras Government Oriental Manuscript Library belongs to a period 500 years earlier.

The M1 Malayalam script was written in the Kollam year 865 (1690 AD).[18] When examining these, it becomes clear that the G3 Grantha script and M1 Malayalam script are the oldest among the Southern Recensions of Valmiki Ramayana available so far. That is to say, it becomes confirmed that by fifteenth century AD the Valmiki Ramayana in vogue in the south contained the version 'shilabhutva'.

The reason for dwelling on the Vanmikam scripts in such detail here is that according to the Northern Recension, Ahalya is cursed as follows: 'Living on nothing but air, thou shalt remain on a bed of ashes in mental distress.' In the Southern Recension, as indicated above, she is cursed as follows: 'Living on nothing but air, becoming a stone ... thou shalt remain.' While all the Northern Recension scripts and a few Southern Recension scripts have the version 'niraahaaraa', how is it that some of the Southern Recension scripts alone should have 'shilabhutva' (in the form of a stone)? The reason is not discernible from the research studies so far conducted. Therefore, we come to know that there are two different kinds of views as far as Valmiki Ramayana is concerned, viz. according to the Northern Recension she remained without consuming any food whereas according to the Southern Recension she lay petrified.

In many of the Ramayanas composed after Vanmikam, in Sanskrit as well as in other Indian languages, it is mentioned that Ahalya was cursed to turn into a stone. The texts are as follows:

    Raghuvamsa (11:34), Narasimha Purana (ch.47), Skanda Purana (Reva Kaandam 136, Nagara Kaandam 208), Janakiharan (6:14), Katha Charit Sagar (3-17),

---

18   UP Shah, p.95.

Maha Natakam (3:17), Udara Raghava (3-29), Kamba Ramayanam (1,9:22), Ramayana Manjari (Uttara Kaandam 647-648), Ranganatha Ramayanam (1-29), Padma Purana (Uttara Kaandam, 269), Assamese Ramayana (9:466), Ananda Ramayana (1.3:16), Krittibasi Ramayana (1-59), Torave Ramayanam (1-12) Ramcharitmanas (1-210), Bhavartha Ramayana (1-14), Tatva Sangraha Ramayana(1-25).[19]

Bhaskara Ramayanam, Molla Ramayanam, Adhyatma Ramayana, Ramalingamrutam are also texts which narrate this matter.

While narrating Ahalya's curse Kamba Ramayanam says that Gowtama cursed her as follows:

> He frowned at the delicate woman and cursed her, saying:
> 'You too, like a whore, become a stone.'
> She was then petrified as a rock.
>
> (1.9: 22)

It was pointed out earlier that in Sanskrit it was Kalidasa who for the first time stated that Ahalya was cursed to be a stone. It is not possible to find out on what basis Kalidasa effected this change. He might have presented it on his own imagination. Further, it is not possible to find out if Narasimha Purana, following Kalidasa, narrates Ahalya turning into a stone, or it does it on its own.

In this connection, one feels like reflecting on the possible basis for Kamban to compose the phrase (become a stone). We find that in the Tamil tradition, even before Kamban, Paripadal had given a literary expression to this matter in verse 19.

> This is Indra in cat form
> This woman is Ahalya, Gowtama's wife

---

19 Bulcke, p.302.

> He who stands at some distance is Sage Gowtama.
> Irate at the deceit of Indra and the conduct of Ahalya
> He cursed her to turn into a stone.
> Here lies she in punishment.
> So explains he to her.
>
> (50-52)

At a time when Ahalya's story had become the subject of a painting, this poem in Paripadal is composed in the manner of a protagonist pointing it out and explaining to his beloved. Therefore it becomes evident that even before the period of Paripadal, this part of the story was widespread among the Tamil people. Hence it strikes one that Kamban might have effected this change following his own (Tamil) literary tradition.

It is not possible to figure out whether the Telugu and Kannada Ramayana texts, supposedly following Valmiki, narrate the story of the curse of Ahalya turning into a stone in accordance with Sanskrit texts such as Raghuvamsa, or present it toeing the line of Kamban.

Even with regard to Kamban it is not possible to assert whether he was following Paripadal or some folklore, or Narasimha Purana. Whichever may be the source, there is no doubt that, among the Ramayanas in languages other than Sanskrit, it is Kamba Ramayanam in Tamil which for the first time gives the detail of Ahalya turning into a stone.

Now the question arises, on what basis some of the Southern Recensions of Valmiki Ramayana added Ahalya being cursed to turn into a stone. The Baroda edition mentions that this detail is exclusive to the southern scripts. It is not possible to construe that they might have effected this change following either the Raghuvamsa or Narasimha Purana, or for that matter Janakiharan. It is because even the Northern Recensions of Vanmikam have not followed these Sanskrit texts; nor do the Telugu Vanmikams or Eastern Devanagiri Vanmikam among the Southern Recensions of Vanmikam follow them. When such is the case, the question arises about the reason for which the Grantha Vanmikams which were in vogue in the Tamil region (G1,2,3) and a few of the Malayala Vanmikams (M1, M2) inserted this textual variation. Until other clear sources of evidence become available, one has to venture to say that Vanmika Ramayanas which were not transliterated in the south, particularly in the Tamil region, provided the text following Kamba Ramayanam regarding the detail of Ahalya being cursed to turn into a stone, by interpolating 'shilabhutva' in place of the foot 'niraahaaraa'.

The moment the word 'Vayubhaksaa' is uttered, we get the meaning of one living on air and hence the term 'niraahaaraa' meaning 'without food', strikes us as tautological. These Ramayanas might have accepted this version because of this and also because of the additional detail, in the 'form of a stone'. Viewed this way, the suspicion whether Kamban's idea might have become the text of Vanmikam gets reinforced.

Account of Gowtama's curse

In the Mahabharata there is no mention of Ahalya being cursed. Hence there is no mention of redemption from the curse either.

Valmiki Ramayana narrates in a detailed manner the episode of Ahalya getting redemption from the curse through Rama:

> On account of Gowtama's curse, Ahalya, who remained formless and not visible to anyone in all the three worlds, appeared in her old form to the eyes of Rama and Lakshmana at the end of the curse.

Both the Northern Recension of Vanmikam (I.48:15-16) and the Southern Recension of Vanmikam (I.49:18) describe the redemption in exactly the same manner.

Both the Recensions of Vanmikam state (I.47:30,31), (I.48:35) that soon after cursing Ahalya and even without her appealing, redemption from the curse was granted by Gowtama saying that, 'The moment Rama sets foot in this hermitage, you will be purified and appear to his eyes in your former form'. That is, even those Southern Recensions of Vanmikam (Dharmalaya edition) which have 'transformed into a stone, living on air, thou shalt remain in the bed of ashes not visible to anyone', do not state that at the touch of the dust of Rama's feet, Ahalya attained redemption from the curse with the disappearance of the form of stone.

> 'Forgiving people's errors is the duty of the elders; be kind...and grant me an end to this', when Ahalya pleaded thus,
> 'When you clutch the feet of one Dasaratha Rama, you will come out of this stone form',
> thus Gowtama granted the redemption from the curse,

says Kamba Ramayanam (I.9:23).

All those texts of Ramayana which state that Ahalya was cursed to turn into a stone, do say that the moment Rama's feet touched her she regained her old form. As examples we may cite Kamba Ramayanam, the Telugu Ramayana texts, Torave Ramayanam, Maha Natakam, Ananda Ramayana, Udara Raghava and such other texts. If all the Southern Recensions of Vanmikam contained at the source itself the reading 'shilabhutva' in the sense of 'turning into a stone', they could not have narrated the redemption of the curse as shown above. Those who altered the curse as 'shilabhutva' perhaps forgot to alter the redemption of the curse also. Hence as discussed above, the surmise that it is because of the influence of Kamba Ramayanam that the changes might have been effected in Vanmikam scripts of G1, G2, G3, M1, M2 and Grantha, Malayala lipi, roughly around fifteenth century AD or a little before that, gets reinforced. Such a counter influence which alters the very source text is indeed astonishing and not found anywhere else.

Sita's Birth
Daughter of Janaka

It appears that in ancient narratives as well as in the Aadi Ramayana (Primal Ramayana), Sita must have been referred to as Janaka's daughter. In Mahabharata too and also the Harivamsa (1:41) and *Koorma Purana* (part 1 ch.21,18), Sita is said to be none but Janaka's daughter (*Janakatmaja*). In these works, it is never said that Sita was a super human being, an *ayonija* (not born of a womb).

In many places in Valmiki Ramayana too, Sita is described as the darling daughter born into Janaka's clan.[20] In the Jain Ramayana text of Pauma Chariyu too, Sita is said to be born to Janaka's wife Videhi (Parva 26).

In the folk songs too, the statement that Sita was Janaka's daughter is found. For example, we may cite what an oral folksong in Braj Bhasha says:[21]

> Sita is the daughter of a minstrel called Janaka. She got acquainted with Rama when he went hunting. He then speaks to his father Jasrathan and asks him to write a letter to Janaka. While replying to that letter, Janaka says, 'I am just a poor minstrel who lives on alms every day. Thou art

---

20   1, 1: 25 (Poet's statement); 11, 28:3 (Rama's statement); 111, 47: 3 (Sita's statement); V, 13:14 (Hanuman's statement).
21   Bharatiya Sahitya, Agra, year 2, issue 3, p.74. cited in Bulcke, 361.

of royal lineage. Given this situation, how is it possible to have any alliance between me and yourself?'

From this folk song, we come to know that Sita is a human girl child; and that Rama's father is of a much higher social status than Sita's father.

The Girl Child Found in the Furrow

Although Mahabharata and such other texts as also folk songs say that Sita was Janaka's own daughter, all the Valmiki Ramayana texts which are in vogue today emphatically say that Sita was found by Janaka in the furrow of the field.

According to **Vanmikam,** Janaka says, 'Once in the past when I was ploughing the land for performing a Yagnam, a girl surfaced from the coulter line of the plough. Picked up by me while I was purifying (the land), and given the name of Sita, she lives in glory. Not emerging out of the womb but from the soil, this girl too is growing up as my daughter' (Southern Recension I.66: 14, 15; Northern Recension I.65: 14, 15).

In the Vishnu Purana (fourth century AD) Sita is described as Ayonija (IV: 5). It is only in the Bhagavatam, which must have been composed during the seventh century AD that, for the first time, it is said that Sita is an incarnation of Goddess Lakshmi (IX: 10,11). Adhyatma Ramayana describes Sita as the incarnation of Prakriti (nature).[22]

According to Vasudeva Hindi, a girl child born to Mandodari is encased in a jewel box and handed over to the minister with the injunction to throw it away. That minister takes the child to Janaka's country and hands her over to Janaka

---

22 AN Jani 30-32,42.

and tells him that while ploughing his sacrificial land he found her and picked her up. Janaka gives the child to his royal consort Dharani and brings her up.[23]

The baby (the girl child born to Mandodari) is handed over to Maricha who is asked to throw it away because of the warning by the astrologers that through the girl child born to Mandodari, Ravana might come to doom. He, in turn, places it in a box and buries it in the town of Mithila. While ploughing the land the baby that was found from deep within the soil was handed over to Janaka. He named the child Sita and brought her up. So says Gunabhadra's Uttara Puranam.[24]

The Tibetan Ramayana **Tun Huang** says, to 'the Ten-headed' (Ravana) is born a girl child. Taking in the astrologer's prediction that because of that baby, Dasagriva and the *Rakshasa*s (demons) will be destroyed, that child is put in a copper casket, with the lid closed and is left to float in the sea. An Indian farmer finds it and takes the baby out and names it 'Found in the furrow' and brings her up; he gifts her to Ramana (Rama) who in turn gives her the name Sita Rani and makes her his wife.[25]

The **Dashavatara Caritam** says that when Ravana was doing penance at the bank of a pond, one day he found a beautiful baby in a lotus flower. He brought it over and gave it to Mandodari. When Mandodari was bringing up the child, Narada came there and said, 'When that baby grows up, she will be sought in love by Ravana'. At once Mandodari wrapped

---

23 Ibid. pp.64. It is Vasudeva Hindi which for the first time claims that Sita is Ravana's daughter and was born in Lanka.
24 Ibid. p.72.
25 JW De Jong, 'The Story of Rama in Tibet'. *Asian Variations in Ramayana*, pp.164-165.

the baby in a silk cloth, placing it in a golden casket, she buried it in a pit close to the sea. Later one day, when Janaka was ploughing the land for performing a Yagnam, he discovered that baby and named her Sita (V Raghavan, pp.146-47).

Kamba Ramayanam, following Vanmikam, presents Sadananda as saying that when Janaka was ploughing the land for a Yagnam, a beautiful girl-child emerged just as Goddess Lakshmi had appeared along with the nectar when the ocean of milk was churned. She was named Sita by Janaka who brought her up (1,12:17).

According to the Laotian Ramayana **Gvay Dvorabhi**, Ravana, who disguises as Indra, rapes Indra's royal consort Sujata. In order to take revenge on him, Sujata is born as Ravana's daughter. Coming to know from the astrologers that she was a child born to destroy him, Ravana puts her in a golden casket, closes the lid and sets it afloat on the sea. The casket, which floats down and reaches the shores of Jambu Dwipa which is Bharata Kanda (continent of Bharata), is sighted by Sage Kasappa. He opens the casket and finds the baby wiping its eyes with its hands and for that reason names her Sita (Si-wiping, ta-one's eyes) and brings her up. Another longish Laotian Ramayana **Phra Lak Phra Lam**, which is an epic, and **The Ramakien,** which is the Thai Ramayana, say that Sita was Ravana's daughter.[26] The Cambodian Ramayana **Reamker** says that it was Indra's wife who was born as Ravana's daughter to take revenge on him.[27]

---

26   Kamala Ratnam, 'Socio-cultural and Anthropological Background of the Ramayana in Laos'. Op.cit p.236 and p.10.
27   F Bizot, 'The Reamker', op.cit, p.267.

In the Kashmiri language, Ramayana texts appeared only in the mid-nineteenth century. Even so, the Ramayana stories have been in vogue in folktales and songs for a very long time. The Ramayana has remained a narrative intimately connected to the people in the Kashmir region. As a result, words associated with Ramayana but invested with new meanings are in usage. For eg., the term Ramayana in Kashmiri language connotes 'a long tale narrating untold sufferings' while the term 'Ravan' besides referring to the character is also used as a verb meaning 'be doomed'. The very mention of the phrase 'Ramayana katha' brings the widely prevalent feeling among illiterate people that it is something which someone listens to unwillingly:

> All through the night I explained to you in detail the story of Ramayana. But when dawn breaks you ask me what is the relation of Sita to Rama.

The first Ramayana to appear in Kashmiri language (1843 AD), **Sankara Ramayana** (Kaandam 1, Adhyaya 6) says that since it was predicted by astrologers that Sita was sure to bring in evil consequences, she was buried in the town of Mithila during a famine and sighted by Janaka while ploughing the field. The highly acclaimed **Prakash Ramayana**, which came up following Sankara Ramayana (1846 AD), says that Ravana's daughter was placed in a casket and was thrown into the river and that when the casket reached the banks, a washerman chanced upon it and handed it over to Janaka. The other Kashmiri Ramayana texts like **Vishnu Pratap Ramayana** also say that Sita was born as daughter to Ravana.[28]

---

28   PN Pushp, 'Ramayana in Kashmiri Literature and Folklore', *The Ramayana Tradition in Asia*, p. 535.

Tulsi Ramayan presents Sita as an incarnation of *Maya* (creative power) and power of *Brahman* (the Absolute). Adhyatma Ramayana, Odisha Ramayana,[29] Gujarati Ramayana, all these texts present Sita as the incarnation of Goddess Lakshmi or power of Brahman, following Tulsi Ramayan.

Janaka's Foster Daughter

As far as the incidents of Ramakatha are concerned, all the Ramayana texts in vogue in India uniformly hold the view that Sita is the foster daughter of Janaka.

Moreover, they are also one in saying that while Janaka was ploughing the land designated for performing a yagnam, he found her in front of the coulter end of the plough.

While the Tibetan Ramayana says that an Indian farmer found the baby in the sea and brought her up, the Thai, Laotian and Cambodian Ramayana texts say that Sage Kasappa, living in Jambu Dwipa, found the baby, named her Sita and brought her up.

Incarnational Birth

Vanmikam, Vishnu Purana, Kamba Ramayanam and such other texts say that Sita is one who is not born of a womb *(ayonija)*. Accepting this idea, some Ramayana texts say that Sita's is an incarnational birth. It is Bhagavatam which for the first time states that Sita is an incarnation of Goddess Lakshmi. Tulsi Ramayan talks of Sita in two ways: as an incarnation of the power of Maya and as an incarnation of the power of Brahmam. The Assamese, Odisha and Gujarati Ramayanas too

---

29 Ambaprasad Suman, pp.114-119.

have depicted Sita as the incarnation of Goddess Lakshmi or the incarnation of *Shakti* (Goddess of power).

The Jain texts such as Pauma Chariyam, Vasudeva Hindi and Uttara Purana do not refer to Sita as an incarnation.

Dasaratha's Daughter

In some texts, it is also said that Sita is Dasaratha's daughter. To the first royal consort of Dasaratha were born three children, Rama, Lakshmana and Sita. After that queen died, Bharata was born to the newly-crowned queen, says Dasaratha Jataka. That Sita is Dasaratha's child is mentioned in the Javanese Ramayana *Ram Keling*, as well as the Malaysian Ramayanas (Hikayat Seri Rama and Hikayat Maharaja Ravan).

This statement is not found in other texts. Scholars like Professor Weber consider the Jataka tale as the source for these. But refuting this, Camille Bulcke holds that these versions were all created by the writers' imagination and are only slight variations of Valmiki's tale of Vedavati (pp.374-375).

The Ramayana Culture

Scholars have shown that after Ashoka conquered Kalinga, the people of the Odisha country who migrated to Burma, Thailand and such regions, carried with them, for the first time, Valmiki Ramayana; and that after seventh century AD, when Hindu kingdoms were established in those areas, the other Ramayana texts and Puranas too migrated there; and that during the medieval age, texts like Kamba Ramayanam and Tulsi Ramayan too spread to these countries.

As a result of this, we know that those countries which adopted Buddhism as their religion, interwove the Hindu and Buddhist religious thoughts in their creation, when they composed the Ramayana story in their languages. It is on this basis that all the South Asian Ramayana texts have created their respective Ramayana works.

Despite accepting the idea of Sita being a human child of Mandodari, they also add the doctrine of rebirth saying that she was born as Ravana's daughter to wreak vengeance on him for harming a woman in his earlier birth, disguised as Indra and someone else.

Ramakien, Reamker, Phra Lak Phra Lam, Gvay Dvorabhi and the Kashmiri Ramayanas, all of them are seen to have absorbed the doctrines of the two religions as shown above.

The South Asian countries follow Buddhist and other religious doctrines in consonance with their religious ethos. Even so, they have kept Ramayana and the Mahabharata as the basis of their tradition and literary culture; the above mentioned Ramayana texts make this sociological truth about life crystal clear.

Sita's Wedding

The Victor's Reward

All the Ramayana texts known to us so far, both Indian and foreign, say with one voice that Rama wedded Sita as a prize (*Virya Sulkam*) for bending the bow.

As Sita is sweeping (the floor) in order to tidy up the house, she lifts the gigantic bow kept there with her left hand, cleans that spot and places the bow back. Observing this, Janaka is completely surprised and concludes that 'She is undoubtedly the incarnation of Shakti (goddess of power). She will become the wife only of the man who lifts up the bow and bends it.' So says a folk song in **Braj bhasha**.

A **Pulanthashakar** folk song says, as Rama approaches the bow in the bow-bending event, Sita prays to Parvathi to reduce the weight of the bow.[30]

Ravana at the Bow Festival

Vanmikam and several other Ramayana texts, in general, say that Janaka invited all the kings to the bow-bending event. Tulsi Ramayan and the Burmese Ramayana Rama Vatthu, besides Krittibasi Ramayana and the Malaysian texts also say that Ravana and Banasura too had come there for the *swayamvaram*. While Tulsi Ramayan says that the two of them could not even move the bow, Rama Vatthu states that Ravana alone lifted the bow but could not string it. Scholars consider that the Sanskrit dramatic works *Prasanna Raghavam* and *Bala Ramayanam* stand as the source for Tulsidas's claim.[31]

Sita in the Swayamvaram Hall

Texts like Vanmikam and Kamba Ramayanam say that the news of Rama breaking the bow is sent to Sita through her female companions. Tulsi, on the other hand, says that Sita was very much present in the *Swayamvaram* hall, praying within herself for the weight of the bow to be lessened in order to make it easier for Rama to handle, and that as soon as Rama broke the bow, she adorned his neck with the garland of victory. What Valmiki, Kamban and others show as Virya Sulkam (reward for valour), Tulsidas chose to depict as a swayamvaram.

---

30 Omkar Kaul, pp. 13-14 (Hindi Footnote).
31 Shankar Raj Naidu, pp. 133-134, Rev. Camille Bulcke, 'Rama Charitamanasa and its Relevance to Modern Age'. *The Ramayana Tradition in Asia*, p.63.

Scene of Clandestine meeting of Rama and Sita

In Vanmikam, Rama meets Sita only after breaking the bow and then marries her. Bhavabhuti's Sanskrit play *Mahaviracharita* (eighth century AD) is the work which, for the first time, mentions the meeting of Rama and Sita. Kamban (tenth century AD), following the Tamil tradition of *Aham* poetry (poetry of the subjective sphere), mentions that Rama and Sita see each other and fall in love even before the breaking of the bow. Prasanna Raghavam (twelfth century AD) and *Mythili Kalyanam*, a play composed in 1290 AD, too narrate in detail the scenes of the tryst of Rama and Sita.

'Mother, if I tell you, you will be cross with me. You may even drive me out of the house. I met Rama in our garden. He gathered me in his arms and embraced me.' At once her mother said, 'Daughter dear, I shall not be angry with you. I shall not scold you; nor will I send you out of the house. Rama is the most suitable husband for you. We shall marry you to him alone', so saying she embraced her daughter affectionately. A folk wedding song in the **Mythili language** narrates this.[32]

The Tamil Bow-song Sita Kalyanam too elaborates the clandestine meeting according to the Tamil tradition. In the North Indian village songs too, there are scenes of Rama and Sita conversing with each other. However, such conversations do not find a place in the written texts of Ramayana works. Some folk songs say, Rama and Sita met each other, loved and married while some others say that their parents arranged the marriage.

Tulsidas sings in great detail of the meeting of Rama and Sita. Some scholars are of the view that Tulsidas, who for the most part walks in the footsteps of Adhyatma Ramayana,

---

32 Vidya Nivas Mishra, 103.

Assamese Ramayana and Odisha Ramayana and such texts, has but followed Kamban in constructing this clandestine meeting.[33] Scholars generally consider that from as early as eighth century AD, the incident of the clandestine meeting of Rama and Sita is found in the Ramayana works[34].

Now, the Ramayana scholar, Camille Bulcke, holds that the Sanskrit plays on Rama such as Mahavir Charitam and Prasanna Raghavam are the reason for Tulsidas's depiction.[35] Be that as it may, there is scope for surmising that since the Sanskrit plays, folk songs and Kamban's epic had appeared before Tulsidas's creation, one of them or perhaps more than one of them, must have been a model for Tulsi.

The Ramayana texts of Thailand and Laos and such countries have also depicted the meeting of Rama and Sita. These two were works which came up in the eighteenth century AD. Much before Tulsi, many a folk song in Mythili, Braj and Hindi had sung of this scene.

Some folk songs which have incorporated Rama's story are constructed in the manner of highlighting the travails experienced by parents who have begotten female children:

One day, Dasaratha who comes to Mithila, meets Janaka and enquires about his welfare. To which Janaka replies ruefully, 'I who have begotten four girls, am worrying, to whose household I should send which girl as a daughter-in-law. When such is my plight you want to know the welfare of my state?' Dasaratha responds saying, 'I have four sons. Why don't you happily give your four daughters to those four?'

---

33   Shankar Raju Naidu, pp. 133-134.
34   Kamala Ratnam, p.240.
35   Camille Bulcke, p.63.

Janaka, who hears this, says in sheer frustration, 'There is neither salt nor oil in the house. No grains in the granary either. No containers, no vessels. How can one hope to conduct the marriage joyfully?' Dasaratha responds saying, 'I shall provide you with salt. I shall supply oil too. I shall fill your granary with grains to the brim. You please give Sita in marriage with a joyful heart. We will take her to Ayodhya with great happiness'.[36] Thus he cheers up Janaka.

The Challenge of Parasurama

According to the Southern Recension of Vanmikam, Parasurama stood, holding the bow of Vishnu, in great rage. The ascetic sages who accompanied Dasaratha, welcomed Parasurama with smiling faces uttering 'Rama, Rama'. Much pleased with the welcoming of the sages, Parasurama turned to Dasaratha Rama and uttered the following (I,74:26,27):

> Oh Rama! Son of Dasaratha! I heard about your stupendous prowess. I too heard the sound of the breaking of the bow. Your valour in breaking the bow is astonishing. On hearing that, I have brought yet another mighty bow. Come and string this dreaded bow and fix the arrow and show your prowess and make me witness it with my own eyes. Or else, throw down the bow saying, 'I deem myself as the one defeated out of fear'. Or else you fight with me (1.75: I, 2,3,5).

Dasaratha, who listened to this, became frightened. Folding his hands in veneration, he addressed Parasurama:

---

36   Rajarani Varma, *Hamare Samskar Geet*, pp. 163-165, quoted in Omkar Kaul, p.14. (Hindi footnote).

You who had given up your animosity against royal clans, you who refrained from putting on the armour, you who stand by the codes of righteousness, you have now come again to wipe me out completely. For, after Rama dies, none of us will survive.

Ignoring the words spoken by Dasaratha, Parasurama looked at Dasaratha Rama and narrated in great detail the history of the two bows – the bow of Siva which Rama broke at Mithila and the bow of Vishnu which he was himself holding then in his hand – and said to him,

> If you are man enough, you may bend this bow of Vishnu and fix the arrow. We can then fight with each other (1.75: 12-13).

Listening to Parasurama's words of audacity, Dasaratha Rama replied in humble words befitting his father's dignity:

> 'Oh! Brahmana, born of the Bhrigu dynasty! I have heard about the acts you have performed for the sake of your father. You have humiliated and dismissed me as one lacking in virility and one without any ability. You may now witness, Sir, in person, the power of my shoulders befitting the Kshatriya clan (royal clan).' So saying, he, enraged, took the bow from Parasurama's hands into his own with absolutely no effort and stringing it he looked at Parasurama and said: 'Oh Parasurama! I have no desire to kill you who are a Brahmana and a close relation of my revered guru Viswamitra; however, this arrow of Vishnu will not return without hitting the target, being meant for destroying that power which is used for evil designs; therefore you may yourself mention the fit target for it' (76:1-8).

Witnessing Rama's valour with his own eyes and listening to what he said with his own ears, Parasurama spoke thus:

'Dasaratha Rama, please listen to what I have to say and grace me. I have gifted away the country which belonged to me to Sage Kasyapa. Now all that I have left is the ability to go to the worlds I wish to and the many worlds I have seized by the power of my penance. Among these, you may please grace me by keeping the last-mentioned as the target; let me go to Mount Mahendra and perform penance. When I see this act of valour you have performed, I am able to recognise you as Lord Vishnu.' Thus he praised and blessed him. At once when Rama dispatched the arrow and obtained the target, Parasurama set out for the Mahendra Mountains (I.76:13- 19, 23- 24).

The Northern Recension of Vanmikam also more or less says the same thing regarding the challenge of Parasurama in sargas 73, 74 and 75.[37]

The **Buddhist** and **Jain Ramayana** texts leave out the episode of the challenge of Parasurama. Therefore, the Kannada Pampa Ramayanam too does not sing of this episode.

In great fury, Parasurama intercepts Dasaratha and the others who are returning to Ayodhya along with Rama and Lakshmana and the retinue, after the wedding with Sita is over.

At that time when Dasaratha pays obeisance to him and attends to him with due honour, Parasurama, with unabated fury, turns to Rama and says, 'I am aware of the power of the bow you broke. I am desirous of knowing the power of your shoulders. This is the reason for my arrival'.

---

37 It is not clear on what basis Padmanabhan Thampi claims that the episode of Parasurama getting vanquished by Rama is not mentioned either in Valmiki Ramayana or in the Sanskrit Adhyatma Ramayana (*Ramayanas of Kampan and Eluttacchan*, Trivandrum, 1996, p.31).

Dasaratha, very much frightened, politely pleads with him: 'It is righteous to fight with someone who is your match; is it right for you who conquered the world to attempt to fight with lads who are so young? If my innocent son Rama's life is lost, we shall all perish as a whole clan. Therefore I pray, bless that my dynasty may live.'

Paying no attention to Dasaratha's words, Parasurama looked at Rama and narrating in great detail the history of the bow of Siva which Rama broke and the glory of the bow of Vishnu which was in his hand, he said, 'Don't you be so vain as to regard the breaking of a disabled bow as a great feat of valour. Moreover, I have a long-standing enmity with your clan. I heard the sound of your breaking the bow and came in rage. If you are truly powerful, you may take my bow and bend it'.

Rama smiled gently at Parasurama who claimed that he had come in rage, and requested with a face brimming with joy, 'Please do give me the victorious bow of Vishnu'. He took it and bent it effortlessly and strung it. He then turned to Parasurama and asked, 'You are one who has killed many a king in this world; and yet you are the son of a Brahmana sage who was the very embodiment of the Vedas; hence it is not ethical to kill you; however this arrow which has been strung will not rest without hitting a target; what is the target?'

Parasurama, with his rage abated, said: 'I have realised that you are Lord Vishnu who has come down to uphold justice. Whether it is the bow of Siva or for that matter the bow of yours which I gave you, would it make any difference to you? Therefore, take all the tapas (penance) I have done as the target and complete the purpose for which you have come and save the world.' So saying, he paid obeisance to Rama and took leave of him, says **Kamba Ramayanam**.

While returning from Mithila to Ayodhya, Rama encounters Parasurama who is rage incarnate and pays his respects to him. At once Parasurama snarls at him, 'Just because you are paying your respects to me, do you hope that I will spare you?' To which Rama replies politely, 'It was not out of fear that I paid my respects to you. I did so out of regard'. When Parasurama retorts, 'Just because you bear my name "Rama", don't feel relaxed thinking that I will not kill you', Dasaratha intervenes and says, 'He is a young boy. Does it become you, who are a Brahmana and a sage, to fight with him and vent your anger on him? Let me in his place fight with you', and comes forward.

Parasurama answers saying, 'I shall fight only with the one who broke the bow of Siva', and looks at Rama and challenges him, 'Can you bend my bow and string it?' Accepting the challenge of Parasurama, Rama, his face seething with fury, takes Parasurama's bow and succeeds in stringing it. Realising that Rama is none but the incarnation of Lord Vishnu, Parasurama praises him, blesses him too and takes leave of him. Thus, the Telugu **Ranganatha Ramayanam** expounds the encounter of Parasurama and Rama, of Rama chiding Parasurama and subsequently conquering him. Says Ranganatha Ramayanam:

> You don't know who I am or the power of my shoulders.
> I know you and your adeptness with your bow.
> He asked his bow to be brought and
> Turning his head he held the topmost part of the bow and
> Stood angrily.
>
> (Bala Kaandam p.74)

Bhaskara Ramayanam too narrates this incident more or less along the same lines. That Rama in great wrath, as if it were the time of deluge, strung Parasurama's bow is denoted by the phrase *pralaya darogram kopamuna*.

Molla Ramayanam says that, looking at Parasurama, who without any provocation challenged Rama for a battle, Rama said, 'It is unbecoming of Kshatriyas (the royal caste) to fight with you, a Brahmana, who is well-versed in the sastras; will it behove me to fight with such a wise and great soul like you?' To which replied Parasurama: 'I am not just schooled in sastras, I am trained in archery too. When you say, "Rama", it is only me. When I am there how can there be another Rama? Don't feel intoxicated with pride, for having broken a worthless bow. Look, try to break the bow in my hand and then we shall see.' Thus spoke Parasurama, his overweening pride going to his head. Without responding in word, Rama quietly took the bow and strung it, says Molla Ramayanam (Bala.83-96).

Malayala Ezhuthachan's Ramayanam narrates the challenge of Parasurama, following the footsteps of Kamba Ramayanam.[38]

According to **Torave Ramayanam**, Dasaratha's forces trembled in fright looking at Parasurama arriving in great wrath. Rama confronted him angrily and asked, 'Why do you hate the Kshatriyas? Why do you oppose them?' He goes on to say, 'It is proper for Kshatriyas to fight; to perform sacrificial rituals and such acts is proper for Brahmanas. If you had fought against some kings and defeated them, they were all weaklings. Your valour will not hold water with me. You will do well to retreat without trying to pick up a fight in vain.' He advises him thus: 'Should you desire to fight a battle, you may engage in a debate with the best men in intellectual fields such as Vyakarana. You are unfit to fight in a battle which involves handling arrows in a professional manner. You are not my equal.'

---

38 Padmanabhan Thampi, *Ramayanas of Kampan and Ezhuttachan* p.31.

Outraged, Parasurama challenged him by saying, 'Let us see what happens when a pond rises to fight an ocean even as we shall see what your plight will be when I fight with you', and flung his axe at Rama. The celestials and others shuddered in fright to see that axe soaring, emitting flames of fire. 'Our line is finished with this', rued Dasaratha and wailed. Rama pacified him saying, 'Fear not', and dispatched an arrow to counter the axe. Parasurama, who again became incensed, got ready to unleash an arrow from his dreaded bow of Vishnu by stringing it. Everyone, including Dasaratha, stood in sheer fright. Smiling to himself Rama got off the chariot and pounced on Parasurama and grabbed that bow.

'It is not proper for us to torment Brahmanas. You deserve to be worshipped by us. Hereafter, it will be better for you to refrain from activities like battles but instead be engaged in penance and such other acts as befit you and lead a peaceful life; kindly go away from this place', Rama uttered these gentle words with a kind face. Parasurama thought, 'The mere sound of my bow would be enough to abort the pregnancy of queens; there are no kings who have fought with me and won'. Feeling happy after realising that this situation had changed on account of Rama, Parasurama decided that his incarnation had come to an end and the incarnation of Rama had begun. He embraced Rama and gave him all the arrows in his quiver and started walking towards his ascetic abode (I,17:3-19).

In **Bhusundi Ramayana** and **Tulsi Ramayan**, the challenge of Parasurama takes place in the swayamvaram hall itself. As soon as Rama breaks the bow, the kings who have assembled there, all band together and oppose Rama and Lakshmana, fight with them and try to abduct Sita. Just then, roaring like thunder, Parasurama appears there in a fierce rage. The moment they see Parasurama, all the kings stand shivering in their shoes. Janaka pays his respects to Parasurama and makes Sita too pay her respects to him. Viswamitra introduces Rama and Lakshmana to him and directs them to pay their respects to him. They too humbly prostrate before Parasurama and rise.

Somewhat pacified by all these prostrations, Parasurama turns to Janaka, and noticing also the broken pieces of the bow lying scattered there, asks angrily, 'Who was it that broke this bow?' Lakshmana came forward and said, 'This is a very old rotten, moth-eaten bow. The moment Rama touched it, it broke. Why are you so incensed by this?' At once, his wrath redoubled, Parasurama bellowed: 'Oh! Lad! You speak without knowing me or my greatness. Take a look at this axe. This is a weapon which has slain the thousand-shouldered Karthaviryan.'

Hearing these words, Lakshmana broke into laughter and replied, 'Only now I hear that Brahmanas wield weapons too. Leave it at that. We don't oppose gods, Brahmanas, cows and the devotees of Lord Vishnu. We won't fight with them. That would be beneath our dignity'. Parasurama turned to Viswamitra and snarled, 'Oh sage! Keep this brat under check. Or else he will be despatched to the world of *Yama* (realm of Death) right away'. Rama, restraining Lakshmana who was repeatedly trying to provoke Parasurama and ridicule him, looked at Parasurama and politely said, 'Being a Brahmana, it is not proper for you to get roused into such a rage'. Even so, Parasurama kept dilating on his feats of valour, stacking them one upon the other and said in fury, 'You who broke the bow too will not be spared by me'.

Then Rama said, 'Sir, I tried my best to exhort you, yet you did not pay heed to my words. All right, let us now act as you desire'. Parasurama showed his bow and said, 'If you bend this and string it I shall recognise you for what you are'. Before Parasurama could even finish, the bow on its own accord moved towards Rama and took refuge in his hands. Parasurama, who witnessed this, realised that Rama was none other than the incarnation of Lord Vishnu and paid his respects to him, and blessing him went on his way to perform penance. All the kings who were watching these happenings were trembling with fear and quietly slipped away one by one (268-284), says **Tulsi Ramayan**.

Sloka Variations in Bala Kaandams

According to the critical edition of the Northern Recension, Valmiki Ramayana's Bala Kaandam contains 2,001 slokas (verses) in 76 sargas; while according to the Gorakhpur edition of the Southern Recension, it contains 2,269 slokas in 77 sargas, and according to the Dharmalaya or Bombay edition of the Southern Recension, it appears as containing 2,355 slokas in 77 sargas (see Table).

In all the Recensions, the first four sargas are structured in the form of the book's prologue or preface. They give the following information: Valmiki meets Narada and comes to know of Rama's story. Brahma blesses Valmiki's attempt at composing Ramayana. Valmiki sits in meditation and has a vision of the entire Ramayana story through the inner eye and finishes composing the epic.

Rama, who listens to both Lava and Kusa sweetly singing that epic story, asks them to go over to his court and sing it and they begin to sing and so on. While, on the one hand, there is the prevailing view that Bala Kaandam itself is a later addition, there is no doubt that in Bala Kaandam as it exists today, the aforesaid four sargas have been added much later.

In the portion starting from the fifth sarga till the seventy-sixth or seventy-seventh sarga, the Bala Kaandam events are narrated. In this part alone, roughly about 300 slokas are found in excess in the Southern Recension of Vanmikam as compared to the Northern Recension.

Table 3
Valmiki Ramayana
BALA KAANDAMS

Sarga	Sloka			Sarga	Sloka		
	Critical edition	Gorakhpur edition	Dharmalaya edition		Critical edition	Gorakhpur edition	Dharmalaya edition
1.	79	100	100	26.	25	36	41
2.	41	43	44	27.	18	28	27
3.	29	39	40	28.	20	22	24
4.	27	36	36	29.	23	32	54
5.	23	23	24	30.	23	26	26
6.	24	28	28	31.	22	24	24
7.	17	24	23	32.	26	26	27
8.	23	24	24	33.	20	26	26
9.	32	20	19	34	21	23	26
10.	29	33	32	35	26	23	23
11.	21	31	30	36	31	27	28
12.	34	22	21	37.	24	32	34
13.	46	41	37	38.	26	24	24
14.	21	60	60	39.	28	26	29
15.	28	34	35	40.	26	30	30
16.	20	32	34	41.	24	26	28
17.	39	37	37	42.	24	25	25
18.	20	59	58	43.	20	41	43
19.	25	22	23	44.	27	23	22
20.	19	28	28	45.	22	45	57
21.	19	22	22	46.	22	23	23
22.	19	24	23	47.	32	22	22
23.	30	22	23	48.	22	33	36
24.	19	32	32	49	25	22	24
25.	22	22	24	50.	28	25	28

Sarga	Sloka			Sarga	Sloka		
	Critical edition	Gorakhpur edition	Dharmalaya edition		Critical edition	Gorakhpur edition	Dharmalaya edition
51.	23	28	28	65.	27	40	39
52.	24	23	23	66.	27	26	27
53.	23	25	25	67.	19	27	26
54.	28	23	23	68.	18	19	22
55.	24	28	28	69.	32	19	20
56.	20	24	24	70.	24	45	45
57.	23	22	23	71.	24	24	24
58.	23	24	24	72.	27	25	25
59.	33	22	22	73.	22	40	45
60.	22	34	35	74.	28	24	27
61.	27	24	23	75.	23	28	33
62.	26	28	28	76.	18	24	26
63.	15	26	26	77.	-	29	38
64.	30	20	20		2001	2269	2355
					2001	+268	+354

Bala Kaandams Total Sargas and Slokas

	Sargas	Slokas
Northern Recension – Critical edition	76	2,001
Southern Recension – Gorakhpur edition	77	2,269
Southern Recension – Dharmalaya edition	77	2,355

AYODHYA KAANDAM

Preliminary Remarks on the chapter Ayodhya Kaandam
Dasaratha's Wish and its Consequences
- Realising onset of age
- Dasaratha's dream and the planetary positions
- Dasaratha's wish to lead the life of a renunciant
- Dasaratha's decision and the endorsement of the court
- Invitation to other kings
- Announcing to the Queens
- Advice to Rama

Corruption of Kaikeyi's Mind by Manthara
- Who was Manthara?
- Manthara's hostility
- Manthara's scheming
- Was Kaikeyi the youngest? Or the middle one?
- Kaikeyi's noble traits
- The circumstances of Kaikeyi obtaining the boons

The Story of Dasaratha getting Cursed
- The circumstances of the incident
- Japanese Ramayana and the story of the curse

Dasaratha's Order and Rama's Acceptance
- Rama's state of mind when he heard of the coronation
- Kaikeyi's command and Rama's state of mind
- Sita's resolve to go to the forest with Rama
- Rama agreeing to let Lakshmana accompany him
- Sumitra's counsel
- Some variations in the accounts of the exile in the forest
- The meeting of Rama and Guha

Bharata's Refusal to Ascend the Throne
- The meeting of Bharata and Guha
- The meeting of Bharata and Rama
- Controversies regarding Rajya Sulkam

Content Variations in Ayodhya Kaandams

Sloka variations in the Ayodhya Kaandams

Ayodhya Kaandam

Preliminary Remarks on Ayodhya Kaandam

IN BALA KAANDAM, the first canto of Rama's story, details of the hero's birth, growth, conduct, marriage and valour were lucidly told. In the prefatory portion of Bala Kaandam we had a literary rendering of the essential traits and virtues that go towards making the protagonist a highly-evolved being, an upholder of dharma and an epic hero.

Ayodhya Kaandam includes incidents which put on trial the principles of conduct that enhance the hero's ethical values. That is, we see the manner in which the incidents in Ayodhya Kaandam form the first turn of events in the flow of the narrative of Rama's story.

From the perspective of literary aesthetics, the incidents of Ayodhya Kaandam form the prelude to Rama's story. If the epic were to be dramatised, Ayodhya Kaandam will be the starting point, going by the tenets of poetics. This claim is applicable equally to tragedy and comedy. Since drama begins with complication of the plot and ends with either the complication of the problem or resolution of the complication, this canto represents the beginning of the complication in the epic.

If the incidents of this canto are an indication of the hero's development of an absolute personality, then they can be seen as constituting the prelude to the whole epic in terms of its structure and treatment.

Thus, the incidents of the Ayodhya Kaandam can be viewed as the indispensable stage in the development of the nucleus of the story in accordance with the features of an epic as well as of drama. These incidents and the characters who caused them to happen can be comprehended by dividing them into three categories, viz. Dasaratha's wish and its consequences, Dasaratha's order and Rama's acceptance of it, and Bharata's refusal to ascend the throne.

The point to note here is that the incidents of Ayodhya Kaandam comprise a tripartite division: (i) the political decision which Dasaratha takes and the resultant complications, (ii) Rama's manner of accepting the decision and the temporary resolution of the complication, and (iii) the manner in which Bharata accepted Rama's decision and the final resolution of the political complication.

Certain causal factors and consequences of action form the nucleus of each of these three parts. They can be studied by analysing the nucleus of these episodes and the actions of the secondary characters involved in them. The manner in which Valmiki and other Ramayana texts have given a literary rendering can now be viewed from a chronological perspective.

Valmiki and other Ramayana texts describe the incidents of Rama's story, some from a human perspective, some from the superhuman and certain others from both. These texts, through several devices, reveal how the human characters too are responsible for the complications and their resolutions. These issues are unravelled in this study by relating them to the respective incidents.

Dasaratha's Wish and its Consequences

Dasaratha's decision to crown Rama forms the first important incident in the narrative of Ayodhya Kaandam. Three reasons – the onset of old age, the planetary positions and desire for renunciation – are cited for Dasaratha's decision to anoint Rama as Crown Prince.

Realising Onset of Age

Majority of the Ramayana texts, including Valmiki's, state that Dasaratha realised that he was ageing and spoke about it to his courtiers. Telugu Ramayanas such as Bhaskara Ramayanam and Molla Ramayanam do not mention this, but state that, having attained contentment after ruling for a long period, Dasaratha wished to crown Rama.

Raghuvamsa states that Dasaratha realised the onset of old age by noticing the grey hairs appearing near his ears.

The same view is presented by Tulsi Ramayan. Scholars consider that Tulsidas must have followed Kalidasa and said so.[1]

---

1 Anjani Nandan Sharan, ed. *Manasa Piyush Ayodhya Kaand* (Gorakhpur: Gita Press, 4th edition-1967) p.27 (Hindi footnote).

Two verses are found in some editions of Kamba Ramayanam which refer to Dasaratha's realisation of his approaching old age by the appearance of a streak of grey hair near his ears.[2] The text brought out by the Annamalai University editorial committee and the UV (Uttamadhanapuram Venkatasubbaiyer) Swaminatha Iyer Library edition point out that the scholars who had read Raghuvamsa might have composed these verses about the appearance of grey hair, inserting them in tune with Kamban's views.[3] Citing the reason that the Kamba Ramayanam edited by Venkatachala Mudaliar in 1840 AD does not contain these verses, the above-mentioned editions hold that these are interpolations. The Kamban Kazhagam edition also presents them as superadded verses. But the Vai Mu Go edition has published the text retaining these verses within the work without any note.

We can make a serious study of the claims of the three poets regarding the indication of the onset of old age by the appearance of grey hairs (if we accept the verses to have been composed by Kamban). The three poets do not simply state that the grey hairs appeared, but have added their own imaginative accounts by employing the poetical device of superimposition.

---

2   1. Mannane avaniyai maganuukku eendhu nee
     Pannarum thavampuri paruvam eedhena
     Kanna moolathinil kazhara vandhena
     Minenak karumaipoi veluthathu oarmayir.
     2. Theengu izhai iraavanan seydha theemai thaan
     Aangu oru naraiyadhay anugitru aam yena
     Paangil vandhidu narai padimakk kannaadi
     Aangadhil kandanan avani kaavalan.

3   a) *Kamban Iyatriya Ramayanam:Ayodhya Kaandam* (First Part)
     Annamalai Nagar: Annamalai University, 1959, p.7.
     b) *Srimad Kambaramayanam: Ayodhya Kaandam* (First Part), Chennai:
     Dr U Ve Sa Library, 1972, p.4.

Old age that set in, wanted to convey a message to Dasaratha, but was afraid that it might reach Kaikeyi. Hence it took the form of grey hairs and whispered into his ears, 'Oh King, hand over the reign to Rama'. Thus goes the imagination of Kalidasa.

The grey hairs that appeared near his ears, seem to exhort him, 'Oh King, the time has come for you to do penance after handing over the kingdom to your son', says Kamban, adding that the King looked at the strand of grey hair near his ears in the mirror and it seemed that all the evil deeds done by Ravana together took the form of grey hairs.

Tulsidas says that old age wanted to give a piece of advice to the King and so it appeared as grey hairs near his ears, urging him thus: 'Oh King, obtain the fruit of this birth by crowning Rama at the earliest.'

Of these three, Kalidasa's imagination has political overtones. The apprehension that Kaikeyi might create obstacles to the King's wishes is conveyed by the poet's choice of diction revealed in the term *shankayeva* (as if out of apprehension). There is a hint-within-the-hint, i.e. the poet very subtly suggests that Kaikeyi is likely to prevent Rama from being crowned.

One of the verses of Kamban appears to contain the motif of avatar. The poet says in the manner of superimposition that the evil deeds of Ravana became the cause for Dasaratha's decision.

Kamban has deliberately employed it as a device to associate Ravana with any opposition that confronts Rama. It is worth considering the reference to Tataka as Ravana's grandmother (VI.13:32) and marking the fall of Ravana's flag (1.7:52), symbolically, as an analogue to the fall of Tataka. Here too, the suggestion that the crowning of Rama might be impeded can be implicitly felt. However, Kamban does not seem to be interested in the question as to who will set the impediment and whether it is ethically valid. That is why it is maintained that this verse about the fall of Ravana contains the motif of incarnation.

There is another verse of Kamban in this context which shows a religious perspective: this presents the view that the grey hairs which appeared near Dasaratha's ears seemed to rebuke him for not handing over the kingdom to his son and proceeding to do penance when it was time for it. That is to say, this verse seems to emphasise that the king, having enjoyed the first three of the four objectives of life (purusharthas), should now seek that (the fourth) which would give him liberation by cutting off the cycle of birth.

Tulsidas states that the grey hairs seem to exhort Dasaratha to crown Rama and obtain the fruit of this birth. The poet does not explain how Dasaratha will obtain the fruit of his birth by crowning Rama. The idea that by giving something (the throne) to his son who is divinity incarnate, the King will obtain the fruit of his birth, can be viewed as an expression of *Prapanna bhakti* (total surrender to the Lord).

We must take it that the above-mentioned three poets, each attributed his own reasons for the appearance of grey hairs on Dasaratha's head in accordance with the world view of their times.

Kalidasa belongs to the period (fourth century AD) when notions of incarnation had not entered the literary sphere; therefore Kalidasa's poetry is marked by a politico-historical perspective. Kamban, who came after the Azhwars, named his epic as *Ramavataram* and expounded it with the motive of divine incarnation. The Bhakti movement aimed at experiencing the Divine; later it got enriched as the intellectual movement of the philosophical preceptors; in the end, it got diluted into a movement of congregational chanting and singing, and it was during this period that Tulsidas was born. Hence his conception doesn't have as its aim any historical, political, incarnational ideology or philosophy, but is a reflection of 'Prapanna bhakti'.

Dasaratha's Dream and the Planetary Positions

The Aadi Kavya or the primal epic, Vanmikam, states that Dasaratha was afraid of the portents of a dream he had, and fearing that the planetary position of his horoscope betokened his end, he wanted to crown Rama at the earliest.

The slokas in Valmiki Ramayana which refer to Dasaratha's planetary position are found in both (the Northern and Southern) Recensions (NR II.4:17-20, SR II. 4:17-20).

This idea is not found in the other Ramayana texts which recite the story of Rama.

Dasaratha's Wish to be a Renunciant

Vanmikam does not state that Dasaratha wanted to renounce the kingdom with the motive of attaining liberation. Kamba Ramayanam and Adhyatma Ramayana are the only two texts that put forth this view. Of the two, it is Kamba Ramayanam which talks about it in elaborate terms, in many a verse.

Dasaratha clearly expresses his wish while talking to Vasishta and other courtiers and then to Rama when he conveys his decision to him.

Adhyatma Ramayana just says: 'I wish to perform deeds of merit dear to my soul.' It does not mention going to the forest to do penance. Kamban's Dasaratha clearly expresses this wish:

> I will leave for the forest to perform a penance great
> That will annul the unending cycle of birth once and for all.

It is worth reflecting upon the fact that those Ramayana texts which hailed from the northern region, which is the home of the concept of the four states of human life beginning with bachelorhood, do not express this view. We may take it that Adhyatma Ramayana makes at least a reference to this view because of the spread of Kamba Ramayanam in the North along with other Vaishnavite texts due to the influence of the South. Amba Prasad's claim, that the impact of Ramanuja is noticeable in the entire text of Adhyatma Ramayana, reinforces this idea.[4]

As far as Kamban is concerned, it appears that the rules of poetics of *Tholkappiyam*, Valluvar's section on renunciation, Silappathikaram's portion on *Thaapathar Palli* (referring to the Jains' place of reclusion), and Chintamani's chapter *Mukti Ilambakam* (also dealing with renunciation) might have been the antecedents of this view.

> The couple who hitherto led a life of pleasure
> Must, when age takes over,
> refrain from indulging in ephemeral joys
> and seek that joy eternal and train the being to attain it
> even while living with one's near and dear ones.
> (Tholkappiyam. Porul Adhikaaram 190)

Bhusundi Ramayana says that Dasaratha goes on a pilgrimage with Kaikeyi after nominating Rama as heir to the throne.[5]

---

4   *Tulsi Kaavya-Chintana* p. 112. (Hindi footnote).
5   Bhagawati Prasad Singh, 'Bhusundi Ramayana,' *Ramayana Tradition in Asia*, p. 488.

Endorsement of the Court

All the Ramayana texts which have depicted the scene of deliberations in the court state that the courtiers praised and hailed the decision of Dasaratha. There are no variations to be found on this.

The Telugu Bhaskara Ramayanam alone marks a minor deviation here. That is, it shows that the people do not want Dasaratha to keep away completely from governance and they wish that he should make Rama the Crown Prince and together they should rule the kingdom. Kamban and other poets say that though the courtiers lament Dasaratha's renunciation of the throne, they forget their sorrow by rejoicing over Rama becoming the king.

The reason for this variation is that, in Vanmikam, Dasaratha takes the decision to make Rama just the Crown Prince (II. 2:12, 54; 3:2,4; 4:22). Tulsi Ramayan too presents the same view (II. 2.8; 4.2; 5:3).

However, epics such as Kamba Ramayanam and Adhyatma Ramayana state that Dasaratha decided to crown Rama the king. Dasaratha so resolved, citing old age as the reason for seeking retirement. Poets from Kamban onwards regarded that there was no difference in terms of power between the titles of King and Crown Prince; hence their works have perhaps projected it as a decision to make Rama the king.

Invitation to Other Kings

Dasaratha, who decided to crown Rama, did not send intimation to Janaka and the King of Kekeya, while sending it to other kings. That the coronation was to take place the very next day and that they who were far away would anyway not be able to make it, is the reason stated in Vanmikam.

Also, the thought that Bharata would not be present during the coronation did not strike Dasaratha. However, Vanmikam also mentions Dasaratha assuring Rama that Bharata, being a highly cultured man, would not take it amiss.

Kamba Ramayanam does not relate anything on this in elaborate terms. That intimation to other kings is conveyed by the orders of the King is alone stated there. The Dasaratha that Kamban presents does not say anything about Bharata's absence. On the whole **Kamban seems to maintain a studied silence over this knotty issue.**

Tulsidas too does not talk about intimation being sent to other kings. He states in general terms that the people of the city were very happy to know about Rama's coronation.

Making Rama the Crown Prince is no ordinary matter that can be ignored. Dasaratha ordered that such an important matter be intimated to other kings, but left out Janaka, father-in-law of Rama, the hero of the ceremony and his own father-in-law, the King of Kekeya and the father of his much-beloved Kaikeyi.

Citing distance as the sole reason for not inviting them does not carry conviction. Moreover, despite Bharata being the object of his love and trust, that Dasaratha could not fetch him as he was far away and hence would not be able to participate sounds unconvincing. Vanmikam shows that such a situation had arisen as the coronation had to take place on the very day notified by the astrologers. Dasaratha could have asked for another day to be fixed, considering the status and importance of those who had to attend. Even so, as a matter of fact, **the coronation did not take place on the day fixed by the astrologers**. Instead, as the epic shows, what transpired was Rama's going to the forest. This flaw in Dasaratha's character has come to stay.

It is not clear why Kamban left this knotty issue without unravelling it.

One wonders if Tulsidas deliberately overlooked it. The reason may be that, when Dasaratha asks Vasishta to fix the day for the coronation, the latter, without specifying any day, simply says, the day Rama chooses to go through the ceremony of coronation is the auspicious day. Therefore, it looks as though Tulsidas did not accept Valmiki's views on Dasaratha's action.

Prakash Ramayana, written in Kashmiri, states that intimation was sent to all the kings including Janaka and Kekeya. It even says that Dasaratha sent messages to fetch Bharata and Shatrughna. Here, the poet, it seems, has tried to shield Dasaratha from any blame falling on him, and yet this issue remains unsolved. That is, the epic does not state whether any of them did come to attend the coronation. When the derivative texts are not able to solve the issue found in the source text, what can the poor adapted texts do?

Announcing to the Queens

Kausalya and Sumitra are delighted to hear about Dasaratha's decision to crown Rama and they rush to offer prayers and celebrate. There is variation in the many Ramayanas on who – Rama's friends or the maids in the court or the general public – informed Kausalya and Sumitra of Dasaratha's decision. However all Ramayanas agree in stating that Kaikeyi comes to learn about the planned coronation only through Manthara. They are silent on the question why Kaikeyi was not told about it by the others.

The critic Anjani Nandan Sharan, who edited Tulsi's Ramcharitmanas under the title *Manasa Piyush* along with an elaborate commentary, has raised this question and tried to find an explanation for it. He gives two reasons why the general public had not informed Kaikeyi:

(1) Kaikeyi had great love for Rama. If this news had been conveyed to her, she would also have been elated and, like Sumitra, would have performed many an act of charity and gone to the temple to offer worship; if that had happened, the coronation would have gone off well; if it had gone off well, the objective of incarnation would not have been fulfilled. Therefore, the poet deliberately chose not to make the general public convey the news to Kaikeyi.

(2) However hard Dasaratha had hidden the news of bestowing *Rajya Sulkam* (the gift of the kingdom: *kanyasulkam*) on Kaikeyi at the time of their marriage, people in the palace, with infinite attachment as well as loving devotion to Rama, would not have been ignorant of it. Therefore, it is clear that they did not have faith in Kaikeyi as far as matters political were concerned, despite her great love for Rama. That was why they deliberately chose not to convey the news to Kaikeyi. Or else the fact that when even the women of the palace and the general public knew of the coronation, news of such importance did not reach Kaikeyi, Dasaratha's younger wife, the object of his special love, and that Manthara was the first one to break the news to her loses its credence.[6]

Omkar Kaul, another scholar, levels a charge against Tulsi that his Dasaratha, who had informed Kausalya and Sumitra of the proposed coronation, had refrained from telling Kaikeyi about it.[7] However, there is no such mention in Tulsi Ramayan (II.8). Not only Tulsi, none of the other poets too has shown Dasaratha as informing Kausalya and Sumitra about this matter. Therefore, Kaul's charge does not appear to be valid.

---

6   *Manasa Piyush, Ayodhya Kaand,* II . 8. 4., p. 55.
7   *Kashmiri aur Hindi Rama Katha Kavya ka Tulnatmak Adhyayan,* 73.155 (Hindi).

Advice to Rama

Of all the instructions imparted to Rama, the teaching of codes of political morality appears to be the most important. Only two texts, Vanmikam and Kamba Ramayanam, talk about this.

> Rama, you are naturally endowed with good qualities and good conduct. Yet I will impart to you a few guidelines which can bring good even to noblemen. Always remain as one who has conquered the five senses.
>
> Take care that the seven crimes[8] which are committed by kings due to lust and anger do not approach you. Always uphold without fail the social morals such as protecting those who seek refuge and helping the poor with compassion. Keep ministers and such others ever pleased by being accommodating.
>
> A king who governs the country well, by safeguarding treasuries, arsenals and the granaries, will be well respected by other kings. You should also try to be one such king.

Thus Vanmikam presents Dasaratha as giving counsel to Rama (II.3:42-46).

In Kamba Ramayanam, the instruction that Vasishta imparts is in a very elaborate format (II.2.14-19). Exhortations found in Vanmikam regarding control of the senses, shunning lust and gambling, accomodating the views of the ministers, maintaining friendly ties with other kings, protecting the people as one's own life, husbanding wealth and such other things are also found in Kamban. Although such ideas are found commonly in both the texts, the readers can easily sense

---

8   The seven kinds of crime are: coveting another man's wife, gambling, hunting in violation of rules, addiction to liquor, wasting time in the company of idlers, meting out punishment disproportionate to crime, and wasteful expenditure.

the poetic quality in Kamban bearing the unique stamp of the master poet hailed as the emperor among poets, enhancing the aesthetic delight of literature.

Now, there is one point worth pondering, not found in Vanmikam but presented in Kamban most emphatically i.e. out of the fifteen verses of instructions, four verses glorify the worship of Brahmanas. The Brahmanas referred to here are none but the ascetics; and yet Kamban singing the praise of the Brahmanas in such eulogising terms does not seem to be in the tradition of mere derivative texts.

When Valmiki himself does not extol in elaborate terms the influence of the sages in his times, it calls for reflection whether Kamban, who lived in a society wherein such sages were becoming rarer, was praising them or the Brahmana scholars.

Here are a couple of ancient Tamil verses:

> He (Selvak Kadungo, the Chola king) will pay his obeisance to
> None but the learned, righteous Brahmanas.
> (Pathitruppathu 63.1)

> Oh, Pandya king!
> To righteous rishis, learned in the four Vedas,
> Thou shall pay obeisance
> even before they raise their hand to bless you.
> (Purananuru 6.19.20)

Whether such an ancient Tamil tradition could have helped Kamban in this regard also deserves to be studied. That in Kamban it is Vasishta who imparts the instruction, and the obstacles that Kamban faced at the time of launching his epic as we come to know through hearsay, should also be reflected upon in this context.

Corruption of Kaikeyi's Mind
Who was Manthara?

No one knows the details relating to the place from where Manthara or her parents hailed. Since the original text only said that she worked as a maid in Kekeya's palace and then came to Ayodhya as Kaikeyi's companion, the derivative versions which came up later present all kinds of fictitious accounts about Manthara's birth and upbringing in consonance with the objective of the respective epics.

Texts such as Mahabharata, Padma Purana, Adhyatma Ramayana, Torave Ramayanam and *Govinda Ramayanam* refer to Manthara as an incarnation. It is a general view that incarnation signifies a different birth taken by a noble being to destroy evil. Here the question arises whether it is appropriate to call Manthara an incarnational being since her intrigue, halting Rama's coronation and driving him to the forest, culminates in great harm. However, since Rama's sojourn in the forest ends in the greater good of Ravana's destruction, it is not seriously wrong to consider Manthara as an incarnational being. So, it may be said that there was scope for such a confusion of views to arise due to the mix-up of human and superhuman perspectives.

One wonders if Kamban indulges in superimposition of his own view when he, the emperor of poets, does not show Manthara as an incarnational being but says that Ravana's evil embodied itself in the cruel-hearted *Kooni* (hunchback).

It was virtually an impossible task to vitiate the heart of the noble-minded Kaikeyi, corrupt her thinking to such an extent as to cause the death of her husband, and make her most-beloved Rama give up the throne and go to the forest. We may consider Manthara as one who achieved the rarest of rare feats, by way of a paradox, when later, despite the efforts of many, none could change Kaikeyi's mind again. We may here recall that to bestow superhuman qualities upon those who accomplish impossible deeds which could not be managed by others and to elevate such persons (even if the details of their place, name and birth were known) from the level of a common human to a superhuman one, after attributing to them superhuman qualities, is a feature of medieval culture found in many a work of world literature.

Manthara's Hostility

If Ayodhya Kaandam forms a turning point in the development of the theme of Rama's story, it is clear that the one who was instrumental in making it happen is Manthara, known as Kooni. If we put together the reasons given by the Ramayana texts for Kooni nurturing a grudge against Rama, four kinds of reasons emerge. They are:

- Manthara's natural character traits.
- The childish pranks played by Rama upon Kooni when he was a little boy.
- Acting against Rama after her mind was corrupted by the instigation of the celestials.
- Acting against Rama motivated by sexual attraction for Bharata.

Of these, Vanmikam, the primal epic, points specifically to the first reason. The epithets *Papadarshini* (evil-eyed), *Vakya Visharada* (clever-tongued) and the suggestion that she was an expert at intrigue and had a crocodile-like disposition, reveal to us that her human nature itself lacked graciousness and was prone to causing harm to others. It is inferred that Manthara was someone who by nature would prevent anything which according to her went against the interests of her lady Kaikeyi. Valmiki seems to hold the view that it was Manthara's natural proclivities which impelled her to think of causing harm to Rama.

The Burmese Ramayana, Rama Vatthu, (seventeenth century AD) too shows that Kooni's natural traits were the reason for her antagonism.

Agni Purana (post-eighth century AD) is the first text to state that Kooni nurtured a grouse against Rama because of the various kinds of injuries that he had caused her. But it does not explain what harm he had done. Among the epic poets, it is Kamban who is the first to put forth this reason. Kamban presents as his own view as well as that of Rama that the cause for Manthara's enmity was that in the past Rama had made fun of Kooni, hitting her with darts of clay balls.

It is possible to consider that Kamban might have drawn this idea from the following hymns of Thirumazhisai Azhwar, Nammazhwar and others.

> Thou wearing the cool basil garland laden with honey!
> Aren't you the one who possesses the victorious bow
> with which you aimed the darts of clay balls to
> set straight the hunched back of Kooni?
> (Thiruchanda Virutham 30)
>
> The Lord who loves to reside at Srirangam
> darted a clay ball into the hunch of Kooni
> who was going about, wearing a string of flowers
> swarmed by bees.
> (Thiruchanda Virutham 49)
>
> Govinda! you sent a dart of clayball
> Right into the middle of the back
> To remove the hunch off Manthara.
> (Thiruvaaimozhi 1.5:5)

However, it is not possible to trace the origin of the views of the Azhwars. Perhaps they might have composed them superimposing their own imagination. Thakkai Ramayanam too, following Kamban, cites the same reason. Even **Ramanatakam,** which for the most part follows Vanmikam, toes the line of Kamban in this matter. It is good to keep in mind the chronological fact that Thirumazhisai Azhwar lived in the mid-seventh century AD and Nammazhwar in the early part of the ninth century AD.

The Telugu Ranganatha Ramayanam too cites the same reason that 'When Rama was a little boy, he playfully broke the leg of Kooni. On account of that incident Manthara bore a grudge against him'. Bhaskara Ramayanam, which appeared later, presents the same view. It has not been possible to find the source for the claim made in Ranganatha Ramayanam.

Bhusundi Ramayana is the first text to state that (Goddess) Saraswati, conceding the request of the celestials, came down to earth, entered the mind of Manthara and made her corrupt and distort Kaikeyi's mind to act against Rama. As far as the northern region is concerned, the impact of this text, which appeared after Vanmikam (twelfth century AD), may be seen in many of the Ramayana texts of the medieval period. Following Bhusundi Ramayana, Adhyatma Ramayana, Tulsi Ramayan and Ananda Ramayana, all put forth the same idea.

The Kannada Torave Ramayanam makes a slight deviation from this and says that by the command of Lord Narayana, the entity Maya took birth as Manthara and turned Kaikeyi's mind against Rama. Making a slight modification, it says that since she is said to be an incarnation of Maya, there was no need for her to go to the palace of Kekeya and so she straightaway came to Dasaratha's palace and settled down as a maid. The basis of this premise is that Manthara by nature was blameless but that the Devas (celestials) corrupted her to fulfil their mission and obtained her services.

Madhava Kandali's Assamsese Ramayana shows Manthara as one who had fallen in love with Bharata. Evincing great zeal in Bharata's welfare, she turns Kaikeyi's mind against Rama, with the intention that the coronation should be done for Bharata. Here the reason cited for her scheming is neither any old feud nor the motif of incarnation but Manthara's own self-interest i.e. her passion. No other Ramayana text has depicted Manthara from this angle.

Manthara's Scheming

All the Ramayana texts, more or less in a similar manner, give an account of the evil counsel given to Kaikeyi by Manthara, wishing to turn her mind against Rama. In general, all the Ramayana texts state that Manthara elaborately dwells upon the loss and dishonour that may befall Bharata and the humiliation certain to befall Kaikeyi too if Rama was crowned.

Vanmikam shows that Kaikeyi's mind changed when Manthara said, 'Kausalya, having received the honour of being the mother of the King, will then treat you and your maids as slaves. It is because you yourself have several times insulted Rama's mother Kausalya, being very proud of the fact that Dasaratha dotes on you more than he does on his other wives. Having been humiliated thus, won't she take revenge upon you should an opportunity arise?' (II.8.37,38.)

According to Vanmikam, Kausalya, on hearing from Rama that Dasaratha had decided to crown him the next day, says, 'This has been my fond hope which I have been cherishing for long' and, shedding tears of joy, addresses Rama, 'Child! May you live long! Let not the intent of those who wish to create impediments to you be realised. May you become illustrious by the grace of the Goddess Rajya Lakshmi and keep my relations, and Sumitra's kith and kin happy (II 4.38,39)'. The words of Kausalya deserve to be placed alongside Manthara's argument and pondered over.

By showing that Kaikeyi, who did not give up her good will for Rama even when she was told about the loss and dishonour that may befall her son, changes her mind when she hears how her 'co-wife' will attain the high status of mother to the King, and is sure to take revenge, the poet reveals the sharp intelligence of Manthara who acts with psychological subtlety.

Some poets differ in their stance in projecting the prospect of the elevated status of the first wife and the consequent disgrace to befall Kaikeyi.

> Fearing your husband Dasaratha
> who bears great love for you,
> Janaka, father of the red-lipped Sita,
> has spared your father until now.
> Remember, he is Rama's father-in-law.
> Is there any hope of a peaceful life for your father hereafter?
> Thou stupid fool! Who else is born to bear such a stigma?
> (II.2.82)
>
> Moreover, your father has some other enemies too.
> Should they wage a war with your sire,
> if he (Rama) does not proffer support,
> forget forever the prospect of a glorious victory.
> Have you resolved to bring your father and kinsmen
> to utter rout
> and you yourself to drowning in the scalding sea of sorrow?
> (83)

In these verses of Kamban, Kooni not only refers to the impending disgrace to Kaikeyi; she also points out the probable threat to Kaikeyi's father on account of her folly.

Wives will even put up with those who abuse them. But they will be roused to fury and will not tolerate their in-laws pointing out even a small flaw of their parents and brothers. Kamban's depiction of Manthara as one who exploits the subtle aspects of psychology by projecting to Kaikeyi the prospect of her father's life coming to an end by her complacency, is worthy of appreciation. The poet laments that it is only after listening to this that 'the noble lady's pure mind got sullied'.

The two Telugu Ramayana texts, Ranganatham and Bhaskaram, Adhyatma Ramayana, the Kannada Torave Ramayanam and Tulsi Ramayan – all of them are in conformity with Vanmikam in this regard.

We come to know that Ramayana texts cite four kinds of reasons for Bharata leaving for Kekeya such as

- Dasaratha sent away Bharata in response to the wishes of his grandfather,
- Dasaratha himself sent away Bharata to avoid any impediments to Rama's coronation,
- Kaikeyi, on her own will and pleasure, sent him off, and
- On Kausalya's urging, Dasaratha sent him away.

The Telugu Molla Ramayanam does not mention Manthara's story or her intrigue at all. In this epic, it is Dasaratha who informs Kaikeyi of the decision he has taken. In the same way, the Hindi epic *Ramachandrika*, contemporaneous with Tulsi Ramayan, has left out the references to Manthara's scheming. It is worth reflecting upon the fact that both these Ramayanas have taken Vanmikam as the source text.

Was Kaikeyi the Youngest or the Middle one?

In Vanmikam, it is not explicitly mentioned whether Kaikeyi is the second or the third queen. Yet the idea that Kaikeyi might be the third wife gains momentum due to the fact that Kausalya herself mentions the close relationship between her and Sumitra and also by the reasons cited in the foregoing comparatist study of Bala Kaandam. Kamba Ramayanam, the next complete text of Ramayana after Valmiki's text, refers to Sumitra as the youngest (I.5:105).

Vyasa's Mahabharata is the earliest text to state clearly that Kaikeyi is Dasaratha's third wife and the youngest of them and is also the mother of Bharata (Vanaparva 274-75). Moreover, Kaikeyi is referred to as the third and the youngest of the queens in the Hindi and Kashmiri Ramayanas.[9] It is worth remembering here that Jaga Veera Pandian expressed this idea almost fifty years ago although he did not present relevant evidences.[10]

The Malaysian Ramayana, Hikayat Seri Rama, shows Kaikeyi as the daughter of Dasaratha born to his mistress Balyadari.[11] None of the Indian Ramayana texts presents this kind of an alternative account of the relationship.

Kaikeyi's Noble Traits

Ramayana texts depict well what kind of person Kaikeyi was before and after being instigated by the evil counsel of Manthara. It can be said that Vanmikam, Kamba Ramayanam and Ramcharitmanas in particular have excellently rendered the distinctiveness of this character.

Vanmikam

Kaikeyi is one who, born in a royal family, lives as a wife of a king. Manthara conveys this fact with the hint that one who

---

9   Omkar Kaul, p. 155. (Hindi footnote).
10 *Pulavar Ulagam*. (Kamban Kalai Nilai). Part 4, (Madurai: Varadarajulu Naidu Press, 1945) p. 1349.(Tamil footnote).
11 S Singaravelu, p. 284.

has a royal lineage as a daughter as well as a wife, should also become the mother of a king (II.7:2,3). On hearing of Rama's coronation through Manthara, Kaikeyi rejoices and says that, to her, there is no difference between Rama and Bharata and that she (Manthara) could not have brought her more joyous tidings than that of Rama's coronation (II.7:35,36). Moreover, she dwells elaborately on Rama's glory:

> Rama never transgresses the path of righteousness; has been refined by the elders; knows the value of gratitude; has a heart which does not covet what belongs to others; upholds truth; is the eldest of the four and therefore, in accordance with royal justice, entitled to the crown; protects his brothers like a father; has greater love for me as a mother than even for Kausalya; Bharata is dear to me; yet Rama is greater than him; regards his younger brothers as dear as his own life. Therefore, even though the coronation is for Rama, the kingdom is going to be Bharata's (II.8:14,18,19).

That Kaikeyi is blameless is suggested in a few other places too in Vanmikam:

> Sage Bharadwaja tells Bharata that Rama's exile to the forest will prove beneficial to many people. And so, one should not blame Kaikeyi (II.92;31,32) (Northern Recension of Vanmikam II.86:28).

During the meeting in Chitrakootam, when Bharata denounces Kaikeyi, Rama reminds him of the fact that Dasaratha at the time of the marriage had promised his kingdom as a wedding gift to Kaikeyi (II.107:3) (Northern Recension of Vanmikam II.99:3).

Scripts of North-western and Eastern recensions of Vanmikam state that one day Kaikeyi had spoken ill of a Brahmana and so the enraged Brahmana cursed her saying that she would also be one day spoken ill of and abused (Northwestern II. 11:37-41) (Eastern II. 8:33-37). This matter is mentioned in Ramayana Manjari as well as Krittibasi Ramayana and Balaram Das' Ramayana (Bulcke 397).

Kaikeyi, renowned for good traits and good deeds, became like a little girl lacking in the power of discrimination to distinguish between what is good and what is bad due to the evil counsel of Kooni. Thanks to the malicious counsel, Kaikeyi, becoming headstrong, profusely praises Manthara's sharp intelligence and her beauty from head to foot (II. 9:36,37). Though by Kooni's goading she had resolved to stop Rama's coronation, she was mentally agitated as the thought was contrary to her conscience and, heaving a sigh, she started thinking about the means suitable for the act to be carried out (II.10:3).

Step by step and more or less with the same focus, both the epics of Kamban and Tulsidas describe the mental transformation of Kaikeyi.

The Jain Ramayanas have mostly depicted Kaikeyi as one who has admirable qualities and equally admirable conduct. The Jain Ramayanas say that in order to foil Bharata's attempt to turn a renunciant following Dasaratha, Kaikeyi wanted to set him on the royal throne, and that on account of his love for Bharata, Rama decided to set forth for the forest.[12]

Vimalasuri's Pauma Chariyam depicts Kaikeyi as one who has boundless love for her son, who accepts her husband's renunciation and who is on good terms with her husband and

---

12 HC Bhayani.'The Prakrit and Apabhramsa Ramayanas', *Asian Variations in Ramayana*, p. 81.

son. Moreover, the Kaikeyi of this Ramayana text does not demand Rama's exile to the forest.[13]

The Circumstances of Kaikeyi Obtaining the Boons

Vanmikam

Kaikeyi showed alertness in saving Dasaratha who fell unconscious when hit by the arrows of the enemy in the war between the Devas and the Asuras. Touched by this gesture, Dasaratha then gave her two boons. Kaikeyi said that she would ask for them when the need arose (II.11:19, 25; II.18 :32).

Vasudeva Hindi

Long ago in the past, Dasaratha had given one boon to Kaikeyi, pleased with her zeal and efficiency in extending hospitality to his kith and kin and another for boldly rescuing him from enemy forces. Kaikeyi had told him that she would avail herself of both later.

North Indian Folk Song

When Dasaratha went to cut a bamboo stick from the bush, he winced as the thorn pricked his fingers. Kaikeyi, who had accompanied him, removed the thorn and relieved him of the pain. Hence Dasaratha, highly pleased, gave her a boon.

Adhyatma Ramayana

Manthara tells Kaikeyi, 'You having a sharp intelligence, very boldly put your left hand in place of the broken axel of a wheel and rode the chariot. Dasaratha, who won the battle, bestowed

---

13 UP Shah. 'Ramayana in Jaina Tradition', *Asian Variations in Ramayana,* p. 68.

two boons on you, highly pleased with your courage and sharp intelligence; you said that you would take them when the need arose.' Padma Purana, Ananda Ramayana and Ramakien too narrate it in the same way.[14]

Molla Ramayanam has not depicted a character called Manthara. Therefore, this Ramayana says that Kaikeyi herself sought the two boons from Dasaratha.

Ranganatha Ramayanam, Bhaskara Ramayanam, Kannassa Ramayanam and Ezhuthachan's Ramayanam, all state that Dasaratha had given two boons to Kaikeyi, being pleased with her support during the battle with Sambara Sooran.

Kooni of Tulsi Ramayan exhorts Kaikeyi, 'Have you forgotten the two boons that Dasaratha has given you? Seek them now and assuage your wounded heart'. Tulsidas does not describe the circumstances that led to the obtaining of the two boons (II.22.3).[15]

A Tibetan Ramayana written in 1429 AD says that when the axel of the wheel of Dasaratha's chariot broke while he was participating in the war between the Devas and the Asuras, his younger wife held it tight with her hand, without letting the wheel come off. The King, pleased with her help, grants her a boon. She tells him that she will seek it when the need arises.[16]

---

14 Adhyatma (Chapter) 2:1:66; Ananda 1,1:85; Ramakien, chapter 14.
15 The number of boons that Kaikeyi obtained:
    Vanmikam states that Dasaratha gave Kaikeyi two boons (II.9,17,18). Vasudeva Hindi, Padma Puranam, Ananda Ramayana, Assamese Ramayana, Adhyatma Ramayana, Kamba Ramayanam, Telugu, Kannada, Malayala, Bengali Ramayanas and Tulsi Ramayan – all these in consonance with Vanmikam, say that Kaikeyi got two boons. Dasaratha Jataka, Mahabharata, Pauma Chariyu and the Tibetan Ramayana say that Dasaratha gave one boon to Kaikeyi. Brahmapurana says three boons were given. (AN Jani pp.30-33) (Tamil footnote).
16 JW De Jong, 'The Story of Rama in Tibet', *Asian Variations in Ramayana*, pp. 173-174.

Dasaratha, who was involved in the war between the Devas and the Asuras, was injured by the weapons of the Asuras. After he returned to Ayodhya, his younger wife, called Kaikeyi, treated those wounds which got healed. Dasaratha, pleased by this ministration, granted her a boon – so says another Tibetan Ramayana story written in 1586.[17]

The Story of Dasaratha Getting Cursed

Dasaratha, before dying, tells Kausalya in detail about the curse he had incurred. When he was a prince, before marrying Kausalya, Dasaratha had one day gone hunting and, targeting a noise which sounded like an elephant drinking water, he dispatched an arrow. Contrary to the trumpeting of an elephant in pain when hit by an arrow, he heard a human being cry loudly, and was shaken. On going near, he saw the son of an ascetic pierced by the arrow and writhing in pain.

Immediately after seeing him, when asked who he was, the young man said that he had come looking for water for his blind parents and that, having been hit by the arrow, he might not survive. Then requesting Dasaratha to brief his parents of his condition and to give them water to quench their thirst, he died. Fearing the charge of murder, Dasaratha went to the sage couple with the pot of water, told them who he was, explained to them what had happened and stood there asking for forgiveness; both of them, inconsolable in grief, came to their dead son with the help of Dasaratha. Lamenting in ever so many ways, they died cursing Dasaratha: 'You shall also, like us, die of grief of losing your son.' Thus explaining the curse of the sage, Dasaratha said that his end was certain.

---

17 JW De Jong, p. 178.

And he died thinking of Rama. This is the account obtained from Rama's story.

All the Ramayana texts narrate this incident, yet the context in which this incident is referred to in the epic, the name of the son of the sage, his caste, the culmination of the incident, are the details in which they differ as given below.

The Circumstances of the Incident

Vanmikam states that when Sumantra returned after leaving Rama, Sita and Lakshmana in the forest and told Dasaratha that Rama and the others had not come back, Dasaratha collapsed in agony and narrated this story to Kausalya (II: Sargas 63-64). Following this, the other Ramayana texts such as Adhyatma Ramayana (II.7), Ranganatham, Bhaskaram, Kannassam, Ezhuthachan's Ramayanam and Tulsi's Ramcharitmanas (II.155.2) too show that after Sumantra returned to Ayodhya on the sixth night of Rama leaving for the forest, Dasaratha recounts the incident to Kausalya.

Govinda Ramayana, which appeared in Punjabi, alone refers to this story in the beginning of the epic itself when describing the greatness of Dasaratha's reign. The Telugu Molla Ramayanam does not mention this story at all. Kamba Ramayanam states that Dasaratha narrates this story to Kausalya while Rama is still in Ayodhya and is getting ready to go to the forest along with Lakshmana and Sita after he hears of Dasaratha's orders through Kaikeyi (II.4.72-87).

Dasaratha, on seeing Rama, Sita and Lakshmana mounting the chariot and leaving before his very eyes, turned to Sumantra and said 'Stop'. When Rama said, 'Proceed', Dasaratha collapsed on seeing, with tearful eyes, the chariot disappearing from view. Dasaratha of Vanmikam had the faint hope that, in response to the advice and request of different ranks of people such as Vasishta, Sumantra and the citizens, Rama would come back without proceeding to the forest. Hence Dasaratha, not considering his end as certain, was looking forward to the return of Sumantra. When he returned to say that Rama had not come back, Dasaratha's end now becoming more certain, he, being reminded of the curse of the sage, recounted that story to Kausalya.

In Kamba Ramayanam, when Kaikeyi asks Rama to leave for the forest, presenting it as the command of the King, Rama takes leave of her right away and at that time, does not even go to see Dasaratha, nor does Dasaratha know about it. When Dasaratha hears from Kaikeyi that Rama has left for the forest, he abuses her in several ways, laments and is reduced to a state of exhaustion. When Kausalya consoles him saying 'Rama may come back, Oh King, don't lose heart', Dasaratha narrates the incident of the curse at this point:

> The words of the sage will not fail.
> The noble one leaving for the forest and my life departing,
> will surely happen, one following the other.
>
> (87)

And he says that the sage's curse will not become ineffectual, making it clear to her that Rama's going to the forest and his dying will happen simultaneously. Dasaratha, who was in a stupor until Sumantra returned, died at once when Sumantra came back and told him that Rama had not come back. This is how Kamban depicts the scene (II.5.59).

While Vanmikam shows that Dasaratha was conscious enough to the extent of being able to narrate the incident of his being cursed after he heard that Rama who reached the forest had not come back, Kamba Ramayanam says, 'When he (Rama) left, his (Dasaratha's) life breath also departed (II.5.59)'. We can take it that Kamban effected this change since he wanted to make it evident that Dasaratha considered Rama as his own life and the moment his life breath left, the body too became lifeless. If this extended episode of the epic is dramatised, Kamban's poetic genius and the maturity of his art will easily become evident.

Japanese Ramayana and the Story of the Curse

The story of the incident of Dasaratha's curse in Valmiki Ramayana is depicted with several deviations in a Japanese Ramayana text. This story is presented as a separate narrative in Sambo-ekotoba, a famous Japanese collection of stories which appeared in the tenth century AD.[18] Although Valmiki Ramayana is considered the source, we find that this story is presented in Japanese with many changes in consonance with the Buddhist views, spread wide by the emigration of Buddhists.

---

18   This story in Vanmikam is also found in *Sama Jataka* in the Pali language and *Shymaka Jataka* in *Mahavastu Avadana*. Later it was translated into Chinese Tripitakam by Buddhist scholars. When Buddhism spread to Japan, the story also got translated into the Japanese language. Among the Japanese texts that narrate the story of Rama, Sambo-ekotoba is the earliest. The entire story of Rama does not find a place in this. Hobutsushu, which narrates the entire story of Rama, appeared in twelfth century AD. Although stories in the Chinese language are considered to be the source for the substance of this text, scholars are of the opinion that it should have reached Japan from India or South Asian countries. Moreover *Monyoushu*, the most ancient literary work of Japan, mentions that Bharadwaj Bodhisena, an Indian Brahmana scholar, with his team had gone to Japan to inaugurate the installation of a new statue of Buddha in Nara, the capital of Japan in 758 AD. Therefore, the beginning of the spread of Rama's story right from eighth century AD onwards becomes a historical fact.
See: Minoru Hara, 'Rama stories in China and Japan: A Comparison', *Asian Variations in Ramayana*, pp. 340-356.

Among them here are a few:
- The sage's son is called Semu in this. In some other Japanese stories, he has been given various other names such as Sama, Syamaka and Sen.
- At the end of this story, the sage's son comes back to life by the grace of Devendra. His parents too, the sage couple, get their vision restored and they delight in seeing their son.
- This story has been depicted with the objective of stressing the value of caring for one's parents and of refraining from killing i.e. it has been cast as a moral story and not as an epic.
- At the end of the incident, the King is not subjected to any curse. When, on seeing the sage's son coming back to life by the grace of Devendra, the King wanted to take up renunciation and live with him, he was exhorted to give up hunting, go back to his country and rule the kingdom with love and compassion. The King too, on returning, conducts himself accordingly and teaches his people the moral of caring for one's parents.[19]

This story drives home the manner of cultural exchange through the use of a subnarrative in Ramayana bearing the message 'Reap what you have sown' and 'One has to bear the consequences of one's action'.

They appear as moral fables explicating the truth of Buddhist doctrines such as refraining from killing, caring for parents and perseverance. The story takes multifarious forms in various countries such as China and Japan.

Dasaratha's Order and Rama's Acceptance

The way Rama received what Dasaratha said when asking him to undergo coronation and relieve him of the burden of royal

---
19 Minoru Hara, pp. 353-354.

responsibility; Rama's state of mind later when he had to go to the forest on account of Kaikeyi's intervention; and the features of his character as revealed in his conciliatory efforts when Kausalya and the others were upset – all these aspects of his personality reflect the maturity of Rama's mind. The various narratives of the story of Rama have depicted these aspects each in tune with the cultural milieu of their times.

Rama's State of Mind when He Hears of the Coronation

The Rama of Valmiki, on hearing the news of the coronation, goes back without saying anything. Valmiki does not make any reference to his state of mind then. Kamban presents it as his personal view that when Dasaratha asked Rama to assume kingship, Rama felt that he had to abide by Dasaratha's word without thinking about his own likes and dislikes with regard to the throne since it was the King's command. It appears that Kamban takes it upon himself to cite the reasons and explain the silent acceptance by Valmiki's Rama.

Although the Rama depicted in Adhyatma seems to be more or less in the same state of mind, the significance of his smiling at Lakshmana calls for some reflection. Moreover, the cheerless tone of 'I am told, my coronation is going to take place tomorrow', and the derisive tone of 'they hope it is going to take place', are the suggestions we find resonating in this. When he tells Lakshmana 'I am only the instrument, you are the one to taste its fallout', we find an implicit suggestion that 'this is not going to take place, and you are going to experience the consequences resulting from it'.

Just as Kamban explains the silence of Valmiki, Tulsidas, closely following on the heels of Adhyatma, elaborates the ideas obtained from this suggestion and brings out Rama's disinclination and unhappiness. Rama may not go against the King's command, and hence he thinks of accepting it; therefore Rama is one who has no deceitful thought. It seems that it is Tulsidas's intention that the readers and devotees should realise this for themselves.

The Rama depicted by Valmiki and Kamban seems to have no likes and dislikes towards accepting the kingship and appears as one bound by a sense of duty. In Adhyatma Ramayana, Rama, who hints at his unwillingness to don the mantle, explicitly shows in Tulsi his unwillingness and reveals the impropriety of the envisaged event and regrets his inability to prevent it.

Kaikeyi's Command and Rama's State of Mind

In Vanmikam, when Kaikeyi conveys the King's command to Rama, Dasaratha, Sumantra, Lakshmana and others are present. Rama grieves to see Dasaratha in a state of stupor. Dasaratha, rendered helpless, feels sad to see Rama readily obeying Kaikeyi's command and leaving in the chariot along with Lakshmana and Sita. Adhyatmam, Ranganatham, Bhaskaram, Kannassam, Tulsi and Ezhuthachan's Ramayanam are mostly in line with Valmiki.

Janakiharan says that Rama's coronation got obstructed by Manthara. But in this connection, Kaikeyi's name is not mentioned in this text (V Raghavan. p. 50).

In Molla Ramayanam, it is Sumantra who conveys the command of Kaikeyi to Rama and Rama starts to leave for the forest without even seeing his father.

In Adhyatma Ramayana, as well as in Torave Ramayanam, the pathetic scene of Dasaratha betraying his helpless state while addressing Rama finds a place.

In Dasaratha Jataka, Vasudeva Hindi and Tibetan Ramayana, Dasaratha himself orders Rama to go to the forest. In the above Ramayana texts, which do not subscribe to the Hindu religion, it has been said that Rama was ordained to live in the forest for twelve years.

The Japanese Ramayana, Hobutsushu, (twelfth century AD), offers a new reason for Rama's exile. In this, there is no mention of the boons. Neither Dasaratha nor Kaikeyi gives the orders. Rama himself goes to the forest with his wife to observe the vow of refraining from killing. Perhaps Rama's story, which migrated from India through Buddhist scholars, had undergone such a change in tune with the Japanese culture.

We find that Kamban, who mostly follows Vanmikam, has greatly altered the circumstances of Kaikeyi ordering Rama. Here, Rama comes alone to the palace. Lakshmana does not accompany him. Even before he gets in and reaches the apartment of Dasaratha and others, Kaikeyi intercepts and meets him. The conversation takes place only between Kaikeyi and Rama. Without his ever coming to know anything about the pathetic situation of Dasaratha's helplessness, Rama listens to what Kaikeyi has to say as the King's command and goes back without meeting Dasaratha. Kamban depicts Rama as saying, 'I shall go to the brightly shining forest today itself', and bidding good-bye, he leaves, meeting neither Kaikeyi nor Dasaratha again.

Kamban compresses more or less twenty sargas of Valmiki into nine verses. This compression by Kamban is critical among the numerous instances which establish the fact that Valmiki's work constitutes the primary epic and Kamban's the secondary or scholar epic. The Indian Ramayanas which appeared after Kamban do not seem to have handled the episode with such artistic maturity. There is no doubt that this compression enriches the structure of the epic and enhances the aesthetic delight. What is more, an opportunity arises to make evident aspects of Rama's personality such as his determination, his faith in Kaikeyi, and the graciousness of his heart that wants to avoid giving mental agony to Dasaratha likely to be caused by a moral conflict. Although it is quite natural for derivative texts to acquire such maturity of artistry, and excel the original text if we go by the theory of evolution, it is worth noting that this kind of maturity is not found in any of the Indian epics before and after Kamban. Hence scholars can easily understand that this stands out as a distinctive feature of Kamban.

In this context, the characteristic traits of Rama, as revealed by his words and deeds, and those presented as the poet's statements have come to be critically analysed. Though all the poets have tried to bring out the state of Rama's mind after his listening to the orders of Kaikeyi, it can be said that the three great poets Valmiki, Kamban and Tulsi, deserve to be specially mentioned in this regard.

Valmiki shows that Rama, who considered Kaikeyi's boons to be the command of the King, was not in the least upset that he had to head for the forest so that Bharata could be crowned king. The poet cites people of the city observing and saying that whatever be the circumstances, Rama did not lose his natural spirit of cheerfulness and the brightness of his face which was like the autumnal moon. Therefore, we understand that the poet thus establishes Rama's equanimity of mind.

However, Valmiki also says that Sita was taken aback to see Rama who returned from the palace with his face looking dull and tired, and his body wet with perspiration. Valmiki says that in another instance, on the banks of the river Tamasa, when

Rama was talking to Lakshmana, he expressed his unhappiness with Kaikeyi. On the basis of these instances, some people consider that Rama felt sad over the loss of the kingdom.

It is true that Rama appears to have been lost in thought while returning to his palace. It is equally true that he looks less radiant. But instead of considering the loss of the throne as the reason for these changes, it seems appropriate to say that Rama, while returning, is thinking of how to console Sita, how to part with her and live alone for fourteen years, or what kind of problems may arise if he takes her along, and hence, the brightness of his face is diminished as an outward expression of such self-effacing thoughts.

Yet, in the words Rama spoke to Lakshmana about Kaikeyi's unkindness on the first night of his stay on the banks of the river Tamasa, we find him feeling sorry explicitly about three issues – the death of his father, the prospect of Bharata alone becoming the king and himself going to the forest.

It is incomprehensible why it has been depicted in Vanmikam that Rama, who had spoken to Lakshmana about Kaikeyi's love and the invincibility of fate at great length, is here shown as speaking ill of her.

There is no reference anywhere about Kamban's Rama expressing his suspicion of Kaikeyi nor is there in Kamban any reference to Sita feeling sad to see Rama's face looking weary. Valmiki also states that on hearing Kaikeyi's orders, Rama's face showed no disturbance and that the natural brightness of the face and cheerfulness did not in the least register any change.

The verses in which Kamban depicts the joy that Rama got listening to Kaikeyi's command are the ones that all readers are familiar with. Wishing to show that Rama was even more elated than was his wont, the poet says that he became one with a face brighter than the lotus flower. Thus his elation even surpassing his natural spirit of cheerfulness, Rama went to meet Sita. That is the reason why the Sita depicted by Kamban, unlike Valmiki's Sita, does not feel sorry about the change in Rama's facial expression. If we observe Kamban's depiction of how Sita recalls the cheerful face of Rama when she was alone in the Ashoka woods, lost in the thoughts of Rama and feeling sad, Rama's cheerfulness and Kamban's suggestive observation become quite evident.

> Deeply moved, Sita recalled his face shining thrice brighter
> when King Kekeya's daughter said unto him
> 'This land girdled by the sea is your younger brother's.'
> She remembered his face
> fresh like a newly blossomed lotus in a picture,
> be it when it was said,
> 'The wealth of this world is yours'
> Or when told,
> 'Thou shall renounce this wealth and
> sojourn in the forest.' (V. 3:19, 20)

We find Tulsidas's statement that Rama's face became brighter fourfold than before when he received Kaikeyi's command, 'Head for the forest' is in harmony with Kamban's view.

Moreover, Kamban presents the state of Rama's mind when he felt he was being relieved of the royal burden by comparing it to the joy of a noble ox after it is unyoked from the cart. Kamban's similie is comparable with Tulsidas's analogy of the joy of a juvenile elephant on being set free from the fetters. Both point to Rama's feeling of elation after being relieved of the royal burden by Kaikeyi's command. When we observe how the two great Indian poets of Ramayana who appeared after Valmiki have more or less in the same manner brought out Rama's state of equanimity, we are able to perceive how the two of them have tasted with sheer delight the nectar of the Rama lore.

We can find Rama's equanimity manifesting itself in the situation where he comforts Kausalya and Lakshmana. When Kausalya tells him, 'You need not go to the forest. Why do you want to act according to the command of my husband's other wife rather than mine?' Valmiki's Rama replies: 'I have no authority to disregard the command of my father. I have got ready to proceed to the forest. Bless me and send me off (II.21:31).' When Lakshmana flies into a rage declaring, 'I'll right away kill Kaikeyi, who deprived you of the throne that is rightfully yours and those who were her accomplices in this, including Dasaratha and the others and forthwith conduct your coronation', Rama pacifies him using various arguments.

'Lakshmana, your prowess is something everyone is well aware of. I too know very well that you are capable of conquering all the three worlds together. Truthfulness is the best of the moral dictates of righteousness. Can we afford to go against the command of the father who wants to uphold it? It is only because of father's orders that Kaikeyi gave such a command; what is her culpability in this? Therefore, shun the thought of exercising your prowess against righteousness. Understand that it is righteousness which is supreme, and not valour (II.21. 40-45).'

'The condition that has befallen us is on account of destiny. Otherwise why should Kaikeyi think of creating hurdles for me? Have I ever before felt in her love any discrimination between me and Bharata? What do you think is the reason for Kaikeyi, who has noble qualities and noble conduct by nature, possessing ideal qualities worthy to be hailed by all, to deviate completely from her nature and talk like an ordinary uneducated woman in front of her husband so as to affect my lot? (II.22.16-20)'

'When one cannot figure out the reason for any condition of happiness, suffering, disease, anger, gain, loss, birth or death, then it must be deemed as God's will. When an act that is begun faces impediments and an unexpected event occurs by itself, it is the act of God and nothing else. So, please do not think that Kaikeyi is responsible for the halting of the coronation. It is because Kaikeyi, propelled by destiny, has done something involuntarily against her own wish. Don't you understand that destiny has such power?'

'Lakshmana! Don't feel sorry for my losing the throne. Between the options of shouldering royal responsibility and living as an ascetic in the forest without a care, happily wandering from country to country, the latter is better. Since I am well aware of the dictates of righteousness expounded so far and also of the power of destiny and as one by natural temperament quite mature, the question of perturbation of mind due to the loss of the throne does not arise, and instead I am now one with a greater spirit of ardour (II.22.20-30).'

Kamban holds more or less the same view. Rama consoles Kausalya saying: 'Oh! You of incomparable chastity, would you render our truthful King an untruthful one?' and then addressing Lakshmana who burst out saying, 'I venture to destroy anyone even if they are celestials, who obstruct your being crowned. I am prepared to lay at your feet double the seven worlds':

> When father ordered, 'Accept this crown',
> was it not my fault to have accepted it without reflection?
> Where does the fault of the King lie in this?
> (II. 4:128)
>
> She who has received the boon
> is the one who has the right to rule.
> Now my wealth lies in renunciation.
> What could be better than this? (4:133)

Rama thus clarifies that Dasaratha did not commit any crime; nor did Kaikeyi do any wrong.

> If the spring runs dry, is it the fault of the river?
> What has befallen me today is not father's fault.
> Nor is it the fault of the one who brought us up
> as her own.
> Nor is it her son's fault. It is fate's, my son!
> Why do you rage against it?
>
> (4:129)

Thus, in one verse, with epigrammatic brevity, Kamban compacts what Valmiki has explained in an entire Sarga (II.22); that destiny is the cause for all the incidents that have taken place.

Although this part of the epic may appear as consoling Kausalya and Lakshmana, it is crystal clear that the motive of these two great poets is to show that Rama's equanimity of mind was not in the least affected by Kaikeyi's boon.

Sita's Resolve to Go to the Forest

All the Ramayanas from Vanmikam onwards state that Sita, who was adamant about accompanying Rama to the forest, obtained his consent. Rama's arguments to forestall Sita's going with him to the forest, as well as Sita's reasons for persisting in her decision, which she declares as, 'Come what may, I shall go with you, or else I shall die today itself' are stated in all the Ramayana texts, more or less in a similar vein.

Other Ramayanas from Vanmikam onwards show that, in response to Rama's argument that 'So many problems will arise by your accompanying me', Sita says, 'I will make sure that no problem arises for you on my account. When you are around, what trouble can befall me?'

Sita of Kamba Ramayanam says tauntingly, 'After leaving me will you find happiness?' Here we can see the conventions of *Paalai* and *Marutham* of Tamil love poetics called *Akam* tradition (which deals with the sphere of love) coming in handy for the poet.

In Vanmikam, the arguments and counter arguments relevant to the contemporary society of Rama and Sita delight us. Yet we realise that there is some gap caused by the differences resulting from time, place and culture in this delightful aesthetic experience. Since Tulsidas's Sita is depicted as having the same feelings as the common humanity, the readers are able to identify themselves with her and develop a sense of enjoyment.

When Madhava Kandali's Assamese Sita asks 'When it is the time to indulge in conjugal bliss, why do you try to leave me?' we find the echo of *riti* literary culture, the influence of Krishna cult, and the aesthetic preference of Maha Manikya (the king from the Varaha clan and the patron of the Assamese Ramayana) for the *sringara* (erotic) *rasa*.

Valmiki's Sita says that she had heard from astrologers even when she was a little girl that planetary conditions indicated the prospect of her living in the forest with her husband. Adhyatma Ramayana as well as Ezhuthachan's Ramayanam, which appeared later, conveys the same idea following Vanmikam. Kamba Ramayanam, the Telugu Ramayana texts, Kannada Torave Ramayanam, Malayala Kannassa Ramayanam and Tulsi Ramayan do not present this point. This second astrological view, in which we hear about Sita in the Ramayana texts, we find coming true and getting realised in Ayodhya Kaandam. The first astrological view (that Ravana will be destroyed on account of Sita) getting realised in the Yuddha Kaandam can be seen later.

Adhyatma Ramayana says that Sita took cognisance of the fact that none of the Ramayana texts mentioned that Rama went alone to the forest leaving Sita behind and presents it as an argument in her favour. The world of criticism has considered the flaw of anachronism to be acceptable in genres like the drama. However, the deviation formed by presenting characters who go outside the scope of the narrative and become one of the readers discussing it themselves, is not known to have been effected in the tradition of epics worldwide.

Secondly, the idea that Rama himself heard his own story recited by others is found in the early portion of the version of Valmiki Ramayana existing today. Contradictory views about the originality of the Valmiki text available now are held among Ramayana scholars.[20] There is a prevalent opinion that Valmiki did not write the Bala Kaandam as it exists now; and that the Ayodhya Kaandam was the beginning of the epic; later some others composed Bala Kaandam and added it as an insertion. According to this view, a pundit belonging to the period of Kalidasa's times may have composed and added it. Scholars consider that keeping in mind the part in which Rama listens to his own story, Adhyatma Ramayana may have depicted the above idea. Many scholars have expressed the opinion that this must have been a compilation of ideas found in many works since it is not possible to figure out beyond doubt either the period of this text or the name of the author, although scholars like Amba Prasad cite Rama Sarma as the author of Adhyatma Ramayana.[21]

---

20 'Kaanda Structure of Ramayana', *Purana Bulletin*, Ayodhya Special issue, vol. XXXIII, No. (Varanasi July 1991). pp. 103-107.
21 AN Jani, pp. 40-41.

There are also those who say that the Valmiki Bala Kaandam available now is a compounded text of two layers – the original and the later insertion.

Therefore, it gets confirmed that the genuineness of Bala Kaandam is suspect. It is also a subject for research whether there is any evidence for this view other than that of the newly added Bala Kaandam of Valmiki Ramayana. It is not possible to find out whether this matter is mentioned in Bhusundi Ramayana, the basic text for all the medieval Ramayanas. It appears that this idea, inserted under the impression that it will result in a new aesthetic delight, has given rise to many questions.

It so happens that Sita, who forsook living in her palace in the company of her kith and kin as a matter of right and deliberately sought life in the forest in order not to part with her husband, is destined to live in a grove in Lanka, separated for several months from her dear husband, imprisoned, as she is, among the demons. When we look at the paradoxical turn the epic takes in its course, we get an opportunity to realise the power of destiny or the irony of events in human affairs. Homer's first epic, *The Iliad*, shows that the leaders of the heroic age were involved in a long-drawn-out battle (lasting ten years) for the sake of a woman taken captive, and got split on account of another woman and after destroying the enemy at the end, returned without rescuing the woman which was their objective, with the woman herself not willing to return. In a parallel to this ancient turn of events, we see something similar in recent events also. Everybody knows how the French Revolution, which was launched with the objective of putting an end to monarchy, i.e. the tradition of dictatorship, and usher in the rise of democracy, finally ended up in the ascendancy of a dictator called Napoleon. The astonishment expressed by

Kamban's Rama at the phenomenon of intent and outcome, of objective and ending, contradicting each other, which marks many an event in human life happening time and again, is echoed in the following verse on the nature of this world:

> What can one say about the way of this world?
>
> (I. 9:16)

Rama Agreeing to Let Lakshmana Accompany Him

The reasons put forward by Rama for Lakshmana to stay back in Ayodhya and the counter arguments by Lakshmana are narrated in a similar manner in most of the Ramayana texts. Vanmikam states these elaborately while Kamba Ramayanam does so briefly. In just one verse (II.4.152) Kamban presents Lakshmana's views clearly and firmly. Kamban's poetic genius in depicting Lakshmana's argument in such a way that Rama has nothing more to say beyond that, is admirable. The analogy of fish, which forms the core of this verse, is also found in Vanmikam.

Sumitra's Counsel

Sumitra, whose character has not been delineated much, exhibits her magnanimity even in the limited opportunity given, in such a way as to surpass the kindness of both Kausalya who exemplifies the dictum that righteousness issues from love and Kaikeyi that it is so even for unrighteousness. Sumitra is a character who talks but sparingly; yet a small observation by her, while bidding farewell to Lakshmana, drives home to us the entire significance of Rama's story. We can find that Sumitra's talk at the human level gives the explicit meaning of 'Despite going to the forest, it is Rama who is the King (Dasaratha); where he resides is Ayodhya; Sita herself is the mother; Ramarajya (Righteous reign of Rama) is what you are going to experience'; and the implicit meaning of 'It is this Ayodhya with its glory defamed that is in reality the forest; here is no king who has the authority to command; here are no mothers who have either the love or the power to accompany the son to the forest nor prevent him from going to the forest. What is going on here is no reign either'. We can find Sumitra's talk suggesting that, as incarnations, 'They (Sita and Rama) remain as mother and father to all the living beings. Their abode is the temple (consecrated with the idol). What takes place there is divine reign. If we don't submit to that reign and instead spend our time here, it amounts to committing a fatal error'.

Sumitra, as depicted by Kamban, puts forward another view which has not been stated by Vanmikam. Sumitra's advice 'Don't accompany Rama thinking of the privilege of the relationship of his being an elder brother. Go as a servant to do him service', can be taken as applicable to both the levels as mentioned above.

Some Variations in the Accounts of the Exile

Period of Stay in the Forest

In Mahabharata, Anamakam, Jatakam and Pauma Chariyam, there is no mention of the time limit for the exile in the forest. Texts like Dasaratha Jataka, Dasaratha Kathaanam and Vasudeva Hindi state that the duration of the exile was for twelve years. In the other Ramayana texts from Vanmikam onwards, a period of fourteen years has been mentioned.

Not Living in the Forest At All

As per Gunabhadra's Uttara Purana, Ravana abducts Sita from the Ashoka woods near the capital. According to the Indo-Chinese *Anama Ramayana*, Ravana comes with his army and launches a war against Dasaratha and abducts Sita. Hence, in these two Ramayanas, living in the forest is an event that did not happen[22] (Bulcke 391).

Reason for Stay in the Forest

According to Dasaratha Jataka and Dasaratha Kathaanam, Kaikeyi asks for only one boon, i.e. to give the reign to her son Bharata. But it is Dasaratha who, fearing that some harm may befall Rama and Lakshmana, orders them to go to the forest for twelve years. Hence Buddhist Ramayanas state that it is only because of the fear of cruelty of a stepmother that Rama was ordained to stay in the forest.

Anamakam Jatakam states that Rama, who came to know that his father-in-law was getting ready to invade his country, goes on his own to the forest with his wife in order to avert the war. And Pauma Chariyam says that Rama, who came to know that Dasaratha is going to renounce power and hand over the reign to Bharata, voluntarily sets forth towards the south along with Sita and Lakshmana. The Tibetan Ramayana states that Rama, who comes to know that Dasaratha is confused and upset about deciding on whom to bestow the throne, to Rama or to Bharata, willingly leaves the country, goes to some hermitage and starts doing penance (Bulcke 393).

Those who Opt for Living in the Forest

In Dasaratha Kathaanam, it is only Rama and Lakshmana who go to the forest. According to Anamakam Jatakam, Rama and Sita alone undertake living in the forest.

---

22 Ramayana of Anama region belonging to Indo-China (Bulcke p.268).

According to the Tibetan Ramayana, Rama alone goes to the forest to do penance.

Sinhalese Ramayana states that in order to protect himself from the harmful effects of the planet Saturn's movement Rama alone lives in the forest for seven years, leaving Sita in the capital – so says Camille Bulcke (394).

The Meeting of Rama and Guha

Vanmikam

As soon as Rama reached the banks of the river Ganga along with Sumantra, Rama's friend Guha who was the King of Sringipura and the chief of hunters, came to see him. Going forward along with Lakshmana, Rama welcomed Guha and embraced him. Feeling sad on seeing Rama and Lakshmana clad in tree barks, Guha fetched them various things; Rama looked at them with kindness and, setting them aside as not required for ascetic life, took just water and slept there that night. Guha too joined Lakshmana in keeping vigil through the night. Next morning, all three of them got on to the boat which Guha had brought and crossed the river Ganga (II.50-52).

Kamba Ramayanam

When they reached the banks of the river Ganga, Guha, who wanted to see Rama, met him with the help of Lakshmana and with great joy, offered him honey and fish which he had brought with him. Pleased by his hospitality, saying that whatever was given out of love was indeed pure, Rama requested him to provide him with a boat to cross the river the next morning. With Rama's consent Guha kept watch all through the night staying awake along with Lakshmana, unwilling to take his eyes off Rama. The next day he helped the three of them reach the other bank of the river in a boat and offered to go with them. Then Rama accepting him as his own brother declared,

> You are very dear to me.
> My younger brother is your younger brother too.
> This Sita, with a lovely forehead, is your kin.
> Before we struck a friendship with you
> We were four.
> Now the bond of brothers is endless.
> With you we are now five.
>
> (II.7.42-43)

He said, 'The day I return to the north, I shall surely come to you', and took leave of Guha.

Tulsi Ramayan

After befriending Guha, Rama sent Sumantra back to Ayodhya, reached the bank of the river Ganga, approached a boatman and was about to get on to the boat, but the boatman-hunter said, 'Unless Rama purifies his sacred feet with water I will not take him into the boat; because my livelihood will be lost if his sacred feet that turned a stone into a woman turn my boat of wood also into a woman'.

Smiling, Rama agreed to his wishes and all three of them crossed the river. Later, on reaching Bharadwaja's hermitage, they sent back Guha and started walking towards Valmiki's hermitage.

Bharata's Refusal to Ascend the Throne

We can analyse the measures taken by Bharata, after he was brought to Ayodhya by Vasishta from Kekeya and after he heard about the events that had occurred in Ayodhya, in three stages, namely, Bharata's refusal to accept the throne, the meeting of Bharata and Guha and that of Bharata and Rama.

Bharata who returned from Kekeya, heard about the disastrous events for which Kaikeyi was instrumental and abused her no end. He bewailed his predicament to Kausalya and lamenting, fell unconscious. Later, somewhat recovering by Vasishta's words of consolation, he performed the last rites for his father. Turning down the advice given by Vasishta and others to ascend the throne, he set forth for the forest along with the ministers and others, intending to search for Rama, bring him back and make Rama himself the king.

All the Ramayana texts narrate this matter more or less in a similar manner. Vanmikam elaborately presents the scene of Bharata meeting Kausalya and, being deeply hurt by her harsh words, crying his heart out saying that he did no wrong (Sarga 75). This section, where Bharata takes a vow, is not found to be so elaborate in the other texts. This part is very useful for getting to know about various contemporary social perspectives such as the code of conduct pertaining to governance and related ideas and beliefs expounded in ethical texts. We find that this sarga is laden with the flavour of people living close to the soil.

Vanmikam says that Bharata performed the last rites for Dasaratha. Ramayana texts in other languages too closely follow Vanmikam in this regard. Kamba Ramayanam alone states that by Dasaratha's orders, Bharata was not permitted to perform the last rites and that it was Shatrughna who performed them. Valmiki's Dasaratha says, 'If Bharata deems it right that Rama should go to the forest, then he can't perform the last rites for me (II.12:94)'. Not only does Bharata not accept Rama's departure to the forest, but he also disagrees with the idea of himself being crowned in his place; he, in fact, opposes these steps, as expected by Dasaratha. Therefore, Vasishta feels that it is not necessary to stop Bharata from doing the last rites, and orders that he must perform them. In a later verse, Valmiki himself presents Dasaratha as telling Kaikeyi, 'Since you halted Rama's coronation, you and Bharata need not do the last rites for me (II.14:17)'. Here it is Kaikeyi who obstructs the coronation and Bharata is in no way responsible for it. Therefore, it is Dasaratha's view that 'if Bharata accepts his being crowned in place of Rama, he should not do the last rites for me'. Vanmikam shows that it is also because of this reason that Bharata was not kept out.

In Kamba Ramayanam, Dasaratha turns to Vasishta and says,

> When I deem not Kaikeyi as my wife
> I deem not Bharata too as my son.
> Oh sage! He has no right to perform my last rites.
> (II.4.51)

The implication is that 'Bharata, who comes to crown himself,' should not do the rites for him. Kamban, who realised Valmiki's dilemma, also states it in such a way as to underscore this implication. Yet Kamban shows that Vasishta prevents Bharata from performing the rites.

All the other Ramayana texts from Adhyatma onwards take only Valmiki's first statement as the basis and show Bharata himself performing the last rites.

The Meeting of Bharata and Guha

Guha, who notices Bharata reaching the banks of the river Ganga with an army, at first doubts him; later understands that someone who has great love for Rama has come and feels happy; tells him all about Rama's abode, and about Lakshmana's rare qualities; and helps Bharata and his forces to get across Ganga along with his mothers. Other Ramayana texts explain this incident mostly in consonance with Valmiki.

What is but briefly presented in Vanmikam, Adhyatmam, Tulsi and the Telugu and Kannada Ramayanas – namely the views of Guha voicing his suspicion of the motive of Bharata's arrival – is narrated in Kamban in great detail. Malayala Kannassa Ramayanam does not say anything about the meeting in particular. In the Tibetan Ramayana, there is no reference to Bharata at all. In the Ramayanas of Southeast Asian countries such as Thailand, Malaysia and Laos, these incidents do not find a place at all.

We notice that Kamban has taken much care to present the first incident of Bharata and Guha meeting each other. Bharata, who has some knowledge of Guha through Sumantra, says, as becomes the tradition of authority, 'Let him come', when it is announced that Guha has come to meet him. Then, when Guha arrives with the offerings, Bharata tells him, 'We must know the way to Bharadwaja's abode. Before that, we must cross the Ganga.' Vanmikam states that Guha, by way of reply, tells him, 'You need not worry, Sir. We will help. Before that, there is something that I want to know. Have you come here as one who has love for Rama? I am suspicious because you have come with a huge army' – thus asks Guha (Sarga 85).

Guha, who became suspicious on seeing Bharata's army, kept his own army in a state of readiness at the southern bank and he alone reached the northern bank in a boat to find out the intention of Bharata who was clothed as one doing penance. Bharata and Shatrughna, who had heard about Guha through Sumantra, had arrived at the bank of the Ganga and were waiting to welcome him.

Guha, who reached the bank of the river, prostrated at the feet of Bharata and Bharata too prostrated at the feet of Guha and they embraced each other. Guha, who embraced him, asked him, 'What has brought you to me?' Bharata replied, 'Father swerved from the path of the ancestors. I have come in order to rectify that and take the king along'. So states Kamba Ramayanam (II.12.31-33).

One cannot admire enough the skill of Kamban in depicting very beautifully and movingly in just one verse how Guha fully understood Bharata the moment he saw Bharata and Shatrughna waiting on the northern bank to receive him:

> Behold, the young prince standing at some distance.
> He looks like my lord. The one next to him
> looks like young Lakshmana.
> He sports an ascetic's appearance like his brother Rama.
> His sorrow seems beyond repair.
> He pays obeisance in the direction of Rama.
> How did I think that those born as siblings to my Lord
> can ever commit any wrong?
>
> (II.12.30)

The thoughts presented in Vanmikam in a matter-of-fact manner, got transformed into paintings in words in the hands of Kamban. Bharata's very appearance conveys everything to Guha. In the case of Vanmikam, only after coming to know through Guha of the place Rama slept in and the ordeals he went through, does Bharata put on the guise of an ascetic by wearing the tree barks. How can one not wonder at the artistic maturity of Kamban who goes a step further and lets the flood of sentiments flow in the heart of Guha?

Kamban's unique poetic excellence, which is evident in the way Bharata praises Guha, introduces his mothers to Guha, and the manner in which Kausalya counsels Guha and Bharata, is not explicated here for the sake of brevity.

The Meeting of Bharata and Rama

Vanmikam

On seeing Bharata coming with an army, Lakshmana rose in fury and armed himself for battle. Rama exhorted him in ever so many ways and when he finally said,

> How can a man kill his own brother who is dear to him as his own life? If you are saying this for the sake of the kingdom, I will ask Bharata as soon as I meet him, to give the kingdom to you; and Bharata will also agree to this, I am sure (Sarga 97).

Lakshmana's rage subsided. When Bharata and Shatrughna bow to Rama, Rama embraces them and instructs Bharata in great detail on the ethics of kingship. Later, on hearing about Dasaratha's death, Rama and Sita grieve over it and perform the last rites. Recovering somewhat, Rama greets Vasishta and the others and talks to them. At that time, when Bharata requests Rama to return to Ayodhya and accept the throne, Rama says, 'It is not right to go against the orders of our father, therefore it is but proper that I stay here. You be the King.' Bharata, who does not agree to this, insists, saying, 'If the mistakes of Dasaratha and Kaikeyi are to be rectified, and if they are to be turned into those who have not swerved from the path of righteousness, it is but proper that you should be back and become the King (Sarga 104-106)'. On hearing this Rama says, 'Oh noble-natured one! It is neither father's fault nor mother Kaikeyi's. When our father married your mother Kaikeyi, he assured your maternal grandfather by way of a promise':[23]

---

23 पुरा भ्रातः पिता नः स मातरम् ते समुद्वहन् ।
मातामहे समाश्रौषीद् राज्य शुल्कम् अनुत्तमम् ॥ २-१०७-३
O, My brother! Long ago, when our father married your mother, he promised your maternal grandfather that he would confer his kingdom as an exceptional marriage-dowry. II (Sanskrit foot note) (Baroda edition II. 99.3; Dharmalaya edition II. 107.3).

> 'I will give the kingdom to the son born to your daughter', said Dasaratha.
>
> 'On one occasion, pleased with her service during a battle, our father had granted two boons to your mother. It is in accordance with those that I have come to the forest. The reign has been ordained for you. Therefore, it is not the fault of either of them. Please give up this argument about the eldest having to wear the crown; go back to Ayodhya and, with the help of our younger brother Shatrughna, run a righteous reign.' Thus Rama gives a decisive reply (Sarga 107).

Rama did not agree with the contention of Vasishta who argued that it is but proper for the eldest to rule the kingdom. Finally, yielding to the request of Bharata, Rama set his sacred feet on a pair of golden sandals to make an imprint of them and Bharata received them, as Vanmikam shows, swearing that he would rule as a representative of the sandals; and in case, after the period of stay in the forest, should Rama not return to Ayodhya, he would immolate himself and give up his life. So saying, he returned to Ayodhya (Sarga 111, 112).

Bhattikavyam says that Rama himself told Bharata to rule in his name by keeping his sandals as a symbol representing him. That is, this text states that 'Bharata did not ask for it; Rama himself gave his sandals' (V Raghavan, p. 65).

Adhyatma Ramayana

Rama, who heard Bharata's plea, said, 'Oh Bharata! Our father did not give us the order carried away by the words of Kaikeyi or in a state of stupor. In order to keep his word, he awarded me stay in the forest and you, the reign of the kingdom. When I act in obedience to the orders of our father, how could you alone defy his orders?' At once Bharata said, 'If so, I shall also take up stay in the forest with you and do service like Lakshmana.

Or else, I will give up my life by fasting.' Spreading the *darbha* grass he sat down facing east. Rama, taken aback by Bharata's resolve, and overwhelmed by astonishment, turned to Vasishta who was close by. The latter too explained to Bharata the purpose of Rama's incarnation. Although Bharata, on listening to Vasishta, understood the intention of the celestials, he begged of Rama, 'You should promise that you will get crowned at the end of the period of stay in the forest.' He obtained the golden sandals studded with rubies, imprinted by Rama's sacred feet and saying that he would rule as the representative of the sandals, he returned to Ayodhya.[24]

Malayala Ramayana texts

When Rama of Kannassa Ramayanam said, 'Does it behove us, the sons of Dasaratha, to make our father a perjurer and send him to Hell? Therefore, in accordance with his orders, your ruling the kingdom and me living in the forest are the right things for us', without any further argument, Bharata agreed, received the sandals and got back to Ayodhya. Ezhuthachan's Ramayanam follows Adhyatma Ramayana in this respect.

Torave Ramayanam

In Kumara Valmiki's depiction, Rama, in order to quell the fury of Lakshmana towards Bharata, exhorted him thus: 'Brother! The sun may rise in the west; but Bharata will never turn against us. Control your anger,' and he became pacified. At that moment, Bharata, along with his younger brother and the mothers, arrived there, fell at Rama's feet and paid his

---

24 Natesa Sastri, pp.122-125.

obeisance. Rama, on seeing his mothers shedding tears, asked them, 'Has your blessed married state come to an end?' and wept bitterly for the loss of his father. After the last rites were over, Bharata bowed to Rama and said, 'You are both father and mother to me; please come to Ayodhya immediately and accept the kingship and bring joy to all of us. Otherwise, one of your brothers will be no more.' Although Vasishta and the others compelled Rama to agree to the request of Bharata, Rama did not. Then, Kaikeyi in tears, with an unblemished mind, turned to Rama and said, 'Do forget the wrong I did out of ignorance and accept the kingship. Oh son! Protect the country, won't you?' and pleading thus, she embraced him. Rama said to her, 'I have never gone against your command; but now, if I yield to your request, father would grieve that I have disregarded his word. Is not our King a man of truthfulness?' Then Bharata obtained Rama's sandals and returned to Ayodhya (II.6.30).

Tulsi Ramayan

Tulsi Ramayan narrates the arguments between Rama and Bharata mostly in the same manner as Vanmikam does. Tulsidas, in this place, mentions the arrival of Indra, Viswamitra and Janaka. Bharata, having come to know of the motive of incarnation through Maya's action i.e. by Divine delusion, without compelling Rama any further, obtains the imprint of Rama's sacred feet on the golden sandals and gets back to Ayodhya.

Kamba Ramayanam

Rama, who, by various words of counsel, assuaged the fury of Lakshmana on seeing the army of Bharata, finally said,

> Because of your affection for me
> You have spoken ill of Bharata.
> But he is the very embodiment of dharma.
> How could you think otherwise of such a man
> of uprightness?
>
> (II.13.44,57)

And he comforted Lakshmana thus.

When Bharata reached Rama and bowed to him, Rama embraced him and enquired about the welfare of their father, 'Is our father, the King, in good health?' On coming to know of Dasaratha's death, he wept bitterly and lamented; and then recovering somewhat, performed the last rites and was lost in grief. The next day he asked Bharata, 'Instead of ruling the kingdom, why have you put on the guise of a renunciant?'

> I pray that you return to Ayodhya
> And accept the crown
> to undo the wrong of your sire and
> the evil done by my mother
> and the resultant sorrow, not ever witnessed before.
>
> (103)

Thus requests Bharata. Then Rama chides him, 'On account of the boons mother obtained, and in accordance with our father's command, I have come to the forest. How can it be right on your part to violate the King's command and come here?'

> By virtue of the boon father gave your mother
> The kingdom has become yours.
> You have indeed the right too, to rule.
> Hence, the reign is yours.
> Rule you must.
>
> (111)

Thus he ordered him. In reply, Bharata said,

> You, who are born before me,
> have no equal in all the three worlds.
> If the kingdom where such a one was born is mine,
> I hereby bequeath it to you.
> Hence, Oh King! Accept the crown.
>
> (112)

Rama, who heard this, said decisively, 'Even if the kingdom becomes mine by your generosity, will the period of twice seven years that I have agreed upon, pass by without my living in the forest? Don't think along the lines of how you can rule when I am there. Did I not, out of fear of going against the orders of the King to adorn myself with the crown, agree to it even when the King was alive? Similarly you also don't dishonour my command; instead keep ruling the kingdom until I come back', thus Rama spoke with finality, making Bharata come around.

Though Vasishta said at that time, 'Take it as my orders and get back to rule the kingdom that is rightfully yours,' Rama declined it. In that situation, when Vasishta was at his wits' end, Bharata put an irreversible conclusion to the argument saying, 'If that is so, let whosoever pleases rule the country. I shall live with you in the forest'. Then the celestials realising a situation arising in which their objective would not be fulfilled, said in an astral voice, 'Rama shall uphold the word of his father. Therefore, it is the bounden duty of Bharata to protect the country till he (Rama) gets back to Ayodhya'. Rama, who heard this, made the issue clear to Bharata, asked him to rule the kingdom and Bharata agreed. He swore, 'Should you not return on the day your stipulated period of stay in the forest comes to an end, I will jump into the fire and kill myself. This is certain'. He took the two sandals, saying 'These two alone will keep me alive', placed them on his sacred head and got back to Ayodhya.

Ramayana texts have tried in several ways to solve the problem of how to move the story forward at this juncture. Valmiki says that Bharata, without arguing any further, takes the sandals bearing the imprint of Rama's feet, and goes back to Ayodhya. Adhyatma Ramayana and the texts that follow it say that Bharata, who, through Vasishta, came to know of the purpose of Rama's incarnation, agrees to go back to Ayodhya, whereas Kamban creates an astral voice whose instruction Bharata agrees to follow. In Tulsi, it is due to the celestials' act of Maya that Bharata realises the truth. It is a common convention in world literatures to resolve, by *deus ex machina* i.e. superhuman devices, complications which cannot be resolved at the human level. It can be said that the Indian poets too have employed this technique.

Controversies regarding Rajya Sulkam

Some of the scholars who noted the predicament of Kaikeyi, against whom all the characters of Ramayana except Rama hurled baseless charges and censured her, are of the opinion that she demands what is rightfully hers; and that too, it is because of her concern – stemming from the strength of her chastity – that her husband should not be subject to the infamy of violating truthfulness – that she asks for what she wants. Such scholars, therefore, think that it is a baseless criticism to censure her. Kaikeyi asks only for the boons that Dasaratha has already given her. It is true that this results in a moral dilemma for Dasaratha who has to give it at this point of time. Yet, their argument is that, with the intention of upholding his reputation, even though he is agonised, Kaikeyi has thus compelled him and got the two boons translated into action; or else truthfulness will be shattered. This argument appears to be valid.

In order to reinforce this view, those who take this stand cite Rama's arguments while staying at Chitrakootam. Rama recalled that Dasaratha had promised, at the time of his marriage to Kaikeyi, to give the kingdom to her son. Therefore it was utterly wrong on the part of Dasaratha to try to offer Rama the kingdom which was Bharata's by right on the basis of the promise made to Kaikeyi. Hence, they hold that Kaikeyi is blameless whereas Dasaratha is the one who is at fault.

The third verse in Sarga 107 of Vanmikam forms the basis for this argument.[25] Though Kamban does not state explicitly this view of the primary text, scholars of Kamba Ramayanam support this argument considering the verse beginning with 'The boon by virtue of your father's words', spoken by Rama at Chitrakootam wherein, the phrase 'By your birth, the reign is yours as a matter of right', refers to *Rajya Sulkam* mentioned by Valmiki. The intention of such a critical analysis is to exalt Kaikeyi who takes all the blame upon herself without letting any fall on Dasaratha who has either forgotten or concealed this basic assurance out of the great love he has for his son Rama, and hail her as the paragon of chastity. It has been shown above that one can accept the justness of Kaikeyi's action without reference to the promise of Rajya Sulkam.

There arise some difficulties in accepting the verse of Valmiki cited above. If it is true that Dasaratha had given Kekeya the assurance of Rajya Sulkam, then this statement should have been presented in Valmiki as the utterance of Narada or that of Valmiki, Dasaratha, Kaikeyi, Manthara or Vasishta. For Kaikeyi, who obtained such a crucial pair of boons, there was

---

25   See footnote no. 23.

no need to have any anxiety in this regard. At least Manthara, who knew all the facts concerning Kaikeyi and as one who was interested in her welfare, could have reminded Kaikeyi of this matter. Or Vasishta, who was acquainted with everything and who had been invested with the responsibility of personally conducting the marriage of Kaikeyi, could have reminded Dasaratha of this matter, when the latter thought of crowning Rama and tried to elicit the views of the courtiers; Vasishta could have advised him to crown Bharata. Thus the question arises why Valmiki should have projected it as the utterance of Rama alone and not that of anybody else who is connected with the issue of Rajya Sulkam.[26] There is no reference even in Vanmikam as to who conveyed this matter to Rama.

Rama himself utters this sloka in Chitrakootam, wanting to make matters clear to Bharata. If that is the case, why did he not open up this matter with Dasaratha when the latter told him that he was going to crown him; why did he not say, 'Please give the throne to Bharata, that alone is proper'? The question arises – Is it not unrighteous on the part of Rama, who knew about the gift, to agree to the coronation? The argument that Rama was scared of defying the King's orders and hence agreed to his decision, does not seem to be valid. Later, when Dasaratha, in the palace of Kaikeyi, devastated by her boon and feeling sorrowful, said, 'Rama! Defy my orders and crown yourself. Rest assured that no blame will fall on you on account of this', – why did not Rama agree to it? Therefore, covering up the matter known to him, and consenting to be crowned, renders Rama grossly culpable. What would have

---

26 Sitarama Sashtrigal, *Valmiki Munihradaya Tatvasara Prakasika* (Trichy: United Printers Ltd., 1943) pp.155-173.

happened had Kaikeyi not sought the boon? Would not the eternal stigma of usurping the kingdom taint Rama that he accepted it, knowing full well that it was Bharata's by right?

It is obvious that this view, which will hold Dasaratha, Rama and Vasishta indefensibly guilty, will not acquit Kaikeyi of the charge of deceitfulness. Nor does it appear convincing or appropriate to maintain that Kaikeyi thought of erasing this stigma on Dasaratha. For this reason, it does not seem to be appropriate either to praise the chastity of Kaikeyi who did not break down on seeing her husband give up his life right in front of her, after pleading with her and blaming her. It is worth pondering that none of the Ramayana poets, including Valmiki and Kamban, who have created characters and given life to them, have authorially identified themselves with or approved of this act of Kaikeyi. Though it is true, according to the principles of theory of evolution that the later generations will be endowed with a sharper intelligence than their ancestors, we do not find it apt to consider that the earlier poets of Ramayana, including Valmiki who composed this sloka, levelled a baseless charge at Kaikeyi without thinking along these lines.

No reference to the sloka on Rajya Sulkam, which has thus given rise to controversial opinions, is found in any of the literary works anywhere. In the fourth section of **Satyopakhyanam** or **Rama Rahasyam**, a Sanskrit work, the idea of Dasaratha marrying Kaikeyi, on hearing about her beauty through Narada, is talked about. In the fifth section it has been said that after the conversation between Manthara and Kaikeyi, Kaikeyi reminded Dasaratha of the assurance of Rajya Sulkam.[27]

---

27 *Purana Bulletin* (Ayodhya Special Issue), p.153.

Despite strenuous efforts, it has not been possible for the present researcher to access the source text containing these two references. Nor has it been possible to find out the period of this work, its author etc. In a manuscript compiled by a scholar called Stein and preserved now in the Jammu Museum, Satyopakhyanam has been mentioned in two different ways, (a) as a part of *Brahmandapurana* (p. 207) and (b) as a part of Padma Purana (p. 204). Hence it has not been possible to find out whether it is a complete text or a part of another text.[28]

Therefore, we are not in a position to say anything definite about Rajya Sulkam unless the text in palm leaf manuscript is published in its entirety or becomes accessible for the use of scholars. It has not been possible to find a solution to this complication just on the basis of a later dramatic work, *Pratima Natakam*. We, therefore, have to conclude on a note of doubt as to whether this sloka found in both the Recensions of Valmiki (Southern and Northern) is a statement of Valmiki at all.

Ramayana texts mostly toe the same line in depicting the scene of meeting between Rama and Bharata which takes place revolving around the subject of Rama returning to Ayodhya and ascending the throne. There are several evidences to maintain that it is only Kamba Ramayanam which mostly goes along the lines of the primary text in respect of ideas and portrayal of characters, even though Valmiki is the source for all the Ramayana texts.

The Ramayana texts which have appeared in many North Indian languages have been impacted by Tantric doctrine and Advaita and other philosophical systems and have evolved into

---

28 Dr G Gangadharan, former Professor of Sanskrit, University of Madras.

Bhusundi, Adhyatma and Tulsi Ramayanas; we find the other texts bearing the impact of one or all of the three texts and deviating a little more from Vanmikam.

Though it does not differ much in content from the primary text, Kamba Ramayanam excels in poetic quality without leaning on either Tantric thought or metaphysics; and, despite its theistic objective, it has become ripe as a useful fruit-bearing tree that can be relished by everyone, including the atheist, making a profound impact on all. We find that the Tulsi Ramayan, coming at the fag end of the Bhakti movement, has the motive of lavishing the immeasurable nectar of Rama Bhakti (devotion to Rama) on all – the erudite and the illiterate alike – therefore differing very much from the original in terms of content, thought and character delineation.

We can conclude this section by saying that Valmiki, a treasure house of cultural history by virtue of delineating Rama's story, Kamban a poetical mine deeply relished by the erudite and Tulsidas, an ocean of devotional ecstasy, remain among Indians as the great trinity of the three sublime epics.

Content Variations in Ayodhya Kaandams

There are some differences between the texts of the Northern, North-western, and Eastern recensions and those of the Southern recensions. The details – that Kaikeyi's mother, unmindful of her husband dying, was bent on getting to know the secrets that she wished to learn, – that Sumantra rebukes Kaikeyi saying, 'You too are like your mother, not bothered about the death of Dasaratha' (Sarga 35) – and Rama and Lakshmana along with Sita going to Valmiki's ascetic abode to bow down and seek his blessings – are narrated only in the Southern Recension of Vanmikam (Sarga 56:16-17). Similarly, it is only the Southern Recension which talks about the planetary positions at the time of birth of Rama and the others.

Both the Recensions of Vanmikam state that in the horoscope drawn on the basis of planetary conditions at the time of Dasaratha's birth, his end was indicated (NR.II.4:17-20; SR.II.4:17-20) and that according to Sita's horoscope, the astrologers predicted for her a period of life in the forest (NR II.26: 6-95 SR II.29: 8-11). But the conditions of the planets at the time of Rama's birth are not pointed out in the Northern Recension.

It is not clear why, in a culture where the epic hero's horoscope was not cast, there should be a mention that the horoscopes of his father and wife were cast. Since we come across, in the Southern Recension, the planetary conditions which are the basis of Rama Navami festival celebrated all over the country, it remains an enigma why they are not referred to in the Northern Recension.

Sarga 100, in which Rama instructs Bharata on the moral principles and responsibilities of kingship; Sargas 108-109, which deal with Jabali's atheistic advice and Rama's refutation of it; and Sarga 117, which describes Rama and Sita meeting Sage Athri to seek his blessings, and the sage's wife Anasuya welcoming Sita, hosting her, gifting her ornaments and extending her warmth, Sita narrating her story to Anasuya, are regarded as 'interpolations' by scholars like Jacobi (Bulcke 378-380). These matters are found in both Northern and Southern Recensions.

Sloka Variations in Ayodhya Kaandams

The following table explains the differences in the number of sargas in the Northern and Southern Recensions of Vanmikam and how they differ in the number of slokas too, as far as Ayodhya Kaandam is concerned.

Table 4
Valmiki Ramayana
AYODHYA KAANDAMS

Sarga	Sloka			Sarga	Sloka		
	Critical edition	Gorakhpur edition	Dharmalaya edition		Critical edition	Gorakhpur edition	Dharmalaya edition
1.	37	51	51	25.	15	47	47
2.	34	54	55	26.	22	38	38
3.	32	49	50	27.	33	24	23
4.	45	45	45	28.	20	26	26
5.	24	26	26	29.	27	24	25
6.	28	28	28	30.	24	47	47
7.	31	36	36	31.	37	37	35
8.	27	39	39	32.	22	45	45
9.	47	66	66	33.	19	31	31
10.	41	40	40	34.	36	61	61
11.	15	29	29	35.	38	37	37
12.	24	112	115	36.	17	33	33
13.	28	26	27	37.	28	37	37
14.	27	67	69	38.	20	17	18
15.	14	48	50	39.	16	41	41
16.	61	47	48	40.	30	51	51
17.	33	22	22	41.	33	21	20
18.	40	41	41	42.	26	35	35
19.	22	40	40	43.	15	21	21
20.	36	55	55	44.	27	31	31
21.	25	64	65	45.	24	33	33
22.	20	30	30	46.	79	34	34
23.	34	41	42	47.	33	19	19
24.	19	38	36	48.	36	37	37

Sarga	Sloka			Sarga	Sloka		
	Critical edition	Gorakhpur edition	Dharmalaya edition		Critical edition	Gorakhpur edition	Dharmalaya edition
49.	15	18	18	73.	17	28	39
50.	22	51	51	74.	21	36	36
51.	30	27	27	75.	14	65	65
52.	26	102	102	76.	30	23	24
53.	26	35	35	77.	23	26	26
54.	20	43	44	78.	17	26	26
55.	21	33	35	79.	21	17	17
56.	17	35	41	80.	25	22	26
57.	39	34	34	81.	23	16	16
58.	57	37	37	82.	27	32	32
59.	14	34	38	83.	22	26	26
60.	19	23	24	84.	22	18	13
61.	25	27	27	85.	77	22	22
62.	15	20	20	86.	36	25	25
63.	18	53	54	87.	27	24	23
64.	24	78	80	88.	27	30	30
65.	28	29	30	89.	19	23	23
66.	45	29	29	90.	25	24	24
67.	15	38	38	91.	17	83	84
68.	29	22	22	92.	15	40	40
69.	34	21	22	93.	41	27	27
70.	23	30	30	94.	59	27	27
71.	25	46	46	95.	47	19	20
72.	25	54	55	96.	29	30	31

Sarga	Sloka			Sarga	Sloka		
	Critical edition	Gorakhpur edition	Dharmalaya edition		Critical edition	Gorakhpur edition	Dharmalaya edition
97.	24	31	32	111.	20	32	32
98.	71	18	16	112.		31	31
99.	19	42	42	113.		25	25
100.	17	76	76	114.		29	32
101.	31	27	-9-	115.		24	27
102.	31	-9-	50	116.		25	26
103.	32	49	32	117.		29	30
104.	25	32	27	118.		54	54
105.	24	42	46	119.		22	22
106.	24	35	36				
107.	22	19	20				
108.	26	18	18				
109.	28	39	40				
110.	52	37	36	Total	3,160	4,294 +1,134	4,357 +1,197

Ayodhya Kaandam Total Sargas and Slokas	Sargas	Slokas
Northern Recension – Critical edition	111	3,160
Southern Recension – Gorakhpur edition	119	4,294
Southern Recension – Dharmalaya edition	119	4,357

ARANYA KAANDAM

Preliminary Remarks on the chapter Aranya Kaandam
Journey towards Panchavati
- Meeting Sage Atri and Sage Agastya
- The greatness of Sage Agastya
- Sage Agastya's reception of Rama
- The weapons given by Sage Agastya to Rama
- Ancient myths originating and prevailing in Tamil culture

Life in Panchavati
- Surpanakha's arrival
- Qualities of Rama's character as revealed in the Surpanakha episode
- The killing of Khara and Dushana
- Surpanakha complaining to Ravana
- What happened to Surpanakha?
- Argument between Ravana and Maricha
- Arrival of the illusory deer
- Argument between Rama and Lakshmana
- Argument between Sita and Lakshmana
- Ravana's abduction of Sita
    - The conversation between Ravana and Sita

- The Abduction
- Marvelling at her beauty
- Comparison of Rama-Ravana
- Comparison of Sita-Ravana
- The manner of abducting Sita
- Sita's lament
- Some points for reflection
- Reasons for abduction of Sita
  - Disfiguring of Surpanakha
  - The killing of Sambukumara
  - Ravana's unacceptable lust
  - Ravana's interest in Moksha

Setting out in Search of Sita
- The first meeting of Rama and Jatayu
- The battle between Jatayu and Ravana
- The second meeting of Rama and Jatayu
- The story of Ayomukhi
- The story of Kabandhan
- The story of Sabari

Content Variations in Aranya Kaandams

Sloka variations in the Aranya Kaandams

Aranya Kaandam

Preliminary Remarks on Aranya Kaandam

THE PLOT OF Rama's story has been built with two indispensable turning points. The first occurs when, even as the preparations for the coronation are going on, Rama has to head for the forest without being crowned, on account of Kaikeyi's scheming. This first turning point, at the human level, is something that happens in most royal families – a conflict over the issue of succession to the throne; at the superhuman level, it is a crisis caused by the celestials and the like, using human beings as instruments to fulfil the objective of incarnation.

In the Aadi Ramayana, this turning point has been depicted as a mere human conflict over the issue of succession to the throne. When the doctrine of incarnation took root in society and turned into an ideology, we find this turning point evolving into a complication caused by superhuman intervention *(Deus ex machina)*.

The second turning point occurs in Aranya Kaandam. Rama, who took up residence in the forest after giving up the throne for his younger brother at the command of his father, spent the first ten years of his life peacefully in the forest regions of Chitrakootam and Dandaka. He was living happily, associating himself with the sages living there and being a source of support to them and they in turn acting as his mentors. Intending to go far away from Ayodhya, he crosses many a forest region, journeys southwards and on the advice of the sages he settles down in a place called Panchavati and lives there. It is here that he loses his wife Sita. He, who has to get back to Ayodhya in a few years, is compelled to go further south in search of his wife, fight with Ravana and retrieve her. Thus, the loss of Sita, which happened in Panchavati, constitutes the second turning point.

The motif of journey is one of the devices which the epics of the world have employed; i.e. when complications arise for the protagonists of the epic, it is a kind of technique employed to depict them as undertaking a journey to extricate themselves from them.

This remains so well-known a technique that it can be safely asserted that there are virtually no epics without the journey motif. Most of the world's renowned classical plays too can be seen making use of this technique. Shakespeare's plays are a good example.

Such literary journeys are of many types. Leaving the country and going to the forest, living there for some time and returning to the country after the resolution of the complications and living happily, is one kind; leaving the country and going to other islands, distant seas and returning upon the resolution of the complications, is another; going to superhuman worlds, such as Heaven, and *paataala* (*patala*, Sanskrit: पाताल, pātāla, the underworld or Hades), to resolve the human complications and then returning after obtaining the resolution, is another kind; yet another kind is that found in works where superhuman beings are the chief characters who, in order to resolve the complications, leave the world of the celestials and undertake a journey to the world of the human beings.

After undertaking various kinds of such journeys, happily getting back when the complications are resolved is a possibility. It is just as likely that the journeys undertaken to solve the complications may be the beginning of fresh complications leading to great suffering. *Thus, Rama's sojourn in the forest becomes a journey undertaken to solve a small issue bringing in its trail a more serious crisis.*

In this connection, it is worth reflecting upon the predicament of Kovalan (in the Tamil epic Silappathikaram) when he crossed forests and lands and reached the ancient city of Madurai to be rid of the earthly affliction of poverty but lost his life.

It is Ravana's abduction of Sita, the major event in the Aranya Kaandam, which forms the second turning point.

The abduction of Sita happens in the beautiful forests of Panchavati on the banks of the river Godavari. All the events of Aranya Kaandam are constructed in such a way as to revolve around this incident. Therefore, we can analyse the events of Aranya Kaandam by dividing them into three stages such as those that happen when undertaking the journey to Panchavati; those that happen in Panchavati; and those that happen after Rama and Lakshmana leave Panchavati and go in search of Sita.

Journey towards Panchavati
Meeting Sage Atri and Sage Agastya
Vanmikam

After Bharata returns to Ayodhya with his army, Rama, along with Sita and Lakshmana, leaves Chitrakootam and sets forth southwards. On the way, finding the hermitage of Sage Atri, he pays obeisance to him. Sage Atri, knowing who Rama is, receives him and the others with great joyous regard and extends hospitality to them; as desired by him, Rama spends the night in that hermitage. Then the sage introduces Sita to his wife Anasuya and asks her to entertain Sita with kindness. Anasuya pleases Sita by praising her beauty and fine qualities and gets to know her by enquiring all about her. The next morning, Rama takes leave of Sage Atri and gets ready to continue the journey. Anasuya then gifts Sita lustrous ornaments, silken garments and ever-fresh aromatic substances and sees her off with good wishes. Later, the three of them enter the dense forest called Dandaka.

The slaying of Viradha after entering the forest of Dandaka, the story of Sage Sarabhanga and the story of Rama's stay in the hermitage of Sage Sutikshana are all not directly connected to the plot of Rama's story. It can be construed that they have been employed to serve as means for conveying the doctrine of incarnation.

Even the meeting with Sage Agastya is not one that is directly connected to the plot. Yet we can study this meeting in some detail since Agastya is associated with various ancient tales, myths of Indian culture, particularly in the southern region.

Following the advice of Sage Sutikshana, Rama comes to the hermitage of Sage Agastya and describes to Lakshmana the greatness of Sage Agastya as one 'who, in response to the plea of the celestials, destroyed the two demons Ilvalan and Vatapi who kept killing the Brahmanas by trickery (11:54-67)'. Rama also says that Agastya was the one who, while coming to the south, stamped down Mount Vindhya which stood obstructing him and that it is due to his settling in the south that the southern region remains an abode of peace, free from the troubles caused by the demons. Thus narrating the story of Sage Agastya, Rama reached the latter's hermitage.

Rama, who spent that night with joy and satisfaction in the hermitage, met Sage Agastya the next day and expressed his wish to know the history of the Dandaka forest. Agastya too narrated it as follows: 'On account of the curse of Sage Bhargava and due to the negligence of Dandaka, a king of the Ikshvaku clan, this region became desolate and turned into a wild forest, depleted of its natural resources for several thousands of years with increasing troubles caused by demons and rendered uninhabitable for human beings. Providentially, I came down from the Himalayan region to this place (24). Afterwards, with the rains pouring down, the natural resources multiplied and it became a pleasant area suitable for living. Yet, the troubles caused by the demons have not ceased. After you came down here, they are tormenting the sages even more. You should provide the sages adequate protection. You shall right away destroy the demon folks of this region which has been neglected by your ancestors (SR 13:19-37).'

Rama, who was happy to hear the story of Dandaka forest requested Agastya thus: 'Kindly suggest a good place for me, Sita and brother Lakshmana to live in peace'. Agastya said,

'Panchavati, located to the south of the banks of Godavari, is the region suitable for your welfare and happiness', and described the route to reach that place. Then the three of them started walking towards Panchavati.

Both the Northern and Southern Recensions of Vanmikam narrate the story of Rama meeting Sage Agastya in the same way as mentioned above.

Yet the details regarding the story of the Dandaka forest as narrated by Agastya, on Rama's request, and the claim that Agastya came from the Himalayan region are not found in the Northern Recension of Vanmikam.

Nor are they found in the Gorakhpur edition of the Southern Recension. In the **Dharmalaya edition** alone, which is in vogue in the Tamil region, this story is narrated as above.

In those sargas of Vanmikam which narrate this story, the difference in the number of verses is as follows:

Editions
Critical edition (Northern Recension) – Twenty-five.
Gorakhpur edition (Southern Recension) – Twenty-five.
Dharmalaya edition (Southern Recension) – Sixty-five (+Forty).

The Greatness of Sage Agastya

The following details regarding the greatness of Sage Agastya are presented in **Kamba Ramayanam** as the avowal of the poet.

Long ago, when the celestials requested Agastya to bless them by destroying the demons hiding under the sea, Agastya scooped out a handful of sea water, drank it and made the ocean go dry. Then, at the celestials' entreaty, he spat out the water he had drunk and brought back the sea. Agastya is credited with this kind of greatness.

Agastya is the kind-hearted person who put an end to the sufferings of the Brahmanas by killing the demon brothers Ilvalan and Vatapi, who, by their sorcery, had been killing and eating them up.

He is the mighty one who stamped down Mount Vindhya which had grown sky high, blocking the way for the sages who came southwards from the north, and caused it to sink into the netherworld.

Obeying Lord Siva's command to lower the northern side of the subcontinent, he came down to the south and has ever since been residing at the lofty Mount Podhigai (the Agastyamalai range in the southern tip of the Western Ghats).

He is the one who has given us Tamil, the language blessed by Lord Siva, which is superior even to the four Vedas, by virtue of its provenance in the world and its poetic richness; it is he who has spread it all over the world. He has the distinction of earning eternal fame for himself by uttering Tamil, the immortal language of the South.

He is the gracious one who gave us the perennial Cauvery through his *kamandalam* (ritual water-pot of ascetics) for the prosperity of all the living beings in the eight directions and seven worlds (37-41, 46).

Agastya gave Rama the weapons he had with him saying, 'This bow, which I have been worshipping, was given to me long ago by the Supreme Lord Himself. You take this along with the quiver of arrows; also take this rare sword and the arrow shot by Lord Siva to burn Thirupuram (the three mythical cities of Tripura). [According to the scriptures, the bow and arrow were used by Lord Shiva to destroy Thirupuram, the three cities constructed by Mayasura (the asura architect), which were located on Earth, in the Sky and in Heaven respectively.] (55).

Other Ramayanas

Following a long paean to Rama in the spirit of worshipping the incarnation (3:17-45), Adhyatma says that Agastya gifted Rama a bow handed over by Indra to be given to Rama, besides a quiver and a gem-studded sword and blessed him (3:46-47).

The Telugu Ranganatha Ramayanam says that Agastya destroyed Vatapi and Ilvalan, stamped down Mount Vindhya, which blocked his way, and came to the south and cursed Nakusha to become a snake. This text says that when Rama and the others met Agastya and bowed to him, the elated sage drew Rama close to his chest and spoke highly of his noble qualities. Ranganatham says that he gifted Rama with divine weapons such as the bow, the arrow, the shield and the bow *kothandam*; however there is no mention of the history of the arms.

Gona Budda Reddy says that Agastya finally recounted to Rama the significance of the place Panchavati and advised him to go and stay there and Rama accordingly started walking towards Panchavati along with his younger brother and Sita (pp.131-132). There is no reference in this text to Agastya's scholarship.

Drinking up the sea water to alleviate the suffering of the celestials, destroying the two demon-brothers who were indulging in killing the Brahmanas, arriving in the south after bringing down Mount Vindhya, cursing Nakusha to become a snake, are all narrated as Agastya's glories in Bhaskara Ramayanam.

Bhaskaram states that Agastya gave Rama divine arms such as a sword, Vishnu's bow and arrows. This text says that Agastya advised Rama to stay at Panchavati situated on the banks of the river Godavari in the south (75-100). However, this text does not show Agastya as endowed with scholarly attributes such as creating the (Tamil) language and composing literary works.

In the Aranya Kaandam of Telugu Molla Ramayanam, there is no reference to the story of Agastya or about Rama meeting him.

In Malayala Kannassa Ramayanam, there is no mention of the various glories of Sage Agastya such as his birth nor is there any reference to the works he composed. That he subdued Mount Vindhya is mentioned; but not his coming down south; nor is there a mention of the various miracles he performed.

Kannassam states that Agastya gifted weapons such as the bow of Vishnu, *Brahmastram* (the missile of Brahma), Indra's bow, quiver and sword and wished him success. He then advised him to stay at Panchavati on the banks of the river Godavari.

Ezhuthachan's Adhyathma Ramayanam narrates all the incidents of Rama and the others coming to the hermitage of Agastya and from there, proceeding to Panchavati, while also including a long paean to Rama in the same manner as does the Sanskrit Adhyatma Ramayana (III.221-550).

Tulsidas's Ramcharitmanas follows Adhyatma Ramayana in narrating the story of Rama's meeting with Sage Agastya. Tulsidas calls Agastya Sage Kumbha (Kumbhaja Rishi) whereas Adhyatma does not do so. Manasam does not say that Agastya gave weapons to Rama. Tulsidas has depicted Rama entirely as a divine incarnation (III, 11:1-7; 12:1-9).

Kumara Valmiki's Kannada Torave Ramayanam says that Agastya gave Rama an arrow, a quiver and a sword named after Rama and other such divine weapons. But the history of the weapons is not narrated.

The story relating to Agastya's birth, the details of his coming to the south and the miracles performed by him are not spoken of in this Ramayana. Nor is there any reference here to his proficiency in language and literature.

It is not known if there are references to Agastya in other Indian Ramayanas and Southeast Asian Ramayanas. Scholars like Ohno Toru and Camille Bulcke (407) say that Ramakien states that Agastya gave Rama the shield that had been given to him by Lord Siva.

Sage Agastya's Reception of Rama

Among the Ramayana texts that record this incident, Valmiki's Agastya praises Rama as the king of all the worlds, one who follows the path of righteousness and a valiant hero and thus welcomes him; but he does not worship him as a divine incarnation.

Though the Tamil epic is named Ramavataram, Agastya of Kamba Ramayanam does not receive Rama, hailing him as a divine incarnation. Agastya realised within himself, 'It is very rare that the ultimate reality which even Brahma could not know, should appear in person, rarer still for Him to offer to help'. Yet, Agastya regards him as the physician who has come to nullify the poison in the form of the demons, to put out the fire of the wrath of the demons, just as the rains from above come down to protect the world; also he regards Rama as a mighty hero. Therefore, Kamba Ramayanam shows Agastya addressing Rama as the 'king of mercy'.

But the Sanskrit Adhyatma Ramayana and Ezhuthachan's Ramayanam, which came up following it, and the Tulsi Ramayan, which was drawn to and impacted by it, have depicted Rama entirely as a divine incarnation. The portions containing long hymns to Lord Vishnu in these texts themselves testify to this. Since these texts came up in the fifteenth and sixteenth centuries when the cult of *Bhagavata bhakti* (worshipping the Lord's devotees) was in full flow, it can be said that they have mostly blossomed as depictions of the doctrine of incarnation, i.e. these texts too are the later-day incarnational forms of the source text of Valmiki.

The Weapons given by Sage Agastya to Rama

Vanmikam
1. Vishnu's bow designed and made by Viswakarma
2. The arrow called Brahmadatta given by Brahma
3. Two quivers given by Lord Indra
4. An impenetrable shield given by Indra
5. A golden-sheathed sword
6. Maatali, the charioteer of Indra, and the chariot which materialised the moment you thought of it

Kamba Ramayanam
1. The bow given to Agastya by Brahma, the Primal God
2. A quiver, full of arrows
3. A sword
4. Siva's arrow which had been launched to burn Tripurasura's three mythical cities

Ramayana Manjari
1. The weapons handed over by Indra
2. Indra's chariot
3. Maatali, the charioteer of Indra

Adhyatma Ramayana
1. The bow handed over by Indra
2. A quiver
3. A sword studded with gems

Ranganatha Ramayanam
1. A bow 2. An arrow 3. A shield 4. Kothandam (a bow)

Bhaskara Ramayanam
1. The bow of Lord Vishnu 2. A sword 3. Arrows 4. Quivers

Kannassa Ramayanam
1. The bow of Lord Vishnu 2. Brahmastra (Brahma's missile)
3. The bow of Indra 4. Quivers 5. A sword

Ezhuthachan's Ramayanam
1. The bow of Indra 2. Arrows and quiver
3. A sword studded with gems

Tulsi Ramayan
No reference to weapons being given

Torave Ramayanam
1. A bow 2. An arrow 3. A quiver 4. A sword

Thakkai Ramayanam
1. The bow of Lord Siva 2. The arrow used by Lord Siva

All the Ramayana texts from Vanmikam onwards state that these weapons were given for the purpose of destroying the demons and protecting the Brahmanas and the sages.

While narrating the history of the weapons, a note is found indicating that they are those either used or given by the gods and the celestials. Therefore, one finds the suggestion that gods, celestials and sages like Agastya sought the destruction of the demons and that they wanted to accomplish it through Rama.

When we examine the data given above, there are seven events mentioned as the miracles performed by Agastya. Of these the three mentioned in Vanmikam are found in all the Ramayanas. Adding to Vanmikam another three about Agastya drinking up the water and thus emptying the sea to the last drop, fostering the Tamil language, setting in flow the river Cauvery from the waters of his kamandalam, Kamba Ramayanam makes it six miracles. Ranganatham adds to Vanmikam the episode of cursing Nakusha to become a snake. Bhaskaram adds to what Vanmikam says the two episodes of cursing Nakusha to become a snake and drinking up the sea.

These two Telugu Ramayanas of the thirteenth century alone narrate the story of Nakusha's curse.

At first it was Kamban and later Bhaskara who presented the detail about Agastya's greatness in draining the sea by drinking up its waters.

The two Tamil texts Kamba Ramayanam and Thakkai Ramayanam alone state the following two incidents: Agastya is the one who came down from the North to reside in the Podhigai hills, and he is the one who fostered the Tamil language.

Of the four miracles not recounted by Vanmikam, the Telugu Ramayanas describe two and Kamba Ramayanam the remaining two. The question naturally arises as to what the sources of these are. The first source that comes to our mind is Vyasa's Mahabharata.[1] In this five miracles are stated:

- Subduing Mount Vindhya (III, Sargas 96-99)
- Staying in Podhigai hills (III,103)
- Destroying Ilvalan and Vatapi (Vana Parva Sarga,99)
- Draining the sea by drinking its waters up (Vana Parva Sargas, 101-105)
- Cursing Nakusha to become a snake (III,103)

Setting in motion the river Cauvery and fostering the Tamil language are not stated in the Mahabharata. So it is possible to consider that the story of Nakusha's curse stated by the Telugu Ramayanas could have been drawn from the Mahabharata.

Ancient Myths Originating in Tamil Culture
Podhigai Hills
Kamban says that, at the command of Lord Siva, Agastya

---

1 *An Index to the Names in the Mahabharata*: by Søren Sørensen, New Delhi : Motilal Banarsidass, rpt. 1978, pp. 16-18.

came to the South and stayed in the Podhigai hills. This is a mythological tale. The Saivite saint Appar's *Thevaram* (hymn) saying that Agastya worshipped Lord Siva (5,73:3), and another Saivite saint Sundarar's Thevaram (7,65:5), saying that Agastya claimed that Lord Siva bestowed upon him his abode at the sacred hills of Podhigai, are probably the sources for Kamban. It can be considered that since Paripadal refers to 'the sage at Podhigai (11:11)', this ancient myth could have come into vogue towards the end of the Sangam Age.

As far as the Sanskrit language is concerned, the story is said to be found in Skanda Purana.[2] It is worth mentioning that going by chronology, this work comes later than the two Tamil works cited above.

Tamil

Kamban praises Agastya as the one who earned the reputation of having fostered the Tamil language and made it known worldwide (and as 'one who attained fame by uttering the everlasting Tamil of the South', III 3:47).The first reference linking the Tamil language with Agastya is found in the commentary on the first sutra (formulation) in Irayanar's poetics on clandestine love. Researchers regard this commentary as belonging to the eighth century AD. Kulasekhara Azhwar, who lived more or less in the same period, also refers to Agastya as 'the great sage of powerful Tamil' (Perumal 10:5). On the basis of these references and various other myths, we may say that Kamban may have associated Agastya with the Tamil language. After Kamban, this lore was variously elaborated by many.

---

2 *Puranic Encyclopaedia*, ed. Vettam Mani, New Delhi: Motilal Banarsidass, 1975, p. 8.

The River Cauvery

Kamban says that Agastya produced the river Cauvery through his kamandalam (II;3:46). Neither Valmiki nor Vyasa presents this view. The verse from the epic Manimekalai says:

> The immortal sage, Agastya tilted his kamandalam and let the maiden Cauvery stream eastward (11-13).

The epic tells the history of the river Cauvery which gushed forth when Agastya's pitcher was tilted and surged eastwards. It is not possible to figure out the source for this myth. This idea from Manimekalai may have served as the source for Kamban.

We understand that legendary accounts of Sage Agastya staying at the Podhigai hills in the South at the command of Lord Siva, him being credited with nurturing the Tamil language, and him producing the river Cauvery with the water from his kamandalam, had all acquired the status of myths of Tamil culture. We have to take it that when Kamban came to narrate the story of Agastya, he added these matters as legitimately relating to the sage and sang of them.

Life in Panchavati

Surpanakha's Arrival

Vanmikam

Rama was engaged in conversation with his younger brother and wife at Panchavati on the banks of the river Godavari. At that time, Surpanakha, a demoness who came there by chance, saw Rama, was captivated by his charm and overcome by lust she asked him,

> You, who are attired as an ascetic,
> why have you come here where the demons dwell?
> Speak the truth.

Rama, who never ever liked falsehood, replied that he had taken up exile in the forest along with his wife and brother at the command of his parents and come to the Dandaka forest. Then Rama asked Surpanakha about herself. She said:

> Rama! I will also tell you everything as it is. I am the sister of Ravana, the chief of the demons. My name is Surpanakha. From the moment I saw you, I have come to regard you in my mind as my husband. This uncouth, ugly human female is not suitable for you. It is I who am suitable for you.

So saying, Surpanakha stood between Sita and Lakshmana (NR.III.16;SR.III.17). When Rama heard the words of Surpanakha possessed by lust, he addressed her thus, with a mischievous smile in a derisive teasing tone:

> Oh lady! I am a married man. This Sita is my wife; my younger brother Lakshmana is now alone, without his wife. Try to get him as your husband.

Surpanakha, who took Rama's sarcastic words to be true, went to Lakshmana and requested him to marry her. Lakshmana, who took the hint from Rama, said the following with a smile:

> Oh lady with beautiful eyes! I am a servant of my elder brother Rama. Would you want to reduce your status to that of a maid by marrying me? It is better that you become his younger wife. He will accept you as his wife, giving up this ugly human female. Therefore, you would do well to go to Rama.

The foolish Surpanakha who took his mocking words to be true, went back to Rama and said, 'Isn't it because of this ugly-looking, uncouth woman's presence that you reject me? Right away in front of your eyes I will kill and eat her up and live with you as your sole wife'. Thus saying, she approached Sita. Rama, whose banter turned into anger, addressed Lakshmana and ordered him thus, 'Brother, we should never engage in bantering with wicked people. Save Sita. Disfigure this demonness'. Thus ordered, Lakshmana unsheathed his dagger and cut off Surpanakha's ears and nose. Screaming in grief on account of disfigurement, she ran back the same way she had come. (VR. NR.III.17; SR.III.18.)

According to Vanmikam, the details gathered from the encounter with Surpanakha are as follows:

- When Surpanakha meets Rama and the others she appears in her natural form as a demoness. Recognising her as a demoness Rama talks to her in a derisive vein.
- Referring to Lakshmana, Rama just says that at present he is alone, without his wife. He does not say that he is unmarried.
- Rama himself realises later that talking derisively has been the cause of untoward consequences.
- Rama orders Lakshmana to mutilate Surpanakha.
- It is Lakshmana who chops off Surpanakha's organs.
- Lakshmana cuts off only the ears and the nose.

On the basis of these we can now look at the details in the other Ramayana texts.

Jain Ramayanas

In Buddhist Ramayanas and most of the Jain Ramayanas, incidents of disfiguring Surpanakha are not to be found. In some, there is no mention of Surpanakha's story at all. One or two Jain Ramayana texts alone narrate this incident with a few changes.

Pauma Chariyu

Chandranakha (Surpanakha), who heard of the killing of her son Sambuka, was wandering in the Dandaka forest, distraught with grief. When she saw Rama and Lakshmana at Panchavati, she became infatuated with them. Expressing her desire and pleading with them, turning from the one to the other again and again, she returned to her dwelling without securing their consent – so says Pauma Chariyu (Bulcke15).

Vasudeva Hindi

When Rama and the others were at Dandaka forest, Ravana's sister Surpanakha, who came there, was struck by lust on seeing Rama and requested him to accept her. Rejecting her entreaty, Rama said, 'I am a sworn observer of penance. One who lives with his wife, never desires another man's wife'. Sita, who was disgusted with Surpanakha's conduct, reviled her as a shameless woman. Angered by Sita's abuse, Surpanakha threatened to kill her. As she was a woman Rama did not want to kill her; he cut off her ears and nose and chased her away.

Narasimha Purana

Surpanakha taking the form of a beautiful woman arrived at Panchavati, and overcome by infatuation on seeing Rama, she spoke as follows:

> Oh my beloved! I have fallen deeply in love with you. Kindly take me as your slave. It is a sin not to accept a woman who comes to you on her own.

Rama, who heard this improper plea of Surpanakha, replied,

I have a wife. I do not keep any contact with another man's wife. Go to my brother Lakshmana. His wife is not there with him now. Therefore he may probably accept you.

Surpanakha who heard this, said with joy, 'Good! If so, give me a letter. If he takes a look at it, he will accept me'.

Rama too gave a letter to him which read, 'Lakshmana, cut off her nose. Don't let her off without her nose being cut off'. Surpanakha gave that letter to Lakshmana. Lakshmana held her, hacked off her nose and ears with a sword and chased her away. Thus Narasimha Purana describes this incident (49: 33-47).

Azhwars' Hymns

In the Tamil literary tradition before Kamban, the references to the mutilation of Surpanakha's organs are found for the first time in the Azhwars' hymns. This detail is mentioned in the hymns of five of the Azhwars such as Periyazhwar, Andal, Kulasekhara Azhwar, Thirumangai Azhwar and Nammazhwar. All the five Azhwars say that **Rama** cut off Surpanakha's organs. There is no reference to Lakshmana. The ears and the nose are mentioned as the organs which were cut off. Andal and Kulasekhara Azhwar say that her nose was cut off. The other three say that both the ears and the nose were cut off.

Uttara Purana

King Janaka sent intimation to all the princes for his daughter Sita's swayamvaram. He also sent one to Rama, the King of Kasi. Narada described Sita's incomparable beauty to Ravana and added, 'But King Janaka has not invited you for the swayamvaram'. Ravana, smitten with love the moment he heard of Sita's beauty, thought of going to Varanasi to abduct her. But following Maricha's advice, he changed his mind and sent Surpanakha to find out Sita's views in this regard.

When Surpanakha went to Varanasi, she heard that Rama and Lakshmana along with their wives had gone to Chitrakootam. Immediately, she assumed the form of a beautiful woman, went to Chitrakootam and went around the apartment of the queens. They mocked and laughed at her. Sita said that to be born as a woman is itself pitiable. Surpanakha, who realised that it was not going to be possible to change the mind of Sita in tune with Ravana's desire, returned to Lanka and expressed to Ravana her inability to persuade Sita (Toru 77).

The detail that Surpanakha was mutilated by Rama and Lakshmana is not stated in Uttara Purana.

Ramayana Kakawin

According to Indonesia's ancient epic Ramayana Kakawin (eleventh century AD), Surpanakha, who was wandering in the Dandaka forest, chanced upon Rama and Sita collecting flowers. She saw them going together wherever they went, left them and sighted Lakshmana plucking flowers all alone and fell in love with him. At once, changing her demonic form, she assumed the form of a celestial damsel and approached Lakshmana; she expressed her love and requested him to marry her. Lakshmana sent her back to Rama saying, 'It is not possible for me, an ordinary human being, to marry you who are a celestial beauty. My elder brother Rama, who is a mighty hero, is the one suitable for you. You had better go there'.

With great joy, Surpanakha went to Rama and openly expressed her love for him. But Rama sent her back saying, 'Close by is my wife Sita. I can never even think of marrying any other woman. I shall give you a good piece of advice. You had better marry my younger brother Lakshmana'. She too, going back to Lakshmana with her eyes ablaze with lust, seated herself in front of him. Going by her actions, Lakshmana suspected her to be a demoness and cut off her nose. At once screaming, she ascended the sky, assumed the original form of a demoness, proclaimed that she was Surpanakha the demoness and vowed to get him killed by her brothers. So saying, she disappeared (Toru:72-73).

Kamba Ramayanam

Propelled by cruel fate, Surpanakha, who was wandering freely in the Dandaka forest, reached the dwelling of Rama at Panchavati. On seeing Rama, she stood wonder-struck by his handsome appearance. Then thinking:

> What penance has Penance done
> for this handsome man, assuming an ascetic's appearance
> to be performing penance!

She changed her demonic form into that of a pretty woman, approached Rama and stood coyly like a young deer. Rama was surprised to see her and asked her,

> Oh! graceful one! May your arrival be auspicious!
> Who is your husband? What is his name? Who are your kith and kin? (III.5.:38.)

'I am the daughter of Visravasu; I am Ravana's sister. My name is Kamavalli; yes a maiden', replied the treacherous woman who came as poison. Rama, who could not believe what she said, asked her how she managed to get such a beautiful human form if she was the sister of a demon. Before he could finish, that hypocritical woman, falsehood incarnate, said (39-43):

> I didn't like the life of living with the deceitful,
> powerful demons. I wanted to choose the path
> of righteousness. Therefore, to destroy my evil

past, I did penance and by the grace of the celestials, I got this form. In order to fulfil a mission, I have come to see you.

When Rama asked, 'For what purpose have you come to me, tell me. If possible I will do what I can'. Surpanakha said, 'It is unbecoming of women from good families smitten by love to express their love themselves. Cure me of my affliction of love and save me'. Rama, who realised that she was a demoness, said, 'Oh! You are a Brahmana woman. I hail from a Kshatriya clan. You have said something contrary to tradition', thus declining her request. Surpanakha argued, 'Though my father is a Vedic Brahmana, my mother is from a Kshatriya family. Therefore, you may accept me (44-50)'.

Rama, who realised that she was a deceitful woman and a demoness as well, wanted to mock her and deride her. He said: 'It is not proper for a human being to marry a demoness.' Surpanakha, who saw Sita beside Rama, said, 'She is a cruel demoness; she has assumed a false guise; oh valiant man! set her aside', and frowned at Sita. Realising that even if it is for fun, association with demons will only result in great harm, Rama asked her to leave the place and went inside the hermitage with Sita (51-69).

Surpanakha, who came again the next morning looking for Rama, believed that as long as Sita was there he would not accept her. Thinking that Sita was alone, she followed her in order to ambush her. When Lakshmana, who was guarding Sita, saw her, he came running and warned her shouting, 'Woman, stop!' Seizing her lock of hair he thought, 'it is not proper to kill a woman'. Hence he let her go after cutting off her nose, ear and nipples (92-94).

Surpanakha, who was mutilated, screamed out calling the

names of demons who were her kith and kin such as Ravana and Khara and complained to them and lamented. When Surpanakha saw Rama completing his morning ablutions in the river Godavari and returning to his hut, she fell down before him, shed tears and wailed, saying, 'Oh Lord! Look at my plight for falling in love with your sacred body (115)'.

Rama, realising that her ears and nose were cut off by Lakshmana for some misdeed of hers, asked her, 'Who are you?' because she was now in her original demonic form. On hearing this, she asked him, 'Don't you know me? Didn't I come yesterday too?' Then Rama asked Lakshmana, 'What misdeed did she commit to get such a punishment?' Before Lakshmana could finish saying, 'This wicked woman came to abduct the virtuous Sita', Surpanakha interrupted Lakshmana, retorting, 'Won't my heart boil with fury like a cauldron to see Sita as my rival (116-122)?'

Rama, who was enraged on hearing this, rebuked her saying, 'We have come to this forest for the sole purpose of destroying the clan of demons; therefore I warn you, leave this place before you get destroyed for your evil words and deeds'. Surpanakha, who heard Rama's words of fury, addressed him as follows:

> Celestials like the four-faced Brahma himself are like chieftains paying tribute to Ravana. The ten-faced Ravana will hack off the very tongue of the messenger who informs him that you cut off the nose and other organs of his sister, that is me. You have earned infamy and invited death upon yourself by cutting off my nose. You have spoiled the beauty of your sacred body, oh dear lord! like the milk that got curdled by being poured on the grass (124-125). Women who are firm in their chastity will not talk of their own glory; yet I say a few words out of the great

love I bear for you. If Ravana, who is stronger than the celestials, opposes you, who will be there to protect you? If you bestow your love on me and save my life, I, in turn, will save you.

In great battles I shall shield you; capable of carrying you aloft in the sky. I can fetch you many a tasty fruit. I shall get you whatever you want. Why this revulsion for me who is capable of saving you? Of what use is this fragile, slender-waisted Sita? (127-128)

Why did you insult me by cutting off my nose? Did you make the mistake of thinking that this woman with a beautiful form should always be by your side, that she will not go anywhere if you did this, that others will not desire her? Did not my love for you get doubled by knowing that with such an intention you acted like this? Am I such a foolish woman who could not understand even this? (133)

Rama, who heard the unrighteous but specious arguments of Surpanakha, said,

Don't ever presume that even celestials cannot stand up to the demons and that the two of us are mere human beings. I challenge you to gather all the powerful demons you mentioned and bring them over here; take my word for it, I shall kill them all to your very face. (137)

Surpanakha, who heard, argued that if Rama accepted her at least as his second wife, she would help him in fighting the demons by revealing their tricks and forestalling their acts of cunning. A snake knows the traits of another snake. (139)

Lakshmana, who observed Surpanakha thus arguing with Rama, said,

Brother, if we don't get rid of her now by killing her, she will keep following and harrying us. May I know your mind?

Rama replied,

> Surely, it may happen so, mightn't it? Fine! If she doesn't leave us, you act as you deem fit. (142)

Surpanakha, who understood the brothers' line of thinking, pondered, 'He won't relent even a little bit. If I linger on, I will lose my life'. Vowing revenge, she decided to leave the place and bring her brother Khara. (143)

Bhusundi Ramayana

An account of this episode similar to Kamba Ramayanam is given in Bhusundi Ramayanam also.

Ranganatha Ramayanam

Surpanakha in her original form came towards Panchavati to take revenge on the killers of her son, Jambu/Sambukumara. On seeing Rama, she was captivated by his beauty, forgot all thoughts of revenge and, desiring to have him, asked, 'Who are you?' Rama replied, 'I am the son of Dasaratha. My name is Rama. This is my younger brother. She is my wife. Obeying my father's words I came to the forest.' When asked, 'Who are you?' she replied, 'I am the daughter of Visravasu; I am the sister of Ravana; my name is Surpanakha. You must marry me', – thus she entreated him. Rama said,

> I am a married man. Had I not been married, I would have held your hand in marriage by now; yet you need not worry. That man is my younger brother. He has been wanting to have a beautiful, suitable wife. Therefore, you please approach him.

Surpanakha, who took his words to be true, approached Lakshmana and requested him to marry her. Realising that this must be Rama's mischief, Lakshmana said,

> It was Rama that you sought first. I cannot accept you. Sita is no match to your beauty. So, Rama will reject Sita and accept you. Therefore, Oh beautiful woman, approach Rama.

And thus, Lakshmana sent her back to Rama. She too went back to Rama and requested him to accept her. Rama turned down her request. Since she pleaded with him again and again, he said to Lakshmana, 'Punish her'. Accordingly Lakshmana cut off her nose and ears (pp.137-138).

Bhaskara Ramayanam

Details such as Surpanakha coming to Panchavati, lusting for Rama, introducing herself, requesting Rama to accept her, getting shunted between Rama and Lakshmana and becoming enraged and planning to abduct Sita, are all told in Bhaskara Ramayanam as in Ranganatha Ramayanam. But Bhaskaram states that Surpanakha came in the form of a beautiful woman. When she tried to abduct Sita, Rama held Sita in one hand and Surpanakha in another and addressed Lakshmana, 'We should not indulge in making fun of wicked people. Don't you see its consequences? Disfigure her'. Lakshmana at once cut off Surpanakha's nose and ears and maimed her. Thus mutilated, Surpanakha screamed out in anger with tears rolling down, and departed to complain to Khara (III First Aaswasam 139-156).

Molla Ramayanam

Molla Ramayana too briefly states the incidents connected with Surpanakha as do the earlier Telugu Ramayanas (Aranyam 7-8).

Adhyatma Ramayana

Surpanakha, who was roaming about the forest of Dandaka, happened to see the footprints of Rama with the imprint of a lotus. At once, irredeemably infatuated with the one to whom they belonged, she followed the footprints and reached the place of Rama. On seeing Rama sitting with Sita she asked,

> Whose son are you? What is your name? What are you doing here clad in tree-barks? I am the daughter of the demon-clan. My name is Surpanakha. I am capable of assuming any form I fancy. I am the sister of Ravana, the chief of the demon-clan. The entire forest has been made mine by rights. I am living here with my brother Khara. I kill and eat up the ascetics I come across.
> I wish to know all about you. Tell me in detail.

Thus requested Surpanakha. Rama, who heard what she said, replied thus:

> I am the son of the King of Ayodhya. My name is Rama. This beautiful woman is my wife Sita, daughter of King Janaka. The other one with me is my younger brother Lakshmana. Oh! The world's most beautiful woman! Tell me what you want.

Surpanakha, who was much delighted by the soothing words of Rama, said, 'Oh! Rama with lotus-like eyes! Please, come with me. Both of us shall enjoy all the comforts and luxuries of the forest. I, who am smitten with love for you, will not live without you'. After hearing the words of the demoness, Rama, while looking at Sita from the corner of his eye, said,

> This beautiful lady is my wife. She will not live without me. If I accept you, you can only live as the other wife. But you will not like it. Lakshmana, my younger brother near me, is a handsome one; the right husband for you. Live happily with him in the forest.

Surpanakha heard this alternative suggestion from Rama. With her infatuation reaching dizzy heights, she approached

Lakshmana and entreated him thus: 'Let us follow your brother's words and live as husband and wife; tarry no further please.' Lakshmana sent her back to Rama saying, 'I am myself Rama's servant. Surely you do not wish to be a servant maid, do you? I am suggesting it for your good. You may go back to Rama. It is he who is the leader of all'.

The evil-minded demoness that she was, she went back to Rama in great fury and said, 'Hey! Ungracious, petty-minded Rama! Why do you torment me thus? Look! I shall right away eat up Sita who is the cause of all this', and assuming a huge form she approached Sita.

Lakshmana, who realised that the situation was going out of control, punished her acting on Rama's order by cutting off her ears and nose with his sword. Her body soaked in blood all over, Surpanakha rushed to Khara with a terrible scream (III. 5:2-20).

Ananda Ramayana

Grieved by the news of Rama and Lakshmana killing her son, Surpanakha goes to Panchavati in the form of a beautiful woman. Captivated by Rama's beauty, she makes advances to him and he directs her to Lakshmana, who mutilates her. She then rushes away to complain to Khara and Dushana, says this text.

Kannassa Ramayanam

Kannassa Ramayanam says that Surpanakha came to Panchavati in her original form. Other incidents such as requesting Rama to marry her are narrated mostly as in the other Ramayanas. Kannassa Ramayanam concludes the Surpanakha episode by saying that Rama and Lakshmana thought, 'Enough of this game'. And then Lakshmana, in great anger, cut off Surpanakha's ears and nose.

Ezhuthachan's Ramayanam

When Surpanakha tried to abduct Sita and run away, Lakshmana, on his own, without Rama's orders, cut off her ears, nose and breasts and humiliated her. These two details are not found in the Sanskrit source. Padmanabhan Thampi thinks that Ezhuthachan made these two changes owing to the influence of Kamba Ramayanam.[3]

Torave Ramayanam

In this text also, like Kamban's Surpanakha, she appears as a beautiful woman. She expresses her lust for Rama and argues with him and meets with the same punishment.

Tulsidas's Ramcharitmanas

Surpanakha, who had nails like a winnowing pan, saw Rama and Lakshmana, who were staying at Panchavati; attracted by their handsome appearance, she fell insatiably in love with them. Changing her form into that of a beautiful woman, she approached Rama and expressed her passion for him. Glancing at Sita, Rama just said, 'My younger brother remains without a partner'. Thus, Surpanakha, who was shunted between the brothers, in great fury revealed her demonic form. Noticing Sita shuddering at the sight of her form, Rama gestured to Lakshmana. At once, Lakshmana cut off her ears, says Tulsidas (III.Doha 16. Chaupa {four-line verse} 2-10. Doha 17).

Ramakien

Surpanakha, who had lost her husband, was roaming in the forest of Dandaka. On seeing Rama, she developed an inordinate lust

---

3   *Ramayanas of Kampan and Eluttacchan*, p. 62.

for him and thought of seducing him. To achieve her purpose, she took the form of a beautiful woman, approached Rama and expressed her desire. Being an avowed monogamist, Rama paid no attention to her. Surpanakha, who saw Sita close by, realised the reason for Rama ignoring her.

Thinking that Rama would not accept her as long as Sita was there, Surpanakha assumed the form of a demoness and tried to kill Sita. On seeing this, Lakshmana, who was close by, came rushing to Sita. Since the demon was a woman, he thought that it would be wrong to kill her; instead he cut off her ears and nose and chased her away from there, so says the Thailand Ramakien.[4]

Ramakirti, which is a combination of the dramatic as well as the literary conventions of Thailand, narrates this episode as follows:

> Samanakha (Surpanakha), realising that unless Sita is killed, Rama will not yield to her desire, tried to attack and kill her. When Rama came swiftly, beat Samanakha up and pushed her down, Lakshmana stood on her chest. Both the brothers cut off her limbs, then her nose, ears and lips.[5]

Kashmiri Ramayanas

Among the Ramayanas that came up in Kashmiri, it is Prakash Ramayana which is considered to be the oldest. According to this Ramayana, which appeared roughly by the end of eighteenth century AD, Rama, who saw Surpanakha approaching Sita, shot an arrow at her nose and cut it off. In the other Kashmiri Ramayanas, it is said that it was Lakshmana who disfigured Surpanakha.[6]

---

4   *Sri Ramakirti Mahakavyam*, trans. Satyavrat Shastri. Bangkok: Moolamal and Amarnath Sachdeva Foundation, 1990, pp.250-251.
5   *Ramakien, The Thai Ramayana*. Bangkok: Patamini Ltd., Naga Books, 1993, pp.74-75.
6   Omkar Kaul, p.85. (Hindi footnote).

Summary

All the Ramayanas from Vanmikam onwards point out that the arrival of Surpanakha is the prelude to the imprisoning of Sita and the consequent destruction of Ravana. Most of the Ramayana texts depict this portion, which is an indispensable part of the structure of the epic, in a realistic manner, some with a literary flavour and some soaked in the spirit of devotion. Vanmikam, Mahabharatam, Pauma Chariyam, Ramayana Kakawin and Ranganatha Ramayanam and such texts describe the arrival of Surpanakha, her conversation with Rama and Lakshmana and her getting maimed, in a realistic manner.

Texts like Bhusundi Ramayana and Ananda Ramayana project it from a Tantric perspective while Bhagavatam, Adhyatmam, Padma Puranam, Tulsi Ramayan etc. depict it in an overwhelmingly devotional mode. Kamba Ramayanam presents the episode of Surpanakha as a word picture, exceedingly rich in imagination, as a fusion of literary flavour and human nature interwoven to some extent with the aura of devotion. Thus, we find the Ramayana texts, each of them depicting variously the episode of Surpanakha arriving at Panchavati and going back, in keeping with their respective religious, social and literary conventions.

Rama's Qualities Seen in the Surpanakha Episode

One who disliked uttering falsehoods:
Vanmikam and Kamba Ramayanam.

Avowed monogamist: Narasimha Purana, Vasudeva Hindi, Ramayana Kakawin, Kamba Ramayanam, Bhusundi Ramayana, Torave Ramayanam and Ramakien.

Ambiguities

Vanmikam praises Rama as one who at all times disliked falsehood; and Kamba Ramayanam hails him in the poet's own utterance as 'truthful Rama' and 'the champion of righteousness' and in Surpanakha's own words as 'the hero of righteousness', and as 'one who in his thoughts upholds high standards of righteousness'. The question, therefore, troubles the reader's mind as to why Rama of such a noble nature, knowing Surpanakha to be a demoness sporting a false guise, should mock her and deceive her by uttering falsehoods.

Neither Vanmikam nor Kamba Ramayanam nor the other texts say that Lakshmana is unmarried. Yet, knowing his nature well, why should Rama send her to him saying he is unmarried? Vanmikam says that it was all just to make fun of her (III.17:32 18:13,19). Kamba Ramayanam says that because of 'the innate sense of humour did he indulge in this sport (III.5:51)'. Other texts also state a more or less similar view.

It is but natural that questions should arise in the reader's mind such as, 'Can Rama thus indulge in mocking other women? Wouldn't it sully his principle of righteousness and the image of his incarnation?'[7]

Yet when we come to know that texts from Vanmikam onwards say that Rama himself later realised that 'though they be demons, the temptation on his part to indulge in banter with them will amount to courting trouble', and that he made Lakshmana too realise it, we find the severity of the questions raised above diminishing. Moreover, Rama does not demand the punishing of Surpanakha; since the texts such as Ramayana

---

7 *Many Ramayanas* ed.Paula Richman, Oxford India Paperback, 1992, pp.69-88.

Kakawin, Kamba Ramayanam, and Ezhuthachan's Adhyatma Ramayanam say that Lakshmana took such a decision on his own, Rama's natural quality of compassion comes to the fore. We find that it is human nature to indulge in innocent fun in riling someone without causing harm or to just entertain such an idea. Kamban clearly states that Rama realised the import of the warning of Thiruvalluvar who says 'derision not even for fun' as in the following lines:

> Although it was fun teasing the demons with curved teeth, the valorous one realised that it would bode ill.
>
> (III. 5: 67)

The sport of mocking someone is in itself hypocritical behaviour. Doing it wilfully is undesirable; it does not behove a hero who has been created as an ideal human being. If such a character has been created from the perspective of an incarnation, mockery would be deemed the most unbecoming aspect of such a character. Therefore, if Rama is viewed as an incarnation, his behaviour towards Surpanakha is most inappropriate; it ends up as a flaw in creation.

Even if we consider Rama to be an ideal hero, this action is not in keeping with his idealism. Yet we find such slips to be unavoidable in the life of everyone, from ordinary folk to great men; such moral lapses should be taken in a spirit of acceptance and viewed as inevitable aspects of human life.

We find that moralists such as Thiruvalluvar have realised the pragmatic need for accepting with sympathy such men who are susceptible to this fault. Therefore, *Thirukkural*, perhaps by saying that falsehood can be considered as truthfulness if it is going to result in great good, finds a compromising formula for truthfulness!

There are several instances in the story of Rama where he may be considered culpable. His actions starting with hitting Kooni with clay-ball darts for fun as a little boy to sending his wife to the forest after getting crowned as the king, have made his character a target of adverse criticism. Several scholars have justified as well as blamed Rama from the perspective of an incarnational motif, and that of spirituality, from an idealist as well as a pragmatist point of view.[8]

We know that though there is just one story of Rama, there are several Ramayanas. Each and every creative work can be considered a piece of criticism too; similarly if we take the stand of analysing every piece of criticism as no less a creation, it is not wrong to pass the verdict on Rama that he stands accused as an individual being, be it as a divine incarnation or as an ideal man. However, instead of feeling happy about doing so, if we realise how complicated human life is, how wretched and pitiable, the depiction of this character will be useful as a lesson to us, the readers.

---

8 a. Kathleen M Erndl, 'The Mutilation of Surpanakha' in, *Many Ramayanas* edited by. Paula Richman, pp. 67-88.

8b. i. In many versions of Ramayana, Rama is considered an Ideal Man, with some limitations, if not an incarnation. The different Rama stories show Rama as one governed by the existing social codes. We also find Rama displaying ordinary human qualities, eg. shooting mud-pellets at Manthara, teasing Surpanakha, abandoning Sita on hearsay, his killing Vaali have sparked controversies, depicting changing social perspectives.

—Translators' note.

8b. ii. The Translators' note in the preliminaries says that Prof Manavalan's discussion of Kaikeyi, Manthara, the Ahalya episode and Surpanakha in the various versions set them thinking as women scholars. From the Jataka tales that do not contain the abduction story to the 18th century, the various versions of Ramayana in this study help us understand the complex perspectives on women emerging.

—Publishing Editor

The tragedies of great poets of the world like Euripides, Aeschylus and Shakespeare drive home just this point. Tragic drama does not mean one with a tragic ending; it also means a play that depicts the tragedies of human life. It is because these plays offer us this lesson that tragic plays are more famous than comedies. It is for the same reason that critics regard and praise the end of tragic plays as providing 'tragic pleasure'.

The enduring value of great literature is self-realisation, that is an individual realising the general nature of humanity and reaping the benefits of that realisation. The Panchavati incident relating to Rama makes us realise our power as well as our misery simultaneously.

The Killing of Khara and Dushana

Surpanakha goes to Khara, the head of the demons in the forest of Dandaka and complains to him about the disgrace she has suffered. Khara goes with his brothers Dushana and Trisira and calls out Rama and Lakshmana for a battle in which he and his brothers get killed by Rama. Surpanakha, who witnesses in person the spectacle of Khara and the others getting killed, is struck with unbearable grief and sets forth towards Lanka to complain to Ravana.

All the Ramayana texts from Vanmikam onwards narrate, more or less in a similar manner, the incident of the killing of Khara and Dushana on account of Surpanakha. The incident does not form an important aspect of the plot. It is considered that the presence or absence of this incident makes no difference to the movement of the plot. We find the Ramayana texts differing with one another in referring to the relationship between Khara-Dushana and Surpanakha. Among the South Asian Ramayanas it is Ramayana Kakawin which is the most ancient. We find that this text in many important places is in line with the Indian Ramayanas. Many of the Indian Ramayanas say that Surpanakha, after getting humiliated with her ears and nose cut off, goes to Khara in the Dandaka forest and complains to him. Malayala Kannassa Ramayana says that Surpanakha first complained to Ravana. All the South Asian Ramayanas say that the disfigured Surpanakha straightaway went to Lanka and complained to Ravana.

Akampana's Report to Ravana

Vanmikam

The demon Akampana, who ran away in fright on seeing Khara, Dushana and their army killed by Rama, rushed to Lanka, bowed to Ravana and reported to him what had happened in the Dandaka forest. Ravana became angry when he came to know of the killing of Khara and Dushana who were his kith and kin as well as the custodians of the Dandaka forest. He declared that he would right away proceed to the Dandaka forest to kill Rama. When Akampana heard this, he shuddered in fear and with much hesitation suggested to Ravana, the king of demons: 'It is not possible to conquer Rama in any battle; you should rather go to Panchavati and abduct Sita by trickery. Rama who has immense love for Sita will give up his life, unable to bear her parting.' Ravana accepted his suggestion, reached the abode of Maricha and sought his help in abducting Sita.

Maricha, who heard Ravana's plea was aghast: 'Who is the villain who gave you this suggestion? Consider him your enemy within and forget this treacherous idea meant to ruin you. Do not wake up the sleeping lion in the form of a human being. Do not get drowned in the ocean of Rama which contains the crocodiles of bows, the waves of arrows and the eddies of martial arts. Oh! King of the demon clan! Go back to Lanka and live happily with your wives. Let Rama live happily with his wife in the Dandaka forest.'

Thus, with concern, he exhorted him. Following that suggestion Ravana went back to Lanka (Sarga-31).

This incident of Akampana reporting to Ravana about the killing of Khara and the others in Janasthana in the forest of Dandaka is found only in the Southern Recension of Vanmikam (Dharmalaya: Sarga 31; Gorakhpur: Sarga 31). This matter is not found in the Vanmikam of the Northern Recension, nor in the North-western Recension or the Eastern Recension (the Gowdia Recension).

In many of the Ramayana texts from Kamba Ramayanam onwards taken for study here, except the Malayala Kannassa Ramayanam, the Akampana episode is not narrated. Nor does it find a place in Southeast Asian Ramayanas such as Ramayana Kakawin. Therefore, scholars such as Camille Bulcke and Jacobi consider that the entire Sarga 31 (50 slokas) must be an interpolation (Bulcke 403).

Surpanakha complains to Ravana

Surpanakha, who was shocked and disappointed at witnessing the killing of Khara, rushed to Lanka wailing and reached the court of Ravana. Vanmikam describes the episode of Surpanakha meeting Ravana and complaining to him in three Sargas (Northern Recension: Sargas 30, 31, 32; Southern Recension: Sargas 32, 33, 34).

One of the three Sargas related to Surpanakha narrates the grandeur of Ravana's court and another, Surpanakha abusing Ravana. The third narrates briefly the humiliation of Surpanakha caused by Rama and Lakshmana and the killing of Khara and Dushana (in 13 slokas) and finally, Surpanakha describing in great detail the beauty of Sita and suggesting that Ravana should abduct her and make her his wife (15 slokas).

In the three sargas mentioned above, Surpanakha, who devotes a considerable time in the court of Ravana to narrating the incidents at the Dandaka forest, refrains from disclosing to him her infatuation with Rama and Lakshmana, and her failure to fulfil her desire, however hard she pleaded with them. Insisting on Ravana killing Rama and Lakshmana, thereby avenging the humiliation of her organs being cut off, she does not tell him the true reason for the disgrace she has suffered; instead she utters a lie that when she tried to abduct Sita for the sake of Ravana, Rama and Lakshmana cut off her ears and nose and humiliated her.

In the description of the glory of Ravana's court, as well as in the delineation of how a benevolent rule of the sceptre should be, and how a cruel sceptre brings about the fall of the reign, and in the instance of Surpanakha picturing Sita's beauty, one cannot help admiring the poet's superb descriptive power, the niceties of the similes he summons up, his political sagacity, not to mention the excellence of the four-footed slokas and their fluid motion. They evoke wonder, delight and admiration. This is just one of the instances of the bard Valmiki's poetic excellence shining forth brilliantly. It is noteworthy that this episode is found in all the recensions of Vanmikam.

Kamba Ramayanam

Kamba Ramayanam describes the episode of Surpanakha complaining to Ravana in a canto of 170 verses. Kamba Ramayanam narrates the glory of Ravana's court in twenty-two verses, the grief of Lankan women on seeing the dishevelled appearance of Surpanakha in twenty-one verses, the valour and beauty of Rama and Lakshmana in the words of Surpanakha in six verses and Sita's beauty in fourteen verses.

In keeping with and going beyond the Tamil tradition, Kamban describes in eighty-five verses the lust and agony felt by Ravana on listening to Surpanakha's description of the beauty of Sita, an agony which crossed bounds and became an obsession. We understand that when Kamban devotes exactly one half of the number of stanzas in a canto of 170 verses to describing Ravana's hopeless passion, he means to expose the tragic flaw of the anti-hero and hint at his meeting with an inevitable fall, with no hope of redemption.

Surpanakha, who forgot about the killing of Khara and others but was eaten away by the beauty of Rama, mused, 'I shall go and commend the beauty of Sita to Ravana'. She fell at the feet of Ravana wailing and screaming and rolling on the floor in such a way as to evoke pity and tears from the onlookers. Ravana, who saw the wretched condition of his sister, asked her who had brought her to such a state? Surpanakha replied that two men at the Dandaka forest unsheathed their swords and disfigured her thus. When Ravana heard that it was two human beings who had done it, he burst out in fury with his eyes emitting fire. He said:

> Utter no falsehood, give up fear,
> tell me everything as it happened

(III.7:51)

Surpanakha spoke thus: 'The two of incomparable beauty and valour are the sons of Dasaratha. They have vowed to destroy the demons and protect the Brahmanas. Khara and the others who were outraged on hearing of the dishonour meted out to me, waged war with them but were despatched by the two to heaven within three *naazhigais* (one naazhigai = 24 minutes) with just one bow.'

Ravana, who heard that his younger brother Khara along with his army was destroyed, reached the limits of his wrath and asked her,

> Tell me what offence you have committed.
> Tell me what made them chop off your nose
> and lips.
>
> (III.7.66)

Surpanakha answered, 'The disaster was caused by a woman who is a paragon of beauty by the side of Rama, whose beauty cannot be represented in any picture'. When Ravana asked her who she was, Surpanakha who got the opening she was looking for, described the beauty of Sita in the following fourteen verses:

> Lord! Her name is Sita; can I ever hope to describe her beauty? She has features that cannot be depicted by anyone. Though one can describe them part by part such as the bow-like eyebrows, spear-like eyes, pearl-like teeth, coral-like lips, one can only feel the words but can never hope to realise their significance, even by stretching the imagination. You will see it for yourself very soon. Why am I telling you about this?
>
> (72-74)
>
> Indra got Sasi as his wife; the father of the six-faced god got Uma as his wife; Lord Vishnu got Lakshmi; you got Sita, should one compare, they are not the ones to gain, it is you.
>
> (75)
>
> One man kept his wife on the left side; another kept his in his heart; Brahma kept his on his tongue. If you possess the slender-waisted woman, I am curious to know where will you keep her?
>
> (76)

It is because, the moment you obtain her you will lavish all your great wealth only on her. Oh! Magnanimous one! I, who have presented you with this opportunity, will be a good woman to you; but to the women of your palace, won't I become the wicked woman?

(77)

Make your might known to the world by abducting Sita, the slender-waisted, and enjoy yourself. Give me Rama so that I may enjoy a life full of pleasure.

(79)

When I tried to fetch such a beautiful Sita for you, that younger brother of Rama's came in between, cut off my nose and ears and ruined my life. After conveying this matter to you, I intend to put an end to my life.

(81)

The beautiful image of Sita as described by Surpanakha crept into Ravana's mind little by little, making him gradually lose control of himself. Kamban describes the plight of Ravana thus:

> Khara he forgot;
> the strength of the one who cut off his sister's nose,
> he forgot.
> He forgot the stigma that came of it.
> All because of Manmatha's shaft of love which conquered even Shiva,
> he forgot all the boons he got.
> But forget he could not,
> the woman whose beauty he had just heard of.
>
> (3: 7: 83)

Thus Ravana, who found it impossible to forget Sita, kept her within the confines of his heart just on hearing about her. The poet depicts the plight of Ravana by saying that as a result, the demon's heart started melting like butter kept under the hot sun.

Ranganatha Ramayanam

Ranganatha Ramayanam contains a scene describing the glory of Ravana's court in an excellent fashion. This text shows that even as the courtiers are expatiating upon the greatness of Ravana, Surpanakha enters the court, weeping and lamenting, dishevelled in appearance. 'Your might and reputation will no longer be the same; Rama and Lakshmana, the sons of Dasaratha, have arrived to destroy your might and authority. They are staying at Panchavati along with Rama's wife Sita. Desiring to have Rama when I approached him, I thus got disfigured. They have killed Khara and Dushana who came in support of me. I do not have any other refuge except you.' Thus Surpanakha complained to Ravana.

When Ravana said, 'Tell me in detail all about Rama and Lakshmana. I will kill them and bathe you in their blood', Surpanakha continued:

> 'It is very rare to come across in all the three worlds one as handsome and valiant as Rama. So is Lakshmana. I have not seen anywhere a pretty woman like Sita. Nobody can match her, be it goddesses or celestial damsels or the gandharvas. Your glory and fame will become manifold if you get Sita as your wife.'
>
> Ravana, who heard Surpanakha praising and admiring the beauty of Sita in eloquent terms, was seized with obnoxious lust for her and he approached Maricha, planning to abduct her (Aranya-pp. 146-147).

Bhaskara Ramayanam

Surpanakha goaded Ravana thus: 'There is not a single beautiful woman in this universe to match Sita; even the status of Indra is immaterial to the one who gets her as his wife. Kill Rama and Lakshmana, abduct Sita and keep her as your paramour.'

On hearing the description of Sita, Ravana was irredeemably infatuated with her and decided to deceive, through deception, Rama who had killed even valorous heroes like Khara and Dushana (First Aswasam pp. 274-286).

Molla Ramayanam briefly narrates this episode following the previous Telugu Ramayanas and Vanmikam (pp. 26).

Kannassa Ramayanam

Surpanakha, at first, complained to Ravana that she was thus disfigured by the sons of Dasaratha who bore the guise of ascetics. He forthwith sent a huge army to kill Rama and Lakshmana. Akampana who returned to Lanka in fright after Khara and the others were slain, told Ravana of what had happened. When Ravana declared that he himself would kill Rama and Lakshmana, Akampana exhorted him, 'As long as his wife Sita is with him, you cannot conquer Rama. Therefore you had better abduct Sita and return'. Accordingly, Ravana sought Maricha who gave him wise counsel and sent him back to Lanka. Kannassa Ramayanam fully follows Sarga 31 of the Vanmikam of the Southern Recension, which is regarded as an interpolation, and narrates the story of Akampana.

Surpanakha, who saw Ravana returning to Lanka, again approached him and goaded him saying, 'Sita alone is a match for you. Therefore go and capture her'. When Surpanakha described Sita again and again, infatuation took hold of Ravana's mind and he approached Maricha again and sought his help to abduct Sita by deceit.

Adhyatma Ramayana

When Ravana was alone in his palace, he thought over what Surpanakha had said. 'Rama, who killed Khara and the other valiant heroes, is no ordinary human being. The Omnipotent Himself has come down as Rama. It is therefore good for me to oppose him directly. If I get killed by Rama, I will at once secure my place in heaven; if not killed, I shall live here itself proudly as the chief of the demons. Of the two, the nobler one will be to oppose Rama and fight with him.'

He decided that it would be better to oppose Him and reach His feet than follow the way of devotion which entailed a long period of penance in order to reach Him; and hence Ravana went to meet Maricha (III.5:38-61).

Ezhuthachan's Adhyatma Ramayanam in Malayalam narrates Surpanakha's complaint, following its source text, the Sanskrit Adhyatma Ramayana.

One can easily perceive the impact of the Vaishnavite Bhakti path of devotion on these two texts. The characters of these texts have been depicted as though they knew their past and its consequences in the future and acted with an awareness of their qualities each as a human being as well as an incarnational being; i.e. one tends to think that these texts create an impression in the mind of the reader that Rama's story seems to move away or deviate from being an ancient epic into a work of Puranic or mythological nature.

Krittibas's **Bengali Ramayana** mostly goes in tune with Vanmikam. This Ramayana says that Surpanakha states that desiring to have human flesh, she went near Rama, Lakshmana and Sita and that enraged them and hence her ears and nose were thus cut off by them. She cites this as the reason for her disfigurement.

Surpanakha, who right away went to Lanka unable to bear the humiliation she had suffered at Panchavati and the grief resulting from the killing of Khara and others, fell at the feet of Ravana and wailed. Ravana then asked her the reason for her suffering. To which she replied, 'Rama has got as his wife Sita, daughter of Janaka, whom you should have got. Now he is staying at Panchavati with his wife and brother', and she described the incomparable beauty of Sita in great detail to Ravana.

She said that when she had tried to carry off Sita, convinced that such a beautiful woman was a match only for Ravana, she got her ears and nose cut off by Rama's brother and was humiliated. Surpanakha, who realised that Ravana was totally overcome by lust just on hearing about Sita's beauty, advised him, 'Without thinking of fighting with Rama, you should abduct Sita by some trick. Find out from Maricha the suitable means and justification for this', and sent him off – so says Kumara Valmiki's **Torave Ramayanam**, a little elaborately.

Tulsidas's **Ramcharitmanas** also narrates, as does Adhyatma Ramayana, Surpanakha complaining to Ravana of the humiliation she had suffered at the hands of Rama and Lakshmana; answering Ravana's queries; describing Sita's incomparable beauty to Ravana; Ravana as a result falling in unquenchable love for Sita and thinking of abducting her; Surpanakha's exhortation to him to avoid war and abduct Sita by deceit; Ravana's decision to oppose them in a fight, which would result only in good, be they human beings or divine incarnation (III.21,1-6; 22, 1- 4).

Southeast Asian Ramayanas such as Ramayana Kakawin, Ramakien, and Rama Vatthu narrate the episode of Surpanakha complaining to Ravana, in general terms like the other Indian Ramayanas. Matters suggestive of divine incarnation are not mentioned. These texts seem to be keenly interested in describing Sita's beauty.

Thailand Ramayana Ramakien in particular shows that

Surpanakha (Samanakha), while describing Sita's beauty, not only says that she is the most beautiful of all the women known to her, but also more beautiful than queen Mandodari and goes on to compare each part of their bodies such as their faces, mouths, breasts, hands, wrists and thighs. Moreover, it shows her as saying that all the three goddesses Uma, Saraswati and Lakshmi put together cannot match the beauty of Sita.

The Thai Ramayana says that Ravana, on hearing about the matchless beauty of Sita, set out immediately to abduct her and went to meet Maricha without even listening to Mandodari (Mando) who tried to prevent him from doing so.[9]

Summary

- All the Ramayanas state that it is Surpanakha who narrates the incidents of Panchavati to Ravana.
- Vanmikam of the Southern Recension and Malayala Kannassa Ramayanam say that it is Akampana who first briefs Ravana and later Surpanakha reports to him.
- Since Akampana, one of the spies of Ravana, has directly witnessed the might of Rama, he suggests **abduction of Sita only as a means to conquer Rama.**
- Surpanakha, on the other hand, asks Ravana to abduct her because she thinks that Rama does not accept her since Sita is with him. Only with that motive does she describe in varied terms the beauty of Sita.
- Vanmikam, Kamba Ramayanam and Ranganatha Ramayanam describe vividly and exquisitely the glory of Ravana's political sagacity and the splendour of his court.
- Janasthana, which is part of the Dandaka forest, is under the control of the demons. Khara and the others have

---

9   a. Ohno Toru, pp. 87-88.
     b. *Thai Ramayana* by King Ram I of Siam,
     Bangkok: Chalermnit Book shop, 1982, p. 39.

been assigned the task of protecting that region. All the Vanmikams state that when that is the case, Surpanakha says she fails to understand how Ravana could indulge in merry-making, drowning himself in liquor and women, ignorant of the important events that had happened there such as the decimation of Khara and Dushana, not even taking steps to get to know of them. Surpanakha thus chastises Ravana. This incident is not described in other texts.

- Vanmikam narrates elaborately the episode of Surpanakha's lodging a complaint in three Sargas and Kamba Ramayanam in a canto of 170 verses. In the other texts, this episode is not so detailed.
- Surpanakha does not tell Ravana the true reason for her being disfigured and rendered dishevelled. All the Ramayanas state that Surpanakha told Ravana that on seeing Sita's beauty, she considered her a match only for Ravana and tried to abduct her and that was why she got mutilated and humiliated.
- Surpanakha of Ranganatha Ramayanam alone tells the truth that when she fell in love with Rama and pleaded with him, she got disfigured.
- Surpanakha of Krittibas's Bengali Ramayana says that her craving to consume human flesh and hence approaching Rama and Lakshmana was the cause for her becoming maimed with her ears and nose cut off.
- Vanmikam very briefly refers to the state of mind of Ravana, who allowed his lust to exceed the bounds of righteousness on hearing about Sita's beauty through Surpanakha. Kamba Ramayanam very elaborately presents, in eighty-five verses, the abominable lust of Ravana.
- The poetic excellence of Valmiki and Kamban in describing the glory of Ravana's reign, as well as his meanness in coveting another man's wife, his inordinate lust overpowering him, is worthy of appreciation and admiration.
- 'While abducting Sita, if the situation so arises that I have to fight with Rama, I will fight with him, and if he is a human

being I will kill him and live with Sita; if he is a divine incarnation of the transcendent entity, I will get killed by him and attain liberation on reaching Heaven; therefore, whatever be the end, it is better to abduct Sita.' Adhyatma Ramayana followed by Ezhuthachan's Ramayanam and Tulsi Ramayan state that Ravana, when he was alone in his palace, thus took a decision after much thinking. The impact of the Bhakti movement is discerned in these texts.

- South-Asian Ramayanas like Ramayana Kakawin briefly refer to Surpanakha's complaint in general terms. Kakawin briefly and Ramakien very elaborately describe the beauty of Sita.
- In the Laotian Ramayana Gvay Dvorabhi, Surpanakha is not mentioned as connected or associated with the incident of Ravana abducting Sita. **This Ramayana does not project a character called Surpanakha at all.**[10]

What Happened to Surpanakha?

Vanmikam does not say in detail anything about what happened to Surpanakha after she set ablaze the flame of lust in Ravana's heart. Though Kamba Ramayanam refers to the wicked suggestion of Surpanakha through a few characters while referring to the foolishness of Ravana's desire for another man's wife, Kamban too does not say anything about what happened to Surpanakha.

Krittibas's Ramayana says that Surpanakha wanted to go in search of Sita in the Ashoka grove and kill her, but she refrained from doing so as she was afraid of Ravana (Bulcke 447). Bhavartha Ramayanam says that Surpanakha met Sita in the Ashoka grove and pleaded with her to marry Ravana (Bulcke 416).

---

10   Kamala Ratnam, 'Socio-cultural…in Laos'. *Asian Variations in Ramayana*, p. 251,n.18.

Reverend Camille Bulcke says that the Ramayana plays in Siam and Burma narrate that Surpanakha herself changed into a golden deer and helped Ravana to abduct Sita after Ravana accepted her suggestion that he should abduct Sita (Bulcke 417). Bulcke says (417) that the tribals in Nilgiris even today worship Surpanakha and the women of a Malayala community known as *nathu* call themselves the children of Surpanakha (descendents of Surpanakha). This is mentioned in studies such as:

1. *German Ethnological Journal,* Part 37, p. 734.
2. *Cochin Tribes and Customs,* Part1, p. 29, by Anantha Krishna Aiyar.

Arguments between Ravana and Maricha

Vanmikam

Ravana went to the Dandaka forest to meet his maternal uncle Maricha, keeping in mind the suggestion of Akampana that he should abduct Sita in order to conquer Rama, and that of Surpanakha that he should abduct Sita in order to have her and enjoy her incomparable beauty. Vanmikam elaborately presents, in seven Sargas, the episode of Ravana seeking help from Maricha and Maricha's reply and consent. (NR Sargas 33-39; SR Sargas 35-41, 198 slokas.)

Mounting a chariot drawn by mules, Ravana crossed the sea, reached the other side of the shore and reached a hermitage set in a beautiful and peaceful forest region. There he saw Maricha, the demon-turned-renunciant, clad in the hide of a deer, sporting knotted hair and wrapped in tree-barks, living on a frugal diet (Sarga35). To Maricha, who asked him the purpose for which he came, Ravana replied as follows:

> Sire Maricha! I have come to you with much mental agony.
> I have no other refuge. My brother Khara, Dushana, Trisira

and other valiant heroes, who were living in Janasthana in obedience to my orders, and the 14,000-strong army assisting them, were killed by Rama, who is living in Panchavati.

It is that Rama who was banished to the forest along with his wife by his angry father. He is a man of immoral behaviour; merciless; a ruffian; miser; lacks control of his senses; lacks righteous thinking; takes pleasure in causing harm to living beings.

Such a one, without any cause for enmity, just cut off my sister's ears and nose and mutilated her simply because he was a mighty one. I am going to abduct, from Panchavati, his wife Sita, who is as beautiful as a celestial damsel. I need help from you who knows the means and tricks for achieving the purpose. I have come to you for this sole reason.

You please take the form of a golden deer with white spots and keep running and prancing around the hermitage of Rama so as to be sighted by Sita. She will be attracted by its beauty and ask Rama and Lakshmana to capture it for her. In their attempt to chase and capture it, when they are drawn far away, I shall carry her off like the planet Rahu swallowing up the Moon's radiance. With great ease, I shall slay Rama, anguished as he will be after losing his wife (SR Sarga 36).

Maricha was very much distressed on hearing Ravana's words and with an agitated heart started advising him:

Oh! King of kings! Many are there out to ruin you by their pleasing sugar-coated words; very few will give you good advice though their words be bitter; fewer are there who wish to listen to good advice. People like you who conduct themselves as they please, take to wicked ways and listen to the evil counselling of their friends, will, by their bad conduct, not only be the instrument of utter ruin of their reign and their people but also ruin themselves.

Rama is not one to be abandoned by his father, as you said; he is not one who swerves from the path of righteousness, not even a bit; he is not immoral; nor a ruffian; he is not the one to cause harm to living beings; nor a fool; nor merciless; nor one who lacks control of his senses.

In Janasthana, what is the fault of Rama in killing Khara and others who opposed and violated justice without knowing anything about the crime of Surpanakha? You should avoid telling lies and uttering something not worth listening to. Rama, who has come to the forest of Dandaka with due regard to the words of Dasaratha and Kaikeyi, is an embodiment of righteousness, a man of great ability; don't even think of opposing Rama in battle; there is no greater sin than the sin of ruining the chastity of another man's wife. On account of such thoughts you will only be cursed for bringing about the destruction of the demon-clan (Sarga 37).

Without interrupting me, just listen to the untold suffering I have gone through by opposing Rama on account of my senseless brutishness.

Long ago in the past, I was wandering in the Dandaka forest as a cruel ruler, intimidating all the worlds by wielding a weapon called Parikayudham.

Sage Viswamitra – one of those frightened of me – in order to subdue me, went to Emperor Dasaratha and sought his permission to take his son Rama as an escort with him. He came to the Dandaka forest and started performing sacrificial ceremonies, with Rama standing guard.

Thinking that he is after all a stripling of a boy, just twelve-years-old, not even beginning to sport a moustache, with a tuft, wearing a golden sacred thread and clad in just a single cloth, I foolishly attacked the altar for the yagna which was being guarded by Rama. As a result, I was hit by just one arrow of Rama's and was hurled a hundred yojanas away into the sea. The juvenile lion did not have the heart to kill me and hence I survived and reached Lanka. You had better protect yourself, your wives, your honour and your country from being destroyed by Rama's one such proverbial arrow. If you don't respect this word of mine and entertain thoughts of abducting Sita, you along with your kith and kin will reach the world of Yama (God of death) (Sarga 38).

I will tell you the story of how I, who escaped death by His grace as told above, once again suffered humiliation; just listen to me without interrupting me.

Again taking with me two demons in the form of deer, I went to Dandaka forest and was roaming around, killing the sages, eating their flesh and drinking their blood. At that time I saw Rama clad as an ascetic, the valiant warrior Lakshmana and Vaidehi who was with them. Sheer arrogance made me regard him as just a renunciant, and, unable to forget the old feud, I, who was in the form of a deer, tried to attack him with my sharp antlers. He strung his mighty bow and despatched three dreaded arrows at me. In spite of knowing about his prowess, I foolishly did not correct my ways, but somehow escaped death. The other two demons became victims of his arrows.

I, who had a providential escape, gave up altogether my evil ways, renounced worldly attachments, and have been living here as an ascetic. I am one who is well aware of Rama's glory. Should I act according to your words I will be ruined. Therefore I don't want to act according to your words. Since I love you, I for one would wish only good things to happen to you. Therefore give up the idea of opposing Rama and go back. If you don't act according to my words, you will get killed by Rama in battle (Sarga 39).

Ravana did not follow the advice of Maricha, much like a man who has dared to choose death rejecting the elixir of life. Looking at Maricha, he rebuked him thus, 'Stop giving me advice. As I told you earlier, take the form of a spotted deer and help me to abduct Sita. Otherwise you will be punished by me right now and will meet with your death' (Sarga 40).

Much hurt by Ravana's harsh words, Maricha said to him, 'Sheep won't get anything good from the fox. So also, those living under you will never get anything good from a cruel being like you. They are sure to be ruined. It is a sheer coincidence that my death comes with your arrival; I will get liberation when killed by Rama, the noble man. Once you abduct Sita neither will you prosper; nor I; Lanka will cease to exist; the demons won't survive either. Corpses don't listen to well-meaning counsel of friends' (Sarga 41).

Lamenting thus, Maricha, with no alternative, got on to the chariot of Ravana, reached Panchavati, took the form of a spotted deer and started capering around the hermitage of Rama.

The Northern Recension of Vanmikam too describes the above conversation between Ravana and Maricha without any major variation.

Narasimha Purana states very briefly Ravana's suggestion, Maricha's unwillingness, Ravana's threat fearing which Maricha takes the form of an illusory deer in accordance with his wish and so on, all based on Vanmikam (49:59-70).

Janakiharan

The episode of Maricha appearing as an illusory deer is not narrated in Janakiharan. Ravana himself puts on the disguise of an ascetic and carries off Sita. This text says that the abduction of Sita takes place when Rama has gone hunting (X.77. V Raghavan, p.51).

Ramayana Kakawin

Ravana crosses the sea, reaches the other shore, meets Maricha and requests him to help him in abducting Sita. Maricha says in response to his request : 'I myself have been punished by Rama several times. Rama is a mighty man. Your Chandrahasa sword cannot harm him. He is the one who defeated Parasurama himself. Tataka, Khara, Dushana and Trisira have all been killed by him easily. In Sita's swayamvaram, Ragothama strung the bow which could not be strung by anyone else and broke it. If you fight with him you will also get killed.'

Ravana, who got furious on hearing the words of Maricha, replied:

> Parasurama was an ageing man, but Rama is a young man, therefore he defeated him. Tataka was a woman. No wonder he easily conquered her. Killing Khara and Dushana is no great victory. You seem to wax eloquent over the glory of Rama breaking the bow. That was a very old bow; for a long time it was just lying about without any use; it was moth-eaten and crumbling. What glory is there in breaking it?

After retorting thus to Maricha's words of warning, Ravana threatened him saying, 'If you don't act according to my words I shall kill you'. Frightened by this, Maricha said, 'I shall act according to your words. I shall assume the shape of a golden deer and make Rama and Lakshmana follow me far away from the hermitage. What happens after that depends on your cleverness', – so saying he reached Panchavati, took the form of a deer and pretended to be frisking around Rama's hermitage (Toru-99).

Other South-Asian Ramayana texts very briefly state the conversation between Ravana and Maricha.

Kamba Ramayanam

Kamba Ramayanam describes Ravana's arrival, Maricha's welcome, Ravana's request, Maricha's advice, the punishment he already got from Rama, Ravana threatening him, finally Maricha yielding to him, all much in the same way as Vanmikam. Some of Kamban's ideas and devices, however, invite attention. They can be briefly stated as follows:

> Ravana said, 'The humans who killed my brothers and disfigured my sister are not valiant heroes who can be my equals. Hence not wanting to fight them, I thought of abducting Sita by deceit. Thus to avenge them I came here seeking your help' (III.8:6).
>
> 'Ravana! Did you obtain your might to conquer all the three worlds by your valour? Or did you obtain it by your penance? Have you ventured to lose by unrighteousness all the wealth you have acquired by your righteous deeds?' – Maricha (8:10).
>
> 'Righteousness will destroy those who usurped the countries of others, those who forcefully collected tax by unrighteous means and those who coveted the wife of another man.' – Maricha (8:11).
>
> 'Out of folly you said Sita has the form of a woman; Sita is not a woman; she is the personification of all the sins committed by the demons.' – Maricha (8:23).
>
> 'I have already received punishment in the Dandaka forest. How can I offer any help?' – Maricha (8:34).
>
> 'Sire, I am willing to kill the one who killed your mother. You please help me to abduct Sita by deceit.'
> – Ravana (8:35).
>
> 'There is nothing more to be said. It is better to obtain the consort of the God of protection (Lord Vishnu) by winning the battle. Winning by deceit will only bring you ignominy. Please choose the righteous path of conquering him in the battle and thereby proclaim your valorous act.' – Maricha (8:36).
>
> 'Do you need an army to conquer them? The sword in my huge hand will do. Won't Sita too give up her life the

moment they die? That is why I shall try some trick and obtain her (alive).' – Ravana (8:57).

Maricha thought, 'He gives room for his head to roll even before he dares to touch the goddess'. Wondering who could divine the consequences of Fate, he asked him, 'Tell me what trick I should perform?' Ravana, in turn, asked him to transform himself into a golden deer and tempt Sita (8:38,39).

Telugu Ramayanas

When Maricha is in his hermitage in the garb of an ascetic meditating, Ravana approaches him, and telling him about the harm Rama and Lakshmana caused to Surpanakha and their killing of Khara and Dushana, says, 'In order to avenge them we must abduct Sita. For this purpose you must take the shape of an illusory deer, reach the place of Rama and Lakshmana and trick them into going far away from the hermitage. Then I will whisk away Sita who will be alone'.

Maricha, who was upset and saddened listening to this, said to Ravana, 'I have already experienced the valour and might of Rama and Lakshmana. Even when they were mere striplings, they killed Tataka and Subhahu. I, who was hit by their arrow, escaped somehow and I am spending my time here as a renunciant. After that event, their might increasing manifold, they now possess many divine weapons.

'Surpanakha, who has sowed the seeds of this evil design in your mind, entertains a passion for Rama which is improper, to say the least. It is because of her that Khara and Dushana and thousands of the army of demons were routed. Therefore, give up the idea of opposing them, go back to Lanka and hold a peaceful reign. Refrain from indulging in evil thoughts and live as a good person', – thus Maricha gave him many a word of good counsel. Stung into a rage by this, Ravana tried to kill Maricha.

Maricha, who thought that it was better to face death by the arrow of Rama than to get killed by the wicked creature Ravana, took the guise of an illusory deer as directed by Ravana. Thus, Maricha went over to Panchavati and pretended to be grazing near the hermitage. This is how **Ranganatha Ramayanam** describes the conversation between Ravana and Maricha (Aranyam: 147-149).

Bhaskara Ramayanam too describes this incident in the same way as does Ranganatha Ramayanam. **Molla Ramayanam** too thus very briefly narrates this conversation.

Malayala **Kannassa Ramayanam**, Sanskrit **Adhyatma Ramayana**, and **Ezhuthachan's Ramayanam** and Kannada **Torave Ramayanam** present the conversation between Ravana and Maricha, mostly in keeping with Vanmikam. There are no significant differences. **Krittibas's Bengali Ramayana** and Tulsidas's **Ramcharitmanas** also present this incident in the same way as cited above. **Thakkai Ramayanam** narrates this incident following Kamban.

The Illusory Deer

Many of the Ramayana texts from Vanmikam onwards state that Ravana asked Maricha to assume the form of a golden deer as a strategy for abducting Sita. Sanskrit Adhyatma Ramayana alone states that Ravana asked him to assume the form of a 'strange' deer (III.6:33). In the Laotian Ramayana Gvay Dvorabhi, it has been mentioned that Indra came as a golden deer and deceived Sita (*Asian Variations*, p.240).

Siam and Burmese Ramayana plays and Rama Vatthu state that Surpanakha herself came as a golden deer (Bulcke 417). In the Malay Fairy Tale of Rama, it has been stated that Ravana himself came as a golden sheep to deceive Sita and the others (*The Ramayana Tradition*, p.163).

In Vimalasuri's Pauma Chariyu, there is no reference to Rama killing the golden deer. This change has been effected in tune with the Jain religious doctrine of refraining from killing (*Asian Variations*, p.69). In Kumaradasa's Janakiharan too, there is no episode of the golden deer. Nor is there any such episode in the Japanese Ramayana Hobutsushu. It is also noteworthy that there is no character called Lakshmana in this Ramayana (*Asian Variations*, p.344).

Arrival of the Illusory Deer

The episode of Ravana abducting Sita contains incidents such as the arrival of the illusory deer, the argument between Rama and Lakshmana and the one between Sita and Lakshmana, and of course Ravana abducting Sita.

Vanmikam

Maricha, frightened of Ravana, who would not listen to his advice nor would hesitate to kill him, assumed the form of an illusory deer according to his orders and pretended to be frisking around the hermitage of Rama. Sita, who saw the illusory deer which sported multi-coloured spots and silvery hair, called out to Rama and Lakshmana (VR (SR) III. Sarga 42).

Rama and Lakshmana, who heard Sita's voice, came out of the hermitage and saw that deer. Lakshmana, on seeing the deer, said to Rama, 'Oh! Elder brother! This deer is the deceptive guise of a demon called Maricha. There is no such deer as one decked with gems in the whole world. This is nothing but an illusion. No doubt about it'. Sita immediately interrupted him and requested Rama, 'Oh Aryaputra! (Scion of the Aryan race) this deer captivates my mind. I have never before seen such a deer. When we return after our exile in the forest, this deer will adorn our Antahpuram.* You please catch this deer and bring it over. If it evades capture, you kill it and bring its hide. I wish to spread it on the darbha grass and sit beside you'.

Rama, who heard the plea of Sita, looked at the deer intently several times and addressed Lakshmana: 'Lakshmana! Look at the desire of Sita for this deer. Is there a match to this deer in the world? It is not surprising that Sita should yearn after this deer. You say this is an illusion caused by the demon. Even if it be so, this deer has to be killed. He has killed the kings who came here for hunting and the sages who have been living here. Therefore, you stay here fully armed, protecting Sita. I will follow the deer, which has run away, and catch it alive; or else kill it and return fast with its hide. Under the care of mighty Jatayu you stay beside Sita and be alert in anticipation of danger confronting you from all the four directions' (III. Sarga 43).

Rama, who gave the orders to Lakshmana as noted above, took the bow and quiver and went chasing the deer. The deer, which made many a deluding appearance, now being near, then far, now alone, then in a herd, took Rama a long distance away from the hermitage. Rama, who closely watched its actions, was irate and despatched a Brahmastra (the arrow of Brahma) towards it. Rising to the height of a palm tree, Maricha fell down with a heavy thud and on death throes shouted, in imitation of the voice of Rama, 'Alas! Sita! Lakshmana!' Maricha, the illusory deer, thus gave up his life. On witnessing

---

*   Antapur or Antahpuram is an Indian language word for exclusive zones for women in a house or palace, inner chambers of a house.

this Rama was reminded of Lakshmana's warning. Realising that something untoward was likely to happen on account of the plaintive cry for help – 'Sita! Lakshmana!' – he took the hide of another deer and rushed towards his hermitage (SR. Sarga 44).

Kamba Ramayanam

Maricha assumed the form of a golden deer and pretending to prance around stood in front of Sita. Sita, who was bewitched by its beauty, said to Rama, 'Here is a deer dotted all over with gems, worth seeing'. Rama too, in admiration of it said, 'This deer is not of this earth'. The younger brother, who was close by, said, 'If you observe its parts and its ability to leap about, you will realise that this is not a real deer; indeed, it is a dissembling one'. Rama, who heard this, turned to his younger brother and explained, 'Oh! Thou young man! Living beings are multitudinous; there is nothing that cannot be; for the nature of living beings no limits are set; no end either'.

Sita, who saw the brothers arguing thus, said sadly, 'Before you both argue over it and reach a conclusion it will go several *yojana*s away and vanish.' Rama, who wanted to fulfil Sita's desire, went over to look at that deer again. To Rama, who did not give the matter a serious thought, the deer looked wonderful indeed. He said to Lakshmana in admiration, 'Brother! Look at this. It is a match only unto itself. Is there any other match to it?' Then Sita said, 'If you capture it and give it to me, I will play with it when we return to our palace after our period of exile in the forest'.

Rama too assured her, 'I shall do so'. When Lakshmana cautioned, 'You will realise in the end that it is a dissembling deer brought about by the trickery of the demon', Rama replied,

'If it is a deceptive deer, it will die by my arrow – i.e. the demon will also die. If it is a real deer, I shall catch it and return. Either way, it is going to be good for us, isn't it?' Realising that it was not possible to stop Rama, Lakshmana said, 'Oh Lord, isn't it better to think seriously before acting? All right! Even if there are many standing behind it or if it is only a deceptive deer, I shall certainly kill it with my arrow. If it is a real deer, I shall capture it and return.'

Then Sita, interrupting their conversation, said to Rama, 'Oh my Lord! It looks as though you won't go and capture it', and with tears rolling down her eyes, she went inside the hermitage.

Rama, who sensed her anger, said to Lakshmana, 'I myself will capture this deer and return. Till then you stay here, guarding Sita', and saying so he took his bow and arrow and hurried forth.

Lakshmana said, 'You will soon realise that it is the same Maricha who came earlier. Sire, you may proceed', and then he stood guard outside the hermitage while Sita remained inside (III.8:43-69). When Rama went towards the deer it ran fast. If he stopped, it too stopped. Realising it to be an illusory deer, he shot a sharp arrow at it. When Rama's arrow pierced his chest, Maricha opened his split mouth, screamed, fell down and died. Rama realised that Maricha crying out imitating his (Rama's) voice was just a ploy. Thinking that Sita would certainly be frightened and that it would be better for him to go before anything untoward happened, he rushed back (70-82).

Telugu Ramayanas

Telugu Ranganatha Ramayanam and Bhaskara Ramayanam, following Vanmikam, briefly present, in a similar manner, the incidents such as Sita asking Rama to capture the golden deer,

Rama and Lakshmana discussing its deluding nature, finally Rama deciding to capture it, and asking Lakshmana to stand guard over Sita and then chasing the deceptive deer. In Molla Ramayanam, the discussion on the illusory deer is not found. The other incidents are narrated as in the previous Telugu Ramayanas, but in a simple style.

Bhusundi Ramayana

One afternoon Rama, Sita and Lakshmana were resting in the hermitage. Then Sita happened to catch sight of a golden deer. She promptly turned to her husband and said:

> Behold, my Lord! How beautiful is the colour of this deer! I would like to make a choli* with the golden hide of this deer. Its flesh will be very tasty. It will be good food for us. Its antlers will adorn your hands.

Rama, who heard Sita's words, addressed her as follows:

> My dear, it looks like an illusory deer. In Janasthana, there are so many demons roaming around in disguise. Just yesterday, we disfigured and humiliated Ravana's sister. Perhaps this could be a demon in disguise sent by Ravana to take revenge. Everything here seems to be so suspicious. Oh Princess! Aren't you the one who spurned the comforts of an empire? You had better suppress this petty desire.

After exhorting her thus he then narrated to her the story of a beautiful woman carried off by a demon in disguise. Yet, realising that Sita was adamant and wondering who could change the workings of fate, he went chasing the counterfeit deer, leaving Sita under the safe custody of Lakshmana. While leaving, he asked her not to come out until he returned.

---

* A wrap or unstiched garment to cover the breasts.

Since the deer could not be caught even after going very far, he shot it down with an arrow. That deer while dying called out three times 'Oh! Lakshmana!' (Bhusundi, Kathavasthu:15).

Kannassa Ramayanam

Malayala Kannassa Ramayanam, following Valmiki, briefly narrates the arrival of the golden deer, the conversation between Rama and Lakshmana, and Rama's decision. Maricha imitating the voice of Rama and crying out, 'Oh brother! save me', when about to die, being hit by the arrow of Rama, is a striking variation found only in this Ramayana.

Adhyatma Ramayana

Maricha, who turned into a golden deer with white spots, was trying to attract the attention of Sita by feigning to play in front of the hermitage (III.6:39-41).

Rama, realising the design of Ravana, called Sita privately, and told her as follows: 'Janaki, listen to me carefully. Ravana will approach you in the guise of an ascetic. You take the form of a **phantom Sita** and stay outside the hermitage. You conceal your original form in fire and remain unseen by anyone for a year. The moment Ravana is killed, you can reach me in your true form.' Sita too, accordingly, remained as the look-alike Sita outside and as the true Sita hidden in fire (II.7:14).

The phantom Sita pointed to the fake deer playing in front of the hermitage and requested Rama to capture it for her. In order to fulfil her wish, Rama took up the bow and arrow to chase the deer and just before leaving, advised Lakshmana, 'Take good care of Sita. In this forest there are several demons adept at wiles. Hence you must be very vigilant and protect Sita.' Then Lakshmana told him, 'It *is* Maricha who has appeared here as a deceptive deer'.

On hearing this, Rama said, 'If it is a deer, I shall capture it and return. If it is Maricha, I will kill him and return. You be very alert and take care of Sita', and went chasing the dissembling deer knowing full well that it was Maricha. Rama, who understood that the deer was dodging him for a long time without being caught, killed it by shooting an arrow at it. Maricha, who was writhing in a pool of blood, changed his voice into that of Rama and cried out, 'Alas! Lakshmana! I am dying. Come quickly and save me'. Then he died (III.7: 5-18).

Living beings just by uttering the name of Rama at the moment of dying, will receive the bliss of attaining His sacred feet. The celestials and others were greatly astonished when they witnessed the blessed soul of Maricha becoming one with Rama after he got killed by the arrow of Rama who stood before him in the corporeal form (III.7:19-20).

Ezhuthachan's Ramayanam

Malayala Kannassa Ramayanam, which mostly follows the Sanskrit Adhyatma Ramayana, narrates this incident, but briefly, in line with its source text. The suggestion that the inner light of Maricha's soul after he dies enters into Rama and disappears is found in the Sanskrit source. But Ezhuthachan leaves it out, not choosing to mention it in his epic.[11]

The **Bengali Krittibas's Ramayana** says that Sita asked Rama to capture the deer as its hide would serve her as a beautiful mat to sit on. There are no other details worth mentioning in this text.

---

11   P Padmanabhan Thampi, p.67.

Ananda Ramayana

Maricha, who took the form of a golden deer, was roaming around in Panchavati so as to be seen by Sita. The illusory Sita, who saw it, drawn by its beauty, asked Rama to capture it for her. Sita also tells him that if it is caught alive she would play with it and in case it dies hit by his arrow, she would make a wrap out of its hide. Rama followed that deer after assigning the task of protecting Sita to Lakshmana. Since it was dodging him and had run far deep into the forest without getting caught, Rama killed it by shooting an arrow at it. The deer at the moment of dying cried out in Rama's voice, 'Oh! Lakshmana! I have been killed in the forest. Come quick', – so says Ananda Ramayana (I.7:88-93).

Kannada Torave Ramayanam

When Rama was getting ready to capture the deer which was playing in front of the hermitage in response to Sita's request, Lakshmana said to Rama, 'This is no true deer but a counterfeit one; this is a result of a deluding scene put up by the demons'. Rama said, 'I have given word to Sita that I will capture it and return and in case it turns out to be a deceptive deer as you affirm, I will kill it and return; till then you stand guard for Sita'. So saying he pursued the deer. As it was dodging him, he shot an arrow and killed it. In his final moments Maricha mimicked Rama's voice and gave out a distress call crying 'Hey! Lakshmana, hey Sita!' and died.

Rama, who heard Maricha's cry, exclaimed, 'Siva Siva Siva, Mahadeva! Great disaster has befallen! Isn't it a wonder that Lakshmana already knew about the matter as it was?' Thus thinking he rushed towards his hermitage. That is how Kannada Torave Ramayanam describes this incident (verses 7-8).

Ramcharitmanas

Sita, on seeing the golden deer, requested Rama to kill it and bring its hide. Knowing all about the deer and the one who sent it and with His will inclined to alleviate the suffering of the celestials, Rama asked Lakshmana to guard Sita and followed the deer. Since it was evading him, he took the bow, strung and kept ready, shot an arrow at it and killed it. Tulsidas in an overwhelming tone of devotion (Bhakti) sings of the 'Bliss of liberation' of Maricha when the deceptive deer hit by the arrow cried out Lakshmana's name and died (III.26:1-9).

Summary

There are no major differences seen in the Ramayana texts in the depiction of Maricha who took the form of an illusory deer. In order to show that it was indeed a wonder not to be found in nature, it has been variously described as a gem-studded deer, golden deer and silver deer. In a **Malay Fairy Tale** version of the Rama story, it is found that Ravana himself came in a different form, that of **a golden-hued goat**, instead of a deer.

Arguments between Rama and Lakshmana

Texts such as Bhusundi Ramayana, Molla Ramayanam, Ananda Ramayana and Ramcharitmanas do not narrate the incident of Rama and Lakshmana arguing about the real nature of the illusory deer. The Rama of Bhusundi Ramayana just says, 'The one that has arrived is an illusory deer; don't set your heart on it'.

Many of the Ramayanas from Vanmikam onwards say that Lakshmana cautioned that the deer that had arrived there was one that could not be found in nature and that it was the demon Maricha who had arrived in this form with an evil design. Therefore, he warned against any attempt to capture it.

Rama, who was very keen to fulfil the desire of Sita, disregarded the warning of Lakshmana. The Rama of Vanmikam and Kamban's Rama both praise the beauty of the deer in keeping with Sita's view.

These two Ramayanas, however, state that Rama, who could not completely ignore the warning of Lakshmana, said to him, 'Brother, if it is a real deer I shall capture it and thereby please Sita. If it is an illusory one, I shall return after killing it. Either way, it is good, isn't it?' and went after the deer. It becomes clear that Rama hopes to fulfil the wishes of Sita, Lakshmana and the sages of the Dandaka forest. Since Rama has been depicted as a valiant hero of humankind, his conducting himself in this manner seems to be appropriate.

The Rama of Adhyatma Ramayana, knowing that the fake deer is none but Maricha, goes out to capture it. Rama here does not disclose to Sita that he knows the truth about the deer; nor does he say it to Lakshmana who cautioned him in this regard. Nor does Rama tell Lakshmana that he ordered Sita to assume two forms – one as the look-alike Sita to the outside world and the other as the true Sita hidden in the fire. Moreover, he orders Lakshmana saying, 'There are several demons in this forest capable of powerful wiles. May you protect Sita from any harm that they might cause her'.

Lakshmana, who was able to realise that the deer which arrived from somewhere out was an illusory deer, was unable to realise that the Sita staying in Panchavati with him was also an illusory Sita. That is, Lakshmana, who could figure out the trick of the demons, could not fathom the trick played by his brother Rama. The elder brother goes out to kill the illusory deer that is Maricha. The younger brother is assigned the task of protecting the illusory woman that is his sister-in-law (Sita).

It is not possible for us to understand the magic of the portrayal of the characters here, namely, the elder brother, the sister-in-law and the younger brother.

Perhaps the author of Adhyatma Ramayana thought that, since the text has been created from the perspective of the path of devotion, it was not necessary to observe verisimilitude with regard to characters such as Rama. The impact of this text is found in the portrayal of characters in Ananda Ramayana, Bhavartha Ramayana and Tulsi Ramayan.

If Lakshmana comes to know the truth that the Sita captured by Ravana is just a phantom Sita and that the true Sita is in the realm of fire, he will not be interested in fulfilling the task of killing Ravana and retrieving Sita. That is why Rama does not tell this truth to Lakshmana; thus argues the scholar Padmanabhan Thampi.[12]

Such a view, implying as it does that Rama was dependent on Lakshmana for the killing of Ravana and for the retrieval of Sita, would certainly call in question Rama's valour and his individuality and therefore does not seem appropriate. It would appear that the poet may have added this detail to indicate the power of Lakshmana's intuitive perception or has followed some literary or folklore convention.

All the Ramayanas present Maricha as calling out to either Lakshmana or Sita. The Maricha of Tulsi Ramayan alone calls out Lakshmana at first in Rama's voice and then in his own voice calls out Rama. We understand from the statement of none other than Maricha of Vanmikam that he prefers to die by Rama's hands rather than get killed by Ravana. This sentiment is found in the later works too. However, Tulsi Ramayan alone

---

12   *Ramayanas of Kampan and Eluttachan*, pp. 67-78.

sings of him saying it explicitly.

Kamba Ramayanam does not refer to Maricha calling out either to Lakshmana or Sita. Kamban just says, 'with his split mouth...calling out... collapsed (III. 8:77)'. Since Rama later says, 'It is true. The wicked man called out in my voice (80)', we come to know that Maricha changed his voice into that of Rama and let out a pathetic cry. It is worth noting that the verses in this canto do not have textual variations.

A few of the Sitas say, 'Capture the deer and return' while many Sitas say, 'Bring its hide'. Except for the Rama of Vanmikam, no other Rama fulfils the wish of Sita; once the deer they kill turns into a demon they return. Only in the case of Vanmikam, when the deer turned into Maricha, Rama killed another deer and brought its hide hung on his shoulders. But, of course, **Sita was not there to receive it.**

Arguments between Sita and Lakshmana

Vanmikam

Sita, who trembled in fear on hearing the distress call of Maricha simulating Rama's voice, asked Lakshmana to rush to Rama, who had called out for help. Lakshmana, in obedience to Rama's orders to be near Sita guarding her, remained where he stood without giving any reply. Sita harshly asked him, 'Lakshmana! What is the reason for your not going to the rescue of your brother despite knowing that he is in trouble? Are you his enemy feigning to help him? Is it because of your desire for me that you remain here without going to Rama's rescue?'

Deeply anguished over Sita's words, Lakshmana tried to pacify her in the following manner:

> Oh! Vaidehi! Your husband is one who has not been conquered by anyone from any race, be it the asuras or the gandharvas or the celestials or the demons or human beings. Your husband will kill that deer and return now. The voice you heard is that of an illusory demon. It is like the city of Gandharvas, a mere hallucination which doesn't exist in reality. I, who have been charged with the duty of guarding you, will not leave you alone in this forest and depart.

Furious with Lakshmana who always spoke the truth uncompromisingly, Sita started abusing him as follows:

> Oh! Thou ignoble creature (*anaarya*)! Perhaps you take the trying situation of Rama as a joyous one for you. It is not surprising that people like you, who nurture enmity within, should behave thus.
>
> Either because of your desire for me or because you are acting as a stooge of Bharata, you are just waiting for an opportune moment to cause trouble for Rama even while deceitfully showing love for him. Oh! Son of Sumitra, take it from me, your cherished dream will not be fulfilled, nor will Bharata's. I will not survive even a moment parting from Rama. Right away, in front of your very eyes I shall give up my life.

Lakshmana was deeply distressed and visibly agitated by the harsh words of Sita. Saddened, he said to her, with folded hands:

> Oh Mythili! You are a goddess to me. I have no right to speak opposing you. It is nothing new to hear improper words from women. Women are given to renouncing righteous ways, disregarding their duty; they are fickle-minded, cruel people; they sow differences and enmities – all over the world, this is how the nature of women is found to be.

Oh! Vaidehi! I will not endure your grating verbal arrows any longer. Let the inhabitants of this forest witness the justice and honesty marking my words. Impelled by the wicked nature so typical of women, you suspect me, who always obeys the words of the elders. Let the nymphs of the forest protect you. Many dangerous ill-omens are appearing. Let only good things happen to you. I shall proceed to where Rama has gone. Let me hope to see you when I return with him.

Sita, who heard Lakshmana's words, addressed him with a tearful face thus:

If I part from Rama I will give up my life; I will jump into Godavari; or else hang myself; or consume potent poison; or immolate myself. I will not touch even with my foot anyone except Rama.

Thus Sita wailed, beating on her chest with both her hands. On seeing her suffering, Lakshmana was deeply hurt within and consoled her. But she didn't even bother to look at the face of her husband's younger brother; nor speak a word with him. Lakshmana, who lingered there for a moment, bowed to Sita and left the place, looking at Mythili again and again (NR III. Sarga 43.SR Sarga 45).

Narasimha Purana

On seeing the illusory golden deer, Sita was drawn by its beauty and told Rama, 'If you capture it I shall play with it after returning to Ayodhya'. Rama left Sita in the custody of Lakshmana and followed that deer. It dodged him and ran towards the forest. Rama shot it down with an arrow. When the arrow hit it, Maricha, who was indeed the deceptive deer, changed his voice into that of Rama and, giving out a distress call, 'Lakshmana! Lakshmana!' collapsed in his original form, discarding the form of the deer.

Sita, who took the pathetic cry of the deceptive deer to be Rama's, asked Lakshmana to rush to his rescue. Refusing to heed the words of Lakshmana that nothing untoward would ever befall Rama, Sita told him, seething in fury, 'I understand your wicked intention. You want to make me your wife as soon as Rama dies. Otherwise why do you hesitate to go to Rama's rescue?' Unable to bear the cruel words uttered by Sita, Lakshmana immediately left the place and went in search of Rama. Thus Narasimha Purana narrates this incident (49:71-80).

Kamba Ramayanam

Sita, on hearing a call of distress, beat herself and fainted; she rolled down like a cobra struck by thunder and wailed saying, 'Asking him to fetch this deer I have, alas, brought about an end to my life'. Then she rebuked Lakshmana saying, 'Knowing that your brother has fallen by the deceit of the demons, you simply keep standing beside me without rushing to him. Oh! Thou younger one'.

Lakshmana calmly answered Sita:

> Why do you wallow in hapless distress thus, unaware of who the dark, lotus-eyed one is? If he rises in fury, all the five elements will be utterly destroyed; the great cosmos will turn topsy-turvy and fall; all the living beings including Brahma (the creator) will be destroyed. Don't you know the might with which he broke the bow of Siva? You lament thus as is wont for women. Why waste words? The demon hit by the arrow of my brother sent out that cry of distress. Please, don't grieve by taking it to be true. Do remain calm (III.9:5-11).

Sita became furious on listening to Lakshmana's explanation and his words of confidence in Rama and, boiling within, she addressed him, in seething anger:

> Your insistence on remaining here and not running to Rama's rescue is not a righteous one at all. Even a few days of association make friends give their life for each other. Despite hearing about the suffering of your mentor, you are not concerned. What more can I say? I shall end my life by jumping into the fire (9:12-13).

Lakshmana, who saw Sita thus lamenting and preparing to jump into the fire, prostrated before her feet and said:

> What is the need for such desperation? I took fright by just listening to your words. Do not be upset. I shall go. Who can conquer cruel fate? Your servant will go. Disaster has befallen. You are asking me to go against my brother's orders. You are alone (9:15,16).

Thus saying, Lakshmana, who left the place, started to wonder:

> If I remain here, she will immolate herself. If I go to Rama's rescue, some harm will surely befall her. What can I do? **Righteousness will protect itself.** She for one would die here. Therefore it is better to leave this place. If any harm befalls her, Jatayu will take care of her (9:17-19).

Thus thinking, Lakshmana left Sita and went in search of Rama as a consequence of the penance of the celestials.

Ranganatha Ramayanam

Sita, who was terrified hearing the pathetic cry, 'Hey Lakshmana!', said to Lakshmana,

> Can't you hear Rama's pathetic cry calling out for help? Or do you pretend not to hear him? Go at once to Rama's rescue.

Then Lakshmana told her, 'Be not afraid, this is a trick of the demons. No one can cause harm to Rama'. Sita, who was livid with anger on hearing this, said,

> Rama trusted you and left me under your custody. But it is sad that you should think of coveting me. I will drown myself in the Godavari and die. No use of talking any further.

Listening to her talk thus, Lakshmana covered his ears and said, 'Oh! Nymphs of the forest! You have heard Sita's cruel words. You are a witness to it. I will go and fetch Rama'. Then he drew seven circles around the hermitage, asked Sita not to come out of the circles, prayed to the god of fire saying 'if anyone crosses the circle, his head will burst into pieces', and went in search of Rama (p.153).

Bhaskara Ramayanam

The view of regarding children of step-mothers as one's enemies can be considered either a detail just added as an innovation or an echo of a contemporary social belief:

> Can the message from moral texts that children
> of the step-mother will be enemies, be ever false? (74)

Books of ethics say that children of step-mothers are one's enemies. Can that be false?

The Sita of Vanmikam does not state this kind of view. Yet, while addressing Lakshmana when he tells her that he will not leave her alone (45: 25, 26), Sita apostrophises him twice as 'the son of Sumitra', thus associating him with Bharata. We cannot but wonder if the poets of Bhaskara Ramayanam read an extra significance into this apostrophe in order to reinforce the perception in communities about the step-mother's children.

Bhaskaram as well as Kannassa Ramayanam does not say that Lakshmana issued any warning to Sita while leaving her at

Panchavati and going in search of Rama.

Bhusundi Ramayana

In this Sanskrit text (twelfth century AD), Lakshmana, who was hurt by the cruel words of Sita, drew a line of safety at the entrance to the hermitage and exhorted Sita not to cross that line and then went in search of Rama.[13]

Adhyatma Ramayana

Sita, in great rage and weeping, told Lakshmana, 'I think you have a wicked motive and want Rama to be killed. You have been sent with us by Bharata who wishes Rama to be killed. You have indeed come with the plan of having me as soon as Rama is killed. Your fond hope will not be fulfilled. Rama does not know that you have come to steal his wife. Save Rama, I will not touch any other man, be it yourself, or Bharata. I will die right away', – saying so Sita wailed, beating herself with her hands.

Lakshmana closed his ears on hearing Sita's cruel words and, overcome by grief, said to her, 'Oh! Wrathful woman! Please don't talk like this. Your indecorous words will hurt none but yourself. You are heading towards ruin'. Then he called out, 'Oh Nymphs of the forest! Save her!' and unwillingly, with much agony, Lakshmana went in search of Rama (III.7:26-37).

Ezhuthachan's Ramayanam

Ezhuthachan narrates the argument between Sita and Lakshmana following his Sanskrit source Adhyatmam.

---

13 Bhagawati Prasad Singh, 'Bhusundi Ramayana... Ramayana Literature', *The Ramayana Tradition in Asia*, p. 489.

Lakshmana, attempting to convince Sita that the voice of Rama that she has heard is actually the deluding voice of a demon, explains to her that Maricha, sent by Ravana, with the intention of abducting Sita, has come in the form of a deer and while dying at the hands of Rama, has let out a pathetic cry. Although not found in the Sanskrit original, Ezhuthachan creates and depicts this scene on his own.[14]

Tibetan Commentary on Ramayana

According to this Ramayana, as found in the commentary on Saskya Pundita's *Subhashita Ratna Nidhi* by his disciple Dmor-ston Chos-rgyal, Sita, on hearing the pathetic cry of Rama, requests Lakshmana to go to his rescue. But Lakshmana hesitates. Then Sita rebukes him saying, 'Are you staying back to capture me as soon as Rama dies?' Lakshmana at once makes a fence around Sita, exhorts her not to go beyond it and then goes in search of Rama.[15]

Ananda Ramayana

In this text also Sita suspects the intention of Lakshmana and accuses him of cherishing a wish to possess her. Lakshmana, who heard this, again turned to Sita and said:

> Oh Mother! Do listen to me. On Rama's orders I stay here for the sake of your safety. But you are tormenting me with your verbal arrows. You will soon face the consequences. However, listen carefully to the advice I am going to give you. I will draw, with my bow, circles along the four directions around you and leave. This will safeguard you.

---

14 P Padmanabhan Thampi, p. 68.
15 JW De Jong 'The Story of Rama in Tibet', *Asian Variations in Ramayana*, p.170.

Wicked people cannot cross it; this will frighten them. Please do not come out of this circle even at the cost of your life.

Thus warning her, he cut out a circle with the tip of his bow and left (1.7:93-100).

Krittibasi Ramayana

Scholars are of the view that Krittibas follows Ananda Ramayana in narrating the incident of Lakshmana forming the magic circle for the protection of Sita.[16]

Torave Ramayanam

Sita spluttered in a severe tone:

> Lakshmana! Does the news of Rama's death give you joy? Has your consciousness descended so low as to think of coveting me? What is the secret of your plot?

In response, Lakshmana explained to her, 'This is the voice of the deceitful deer; not Rama's. Rama is supreme among mankind. Nobody can kill him. How can you utter such indiscriminating words to me?' Even as she was weeping, Sita angrily asserted that she would take a drastic step, should he have some evil design on her.

Lakshmana, who heard this, closed both his ears with his hands and said:

> Oh Mother! Right away I shall go and fetch Rama in half a naazhigai (twelve minutes). Those who are around this place are tricksters. So please be alert and use your powers of discrimination.

---

16 Bijoya Das, 'A comparative study of Krittibasa Ramayana and Kambaramayana', unpublished PhD Thesis, Jadavpur University, Calcutta, p.208.

Thus advising her, he went out fully armed, in search of Rama. Before leaving, he prayed to the five elements to protect Sita. Since he was deeply wounded by Sita's words, he left Sita alone in violation of Rama's orders and went in search of Rama (Sandhi/Chapter-9).

Ramcharitmanas

Sita, on hearing the pathetic cry of the deceptive deer, shuddered in fear and said to Lakshmana, 'Your brother is in great danger; go at once and save him'. Lakshmana laughed on hearing this and replied, 'O Mother! Listen to me. With just the lifting up of Rama's eyebrows, this entire universe will be destroyed. What harm can ever befall him?' Lakshmana became deeply hurt by the bitter words the irate Sita uttered on listening to him. So he left Sita under the care of the nymphs of the forest and went in search of Rama (III.28:1-3). It has been mentioned in Lanka Kaandam that Mandodari, who advised Ravana to restore Sita to Rama and live in peace, mocked at him saying, 'You couldn't even cross the small line drawn by Lakshmana. So much for your valour (IV.36:3)'.

Ramayanas such as the Malaysian **Hikayat Seri Rama** and the Burmese **Rama Vatthu** state that Lakshmana was forced by Sita to go in search of Rama. Before leaving he drew a circle of safety around her, warned her not to come out of it and then left. In the Thai Ramayana, **Ramakien,** and the Laotian Ramayanas **Gvay Dvarobhi** and **Phra Lak Phra Lam** it is not stated that Lakshmana drew circles of safety.

Summary

Sita's Accusation

Taking the voice of the illusory deer to be that of Rama, Sita does not accept in the least the words of explanation offered by Lakshmana. On the contrary, she hurls missiles of abusive words and false accusations at him. This cruel aspect of Sita's character filled with folly is described in great detail in all the Ramayanas from Vanmikam onwards. We also find in these the tendency on her part to link Lakshmana with Bharata and speak abusively of them, clubbing them together as conspirators.

The Sita of Kamba Ramayanam alone, though angry with Lakshmana's composed attitude, does not throw improper charges at him; nor does she wail accusing him of hatching a conspiracy, joining hands with Bharata.

> 'It is not right on your part to remain calm without rushing in panic to Rama's rescue. Despite knowing the danger which has befallen your elder brother, you are not scared. What else can I say? I will jump into the fire and give up my life. That's all.'

The Sita of Kamban says just this much. Lakshmana leaves the premises only on account of his apprehension that Sita will immolate herself if he does not do so. He does not get angry with Sita nor is he upset with her.

Sita at first regrets just her own mistake on hearing the pathetic cry of the illusory deer. Since she realises what her fault is, she rues, 'What a folly have I committed! By insisting on his capturing this deer, haven't I put my life itself in mortal danger?' She, therefore, does not make the mistake of hurling charges at others. This quality of compassion found in Sita of Kamba Ramayanam is not found in any other Ramayana.

One is not able to find even in those Ramayana stories that bear the influence of the Bhakti mode, the depiction of Sita as one who has the trait of 'considering her fault in the same light as the fault of others'.

When viewing some of her accusations, one tends to think that her hatred for Kaikeyi and Bharata and her disappointment that Rama has not become the king remain lodged deep in her subconscious mind. But the reason for her accusation that Lakshmana is waiting to possess her is one that goes beyond all imagination.

One may offer an explanation for Sita's undignified conduct from the point of view of the incarnation-motif: that only if Lakshmana leaves Sita, can the objective of Ravana's destruction be fulfilled; hence Sita has been depicted as deliberately hurling these charges against Lakshmana aiming to hurt him. In fact, such an explanation has been given.

Consider Kamban's suggestion of the incarnation-motif when he says,

> As a result of the penance of the celestials, Lakshmana left Sita and went in search of Rama.

Here the cultural and creative dimensions in the conception of character become clear.

Majority of the Ramayana texts say that after hearing the harsh words of Sita and her unfair accusations, Lakshmana did not offer any reply but, before going in search of Rama, prayed to the nymphs of the forest to safeguard her.

We find that in some Ramayanas, Lakshmana has been depicted as one who retorts by denouncing Sita and as one who under the pretext of referring to Sita, highlights the general weaknesses of women. As examples we can point to Adhyatmam, Ananda Ramayana and a few others. One cannot help finding implicit references to Kaikeyi and Surpanakha in the denigrating remarks of Lakshmana. Perhaps it is not possible for anyone to forget those who have wronged us even after the particular place and time have passed.

Majority of the Ramayana texts say that Lakshmana, before leaving Sita, prays to the nymphs of the forests to protect her even though she had hurt him by hurling harsh words at him. Kamba Ramayanam says that he leaves her in the care of Jatayu. Some Southeast Asian Ramayanas state that he leaves her in the care of the Goddess of Earth. It is worth reflecting upon the fact that it is only Jatayu, to whom the Lakshmana of Kamba Ramayanam prayed, who actually comes to the rescue of Sita.

The Circle of Safety

Bhusundi Ramayana, Ranganatha Ramayanam, Ananda Ramayana, Krittibasi Ramayana, Tulsi Ramayan, Malaysian Hikayat Seri Rama and Burmese Rama Vatthu state that Lakshmana, before leaving Sita, drew **circles of safety** either around her or around the hermitage for the sake of Sita's security and left after warning her not to cross them.

This detail is not mentioned in Vanmikam, Kamba Ramayanam, Bhaskaram, Kannassam, Adhyatmam, Torave Ramayanam, Laotian Phra Lak Phra Lam, Gvay Dvorabhi and Thai Ramakien.

Those Ramayanas which state that Lakshmana drew a circle of safety, place it at the end of the incident of the argument between Sita and Lakshmana at Panchavati in Aranya Kaandam. The motive of Ramcharitmanas in narrating this incident not in that context, but as the words of Mandodari in Lanka Kaandam, is not clear.

The Ramayanas of the medieval period state that Lakshmana left after drawing a circle of protection, be it a line or a fence, impelled by his sense of foreboding that something untoward might befall Sita and hence, he must provide security to her, however much she rebuked, abused and denounced him. By this, his devotion to her as well as his sense of duty to honour the command of Rama is clear.

Abduction of Sita

The Conversation between Ravana and Sita

Vanmikam

Ravana, who noticed Lakshmana leaving Sita, put on the disguise of an ascetic Brahmana; clad in saffron, with knotted hair, holding an umbrella and a kamandalam in his hands, he stood before Sita with much hesitation. Like an abandoned dry well covered over with grass, Ravana, the dissembling villain that he was, addressed Sita thus:

> Oh! *Sundari!* (pretty woman) Are you the omnipresent daughter of the Mountains, Parvati, roaming anywhere she pleases, or the Goddess of Arts, Saraswati, or the Queen of Indra, Sasi or the Goddess of Wealth (Lakshmi), or the Goddess of Earth, Bhoomi Devi; or are you Rathi (the nonpareil of beauty)? Who are you?
> I have not seen in any world a more beautiful woman than you; you, with your slender waist, two thighs, two firm breasts standing erect upwards, your smile, and the eyes with a reddish tint, captivate me. How is it so that you are here all alone, without any fear, in this forest where wild animals roam?
> Who are you? To whom do you belong? Where have you come from? For what purpose are you staying in this forest of Dandaka where demons live?

Sita – thinking that Ravana, who enquired after her thus, was a true ascetic – gave him a seat and offered him a variety of fruits. Ravana, on seeing her and observing her treatment of him with respect, fell passionately in love with her and made up his mind to abduct her (SR.III.46 NR.44). Thinking that if she did not give a proper reply to the ascetic who enquired about her, he would curse her, Sita turned to him and spoke as follows:

Oh! Noble Brahmana! I am the daughter of the King of Mithila. Sita is my name. I am Rama's wife. I lived very happily for twelve years in the capital of the Kings of the Ikshvaku clan. In the thirteenth year, King Dasaratha wanted to perform coronation for Rama. But my mother-in-law Kaikeyi secured orders from the king by virtue of the two boons the emperor had given her long ago to make my husband Rama go to the forest and her son Bharata rule the kingdom. My husband was then twenty-five-years-old. It is said that I was then eighteen-years-old. Kaikeyi said to my husband who was all ready for the coronation, 'Your father has ordered that Bharata should rule this kingdom without any disturbance and that you should go to the forest for fourteen years. Therefore you should leave for the forest at once'. My husband is one who always gives, never receives; always speaks the truth; never utters falsehood at any time. Therefore, when he heard Kaikeyi's words he said, 'I shall do so', and with Lakshmana, son of his stepmother, and me he has been living in this forest, clad in tree barks and keeping only the bow for his defence. He will return here right now after gathering good vegetables and fruits. Oh! Brahmana ascetic! What is the purpose of your coming here alone without any of your disciples? Kindly tell me the truth about yourself (III.47:3-25.NR. 43: 3-19).

Ravana, who heard the story of Sita, introduced himself as Ravana, the chief of the demon clan who had conquered all the three worlds and had Lanka surrounded by the sea as his capital. He then said that the moment he saw Sita he had given up his love for his wives and that Sita should become his enthroned queen. On hearing these words, Sita was shocked and roused to rage; she said to Ravana:

> The mighty and magnanimous Rama is everything to me. The fox that you are, you dare to desire the lioness. You venture to pull out the tooth of the lion. You want to consume potent poison and yet survive, don't you? You are wiping your eyes with a needle. You are tasting the knife with your tongue. You want to cross the ocean with a boulder tied around your neck. You dare to uproot the sun and the moon. You hope to hide in your clothes the fires that rage around you. You want to walk on the tip of iron tridents.
>
> You are a fool who does not know that between Rama and yourself there are as many differences as there are between the lion and the fox, the ocean and the stream, nectar and porridge, gold and lead, sandal paste and slush, the elephant and the cat, the eagle and the crow, the peacock and the waterfowl, the swan and the vulture. Even if you abduct me, as long as such a Rama is alive, the strength of my chastity will never diminish. (SR III.47:27-50. NR 45:22-42).

Wishing to show off his prowess to Sita who did not yield to his wish, Ravana indulged in self-praise thus:

> Kubera, who is my elder brother and the son of my mother's elder sister, is frightened of me and is hiding himself in Mount Kailash. The celestials including Devendra, the Nagas and the five elements are all under my control. The red hot Sun will turn into the cool pleasant Moon the moment it comes near me.
>
> Come to my city of Lanka filled with a variety of riches and enjoy all the pleasures of the world. What kind of comfort are you going to experience with that Rama who is a mere mortal being and a man of poor capabilities and one who, despite being the eldest, gave up the throne, took

up exile in the forest and out of frustration turned into an ascetic and has been living in the forest? Therefore accept me who, by virtue of your meritorious deeds, has been infatuated with you.

Sita, who was all alone, reached the very limits of rage when Ravana uttered improper words to her and she told him firmly,

> Even he who steals Indra's wife Sasidevi may hope to survive; but, oh demon! the one who abducts me, even if he were a celestial being who has drunk the elixir of life, will not survive (SR. III.48.NR 46).

Thus spoke Sita in extreme anger.

The Abduction

On listening to Sita's unyielding words and her turning him down, Ravana unmasked his false guise as an ascetic, assumed his own form as the ten-headed one similar to Yama (the terrible God of Death), and holding a bow, addressed Sita as follows:

> If you want a husband who is renowned in all the three worlds, yield to me. I am the one most suitable for you. Oh! You stupid woman who considers Rama as omniscient and omnipotent; Rama, who, after all, got scared of the words of a woman and giving up his kith and kin and his citizens, has been roaming in this forest! What is it that you find in Rama that you so love and admire him?

Ravana spat away thus. As the time for reaping the consequences of his bad deeds drew near, Ravana approached Sita and grasped her lock of hair by his left hand, lifted her up by holding her two thighs with his right hand and set her down on the chariot drawn by mules. At once the chariot started flying towards the sky.

Sita who was carried away skyward called out to Rama and Lakshmana and, wailing aloud, appealed to them to get her released. She lamented desperately and said that Kaikeyi along with her kith and kin would rejoice that Sita, the wedded wife of Rama who ever walked the road of righteousness, had been captured. Then she addressed all the plants, trees along the way and the nymphs of the forest and pleaded with them to convey the message of her plight to Rama. Finally, on seeing Jatayu perched on a tree, she said, 'Oh! Jatayu! Please convey to Rama and Lakshmana at once that I am being carried away by this king of the demons', – thus crying bitterly she implored him (SR.III.49/NR.47).

Narasimha Purana

Soon after Lakshmana left, Ravana, who had disguised himself as an ascetic and reached Panchavati, said to Sita,

> Bharata has come from Ayodhya to the forest of Dandaka. Right now he is talking to Rama. Rama has sent me to fetch you there. Rama has agreed to return to Ayodhya in response to the request of Bharata. Rama has captured a deer for you to play with in Ayodhya. Your lord and his brother have received permission to rule the kingdom. Therefore get onto this flying chariot (vimana) quickly; Let us join them (49:82-85).

Sita, who mistook the words and deceitful praise of the ascetic to be true, followed him and got on to the chariot. When the chariot started flying towards the south, Sita understood his cunning design and began to wail and cry in grief. Narasimha Purana says that, though Ravana was seated close to Sita, he did not touch her at all (49:86-88).

Bhagavatam

Bhagavatam says that, when Rama had gone very far into the

forest following the illusory deer, Ravana carried her off like the wolf that waited for the opportune moment and carried off the sheep (IX.10:11).

Uttara Purana

In Gunabhadra's Uttara Purana, it is not stated that Rama and Sita ever went to the forest. This text presents Rama and Sita as living in Varanasi and the incident of Sita's capture as taking place in Chitrakootam, the adjoining forest. In this incident there is no reference to Lakshmana. After Rama goes chasing the illusory deer, impersonating Rama, Ravana approaches Sita and tells her, 'I have caught the deer and sent it to Varanasi. It is time we returned home'. Sita, who hears this, gets on to the Pushpaka aircraft parked there, looking like a palanquin, and seats herself (Bulcke 443).

Tibetan Ramayana

Since much time had lapsed after Rama had gone in search of the illusory dear, Lakshmana thought he must be in danger and leaving Sita alone, he went in search of Rama. Dasagriva (Ravana), who was looking for such an opportunity, carried Sita off along with the plot of ground where she was staying, says Tun-Huang, the Tibetan Ramayana (ninth century AD).[17]

In the Ramayana version found in the Tibetan commentary on a grammar text called **Subhashita Ratna Nidhi** (thirteenth century AD), as soon as Lakshmana goes in search of Rama, Ravana assumes the guise of a brahmana and begs for alms from Sita. Sita refuses to come out of the fence put up by

---

17 Dasagriva carries off Sita 'together with a plot of ground'. JW De Jong, 'The Story of Rama in Tibet', *Asian Variations in Ramayana*, p. 165.

Lakshmana. At once Ravana carries her off together with the whole plot of ground where Sita has been staying.[18]

Kamba Ramayanam

Ravana, who was waiting for Lakshmana's departure, put on the guise of an ascetic, mature in age and austerities; chanting Vedic hymns melodiously to the accompaniment of a veena, he approached the hermitage and enquired, 'Who all are living in this abode?' Sita, who heard it, came out of the hermitage and said, 'Please come in'. The man who came in took a glance at the queen of chastity. He thought that even ten pairs of eyes wouldn't be enough to look at the corporeal beauty of this lady which matched that of Goddess Lakshmi and that one would need a thousand eyes. Ravana, who feasted on the very sight of her beauty, thought, 'While the *devas* (celestials) and *asuras* (demons) along with their consorts are under her service when she will be ruling all the three worlds, I shall gladly go about running errands for her. I shall give up my very throne to my sister for showing me such a paragon of beauty'. Sita said to the ascetic Ravana, who stood charmed and wonder-struck by her beauty, 'Please come in, your holy self' (III.9:20-33).

When the deceitful ascetic accepted the invitation of Sita and went near her, she offered him a seat saying, 'Please be seated here'. Then the mountains and the trees shook in fear; the cries of birds slowly subsided; animals were scared; the snakes slithered away with their hoods shrunk.

Taking the seat, Ravana asked her, 'Whose is this seat? Who is the ascetic who occupies this seat? Who are you?' Sita replied:

---

18 Dasagriva carries off Sita 'together with the whole plot of ground' – JW De Jong, Op. cit. p.170.

The son of Dasaratha. One who lives happily with his brother in obedience to his mother's wishes. Oh Venerable Sire! You must have heard of his name, haven't you?

He in turn said, 'Heard of him; but I have not seen him', and then enquired, 'Whose daughter are you?' She said in response, 'I am the renowned daughter of Janaka; my name is Janaki; I am the wife of Kakuthan (Kakusthan was the ancestor of Rama, father of Raghu from whose dynasty Rama hails. Rama himself is called Kakusthan)', and then asked him, 'Oh Revered Sire! Where are you coming from?' Then Ravana, with a scheming mind, started to reply thus:

> He is one who out-Indras Indra. A handsome man (sundara) who cannot be depicted in a picture; descending from the line of the Four-faced God, Brahma; one in whose tongue resides the sacred Vedas; king of all the worlds; one who uprooted Mount Kailash; one who rules Lanka with the celestials in service. Speech falters when expressing his glory. One who is blessed with the boon of eternal life; one who holds the sword given by Siva; a virtuous man; a handsome person marvelled at even by Manmatha (God of Love); one who is so eminent as to be worshipped as 'God' by people like us. All the beautiful damsels in the world long for his love; but without yielding to them he goes in search of a woman dear to his heart. Because he has requested me, I have been staying in his city for a few days. Unwilling to part with him though, I have come from there (9:34-48).

After hearing this long account of self-praise, Sita said in reply, 'Why should you, doing penance deeming the body as a burden, ever have to live in the city of the wicked demons who eat up human beings? Instead of mingling with sages and visiting sacred places to offer worship, why have you been staying with those who cannot do righteous deeds even if they wish to? Oh, how could you do this? How can those who consort with the wicked ever be pure?'

Ravana thought she doubted him. Hence he said, 'How can anyone hope to survive in this world after antagonising the mighty demons?' She replied, 'Rama, who is the champion of righteousness, will root out the demons within the period of his stay here; thereafter there will be no cause for suffering in this world'. Thus Sita spoke, as if to offer him refuge. When Sita said so, Ravana retorted,

> If the demons were to be exterminated by humans, a baby rabbit can kill a whole herd of elephants; it is like a deer killing a pride of sharp-nailed lions.

When Sita heard the disparaging words of Ravana, she said,

> Perhaps you have not heard of the killing of Viradha, Khara and numerous others. The herd of deer which you mentioned all turned into demons. You will watch their annihilation and the celestials rejoicing over it right away; you, the impeccable one, wouldn't you know all? Can evil ever conquer righteousness? (49-57)

Ravana, who heard Sita boasting of one man killing a few, addressed her as 'a naive woman' and said,

> Do you want to uproot Mount Meru? Or demolish the sky? Or stir up the ocean? Put out the fire? Lift up the cosmos? In all these what is it that Ravana cannot accomplish? Who do you think Ravana is?

Thus spoke an incensed Ravana. At once Sita said,

> Of what use are the thousand shoulders well-built? Don't they need the capability to fight? The thousand-shouldered one (Karthaveerya Arjuna) captured the twenty-shouldered King of Lanka. He was overthrown with an axe by Parasurama who was just two-shouldered.

When Sita retorted thus, sparks darted from Ravana's eyes. 'When anger burst forth, the false guise dropped (58-62).' Ravana emerged out of the disguise and said to Sita,

> You dare to call the humans who live in the midst of filthy
> worms of the soil mighty? Being a woman you
> are pardoned! Be not afraid, come with me and live in
> prosperity (65-66).

Sita, who heard this, closed her ears with her tender hands; fury and tears overwhelming her, she flared up, 'What did you say, Oh demon! Do you think I who am the chaste wife of Kakuthan will ever allow the values of my family to be destroyed, fearing after all for this mortal life which vanishes just as the dewdrops on the blade of grass evaporate in no time? Before Rama's deadly arrow kills you, you had better go and hide yourself'.

Sita, who found Ravana not getting over his infatuation despite listening to her harsh words, but shamelessly falling at her feet, was much agitated and called out in anguish, 'Oh, my Lord! Oh, the younger brother!' (71)

Then, Ravana, who recalled a curse he had earlier incurred, carried off, on his shoulder, Sita along with the whole plot of ground on which the hermitage stood, got on to the chariot and flew skyward. Sita, overcome by grief, addressed all the objects of nature such as the mountains and pleaded with them to explain her condition to the warriors.

> Oh, Varada, the giver of boons! Oh, the younger one,
> Oh, the impeccable Bharata, oh the youngest,
> Won't you all become blame worthy? (77)

Thus she called out to the four of them, Rama, Lakshmana, Bharata and Shatrughna. Ravana, who heard it, laughed in derision saying, 'You, with glinting tresses! Do you think those human beings whom you are calling out to so desperately will kill me in war and rescue you?' When Ravana said that, Sita glared at him and raged on with a series of arguments thus:

> By deceit you created a false deer; doing so you sent away Rama who is your god of death; in the meanwhile, you entered the hermitage and are carrying me off. If you don't wish to see yourself killed by them in the battle, stop the chariot (81).
>
> You are not a truly valiant person; you resorted to trickery knowing fully that those human beings who killed your pack of demons in a trice and cut off the breasts and nose of your sister, are present in this forest. Isn't your deceptive act a result of fear?

Ravana, who heard Sita denigrating him thus, said, 'Oh Lady! If I, who lifted up the silvern mountain of Siva who has a third eye on his forehead, should fight with mere mortals, it will be an act of disgrace. Deceit is much better than that'. Sita, who heard Ravana's reply, said,

> Fighting with enemies is an act of disgrace you say! But is abducting chaste women by deceit the greatest feat of valour! For demons, who have no mercy, neither does blame matter nor does sin. (83-84)

Thus she retorted in sorrow.

Bhusundi Ramayana

Ravana masquerading as a Brahmana stopped his chariot near Panchavati and waited near the hermitage of Rama for the opportune moment. Lakshmana, who was hurt by the harsh words of Sita, drew a line with the tip of his bow at the entrance to the hermitage, asked Sita not to come out crossing that line and went in search of Rama. After Lakshmana left, Ravana arrived and stood in front of the hermitage. At once flames flared up along that line. However hard he tried, Ravana could not cross that line (*Lakshman rekha*) and go inside.

Then he begged, 'Mother! Give alms to this poor Brahmana'. Sita, who heard this, hid her true form in the fire, crossed the line drawn by Lakshmana and stood in front of Ravana in her human form for the purpose of fulfilling the motive of incarnation. Revealing his demonic form immediately, Ravana carried Sita in his arms and flew skyward towards Lanka.

Phrases like *Lakshman rekha*, *Chaya Sita* (Lakshmana's Line, Shadow Sita) are found for the first time in this text.[19]

Ranganatha Ramayanam

When Ravana, posing as an ascetic, arrives at the hermitage, Sita takes him to be a true ascetic; she comes out of the circle of safety drawn by Lakshmana and extends hospitality to him. To Ravana who asked Sita, 'Who are you, living alone in this huge forest?' she gives an account of herself and how the three of them happened to come to the forest and in turn asks him, 'Who are you?' Ravana tells her his true story and asks her to come along with him to Lanka and live there as his wife.

Sita, who is outraged on hearing that, nips a stalk of straw and holding it in her hands says, 'How dare you speak like this to me, the wife of Rama? Rama is as different from you as the ocean is from a canal and the eagle from the crow. If you wish to save your life, go back at once to Lanka'.

Ravana, who hears this, assumes his original form and the very moment he looks at Sita, she slumps down in a state of

---

19 (a) 'Sitam chayamayim striyam'(Sanskrit, the false female image of Sita) (I. 136: 102) ed. Bhagawati Prasad Singh, Varanasi: Vishvavidyalay Prakashan, 1975; p. 853.
(b) Bhagawati Prasad Singh, 'Bhusundi Ramayana and its Influence', *The Ramayana Tradition in Asia*,p. 489.

stupor. Immediately, Ravana lifts her up on to his chariot and goes to Lanka skyward on an aerial route (pp.153-155).

Bhaskara Ramayanam

When Sita extended appropriate hospitality to Ravana who came in the guise of an ascetic, he asked her who she was and why she had come to this forest; she narrated her story and also described to him how Rama and Lakshmana had gone in search of the magical deer.

Listening to her, Ravana, who proudly narrated his own history, said that he had arrived there after he heard of Sita's incomparable beauty and asked her to come with him to Lanka and entertain him.

> Sita who heard Ravana's words was terrified at heart and burst out in rage:
> How can you, being the son of Visravasu, utter such unrighteous words? You and Rama are just like the elephant and the mosquito. Have you dared to die by Rama's arrow?

Ravana broke into laughter at this and said,

> This entire universe is under my thumb. I can make deadly snakes spit out venom. I can pulverise the earth so that it is contained in my hands. I can swallow up the sky. I can break all the directions. How dare you speak of Rama's valour to such a person as me?

So saying, he assumed his original form and stood before her. At that sight, Sita fainted and fell down. Ravana slowly lifted up the unconscious Sita and placed her on his chariot and set forth to Lanka skyward. Sita, when she recovered, lamented, 'Ravana the demon is carrying me off. Oh Lakshmana! I abused you out of my foolishness. I am now reaping the consequences of that sin' (Second Aswasa, 82-115).

Telugu Molla Ramayanam very briefly narrates this incident (verses: 37,38).

Kannassa Ramayanam

Sita welcomes Ravana, who has come in the guise of an ascetic and extends due hospitality to him. Ravana extols her beauty and asks her the reason for her coming to the forest; Sita explains the reason for their exile in the forest and enquires about Ravana.

Ravana too tells her his true story and expressing his desire to make her his wife, he invites her to go with him to Lanka. Sita is furious and replies that if her husband happens to know of his diabolical design, he will destroy Ravana and his entire clan. Incensed by her retort, Ravana sheds his disguise, takes his original form as a demon, seizes Sita, seats her in his chariot and flies into the sky.

Adhyatma Ramayana

Ravana, who was waiting for the opportunity of finding Sita alone, put on the garb of an ascetic and approached her soon after Lakshmana left Sita. Mistaking him to be a true ascetic, Sita extended appropriate hospitality to him. Sita responded to the ascetic's query regarding who she was, by narrating the story of her sojourn at the forest of Dandaka and enquired about his story. The ascetic too narrated his true story to her and asked her to go with him to Lanka. Sita, who felt outraged by this, said in a stern tone, 'How dare you say you will carry me away, the consort of Lord Vishnu? The moment Rama returns you will fall a prey to his arrow'.

Ravana, on hearing the words of Sita, assumed his original form. All the nymphs to whom Lakshmana had prayed to protect Sita fled in fright on seeing the form of Ravana. Ravana dug up the plot of ground where Sita stood, lifted her up on to his chariot and flew aloft. The terrified Sita looked at the earth below and cried, 'Ah Rama! Ah Lakshmana!' She kept wailing, 'Oh Lakshmana the devout one! I have hurt you by my unbecoming words. Please forgive me!' (III.7:38-66)

Ezhuthachan's Adhyatma Ramayana narrates this incident following its Sanskrit original; only, while referring to the abduction of Sita, instead of following its Sanskrit source, it states, 'Ravana lifted up Sita, seated her on his chariot and departed' (Thampi,70).

Bengali Ramayana

Ravana, who disguises himself as a simple, aged ascetic, approaches Sita and begs for food to appease his hunger. When Sita, standing behind the circle of safety drawn by Lakshmana, stretches out her hand and offers him a plate full of vegetables and fruits, the ascetic says he is not in the habit of entering the household of anyone and accepting alms. Sita then comes out of the circle of safety. At once Ravana grabs her hands and draws her towards him and flies off in the aircraft. So says Krittibas's Bengali Ramayana.

Ananda Ramayana

After Lakshmana left warning Sita, Ravana transformed himself into an ascetic, reached the entrance of the hermitage at Panchavati where Sita was staying, uttered, 'Narayana Hari' and stood there silently. The 'Illusory' Sita, (I,7:89) who heard this, held out her hands to give him alms. The pseudo-ascetic on seeing this said, 'I don't take alms from those confined within a line. If you are one who upholds the household ethics of Rama, cross the line, come out and offer the alms'.

Sita, who heard what the ascetic said, wondered, 'Will any harm befall me on account of this?' and setting her left foot outside the line and putting forth her hand said, 'Here, receive the alms'. At once Ravana caught hold of her, seated her on his chariot drawn by mules and went back on the same route he came by. Thus Ananda Ramayana describes this incident (I.7: 101-107).

Torave Ramayanam

Ravana, assuming the habit of an aged ascetic, arrives at the hermitage of Sita. Sita extends proper hospitality to him and enquires about his story. In reply he says, 'I am an itinerant ascetic who has been to many countries. The country I wish to visit next is Lanka'. When, captivated by Sita's beauty, his disguise as an old man disappears, he turns into a middle-aged, good-looking ascetic, and describes Sita's beauty in eulogising terms. He then tells her, 'Rama has been killed by Maricha, the illusory deer. The one who has gone in search of him is also dead. That being the situation, how can you live all by yourself? Come, let us go to Lanka'. Sita, on listening to this, suspects him to be a sorcerer. Then Ravana appears in his original form, details his feats of valour and asks her to marry him and live happily. When Sita does not consent to his proposal, he drags her by her lock of hair, comes out of the hermitage, gets her seated in his chariot and leaves. So says Torave Ramayanam (Sandhi/Chapter-9).

Ramcharitmanas

When Ravana, in the cloak of a renunciant, noticed that Sita was alone, he furtively glanced from one side to another and entered the hermitage like a sneaking dog. Reason and capability desert the one who has allowed his mind to go the way of evil.

Ravana, who found Sita ignoring him despite his waxing eloquent about himself and extolling her beauty, threatened her and asked her to become his wife. Looking at him with disgust, Sita said, 'You are a rogue in the garb of an ascetic'. At once Ravana's fake form vanished and he came into his original demonic form. Yet undaunted, Sita turned to him with courage and shot back, 'Oh you base wretch! Just wait awhile. My husband will be here soon. Like a little rabbit desiring a lioness, you have courted your end by your desire'. Ravana who reached the limits of his fury on hearing her words of derision, dragged her on to his chariot and sped away through the sky (III 28: 5-8).

It has been stated in Pauma Chariyu, Vasudeva Hindi, Ramayana Kakawin, Ramakien, Rama Vatthu and Hikayat Seri Ram that Ravana arrived putting on the appearance of an ascetic and Sita, unyielding, shouted at him in fury. Unable to bear being rejected by a woman, Ravana cast off his disguise, resumed his demonic form, got on to the chariot carrying Sita in his hands and flew away towards Lanka.

Summary

Texts such as Vanmikam, Kamba Ramayanam and Ramayana Kakawin narrate the incidents such as Ravana's coming to Panchavati, meeting Sita and asking her the reason for living in the forest of Dandaka, Sita in response narrating the story of their having to reside in the forest, Sita enquiring about Ravana's story after narrating her own and Ravana in turn narrating his – all more or less in the same manner. In Vanmikam, Kamba Ramayanam, Ranganatham and Bhaskaram, these matters are narrated a little elaborately. In Torave Ramayanam alone, it has been stated that Ravana called himself an itinerant and said, 'I have been to most of the countries; I want to see the golden city of Lanka which is considered to be a renowned city'.

Marvelling at her beauty

The incident of Ravana meeting Sita and extolling her beauty in sheer wonder finds a mention in Vanmikam, Kamba Ramayanam, Torave Ramayanam and other Telugu Ramayanas. Vanmikam alone presents in elaborate terms Ravana praising Sita's beauty. Kamba Ramayanam puts it briefly as Ravana saying, 'My ten pairs of eyes won't suffice to marvel at and feast on your beauty. I need a thousand eyes'.

Comparison of Rama - Ravana

In some Ramayanas we find that, when Ravana, captivated by Sita's beauty, suggests that she should come to Lanka and live as the queen there, Sita, enraged as well as frightened, derisively compares Ravana with Rama in various ways.

Vanmikam says that Sita scoffed at Ravana declaring that between Rama and Ravana there exists as much difference as there is between a lion and a fox, an ocean and a brook, nectar and porridge, gold and lead, sandal paste and slush, the elephant and the cat, the eagle and the crow, the peacock and the water-hen, the swan and the vulture.

Ranganatha Ramayanam, following Vanmikam, says that Sita told Ravana that between Rama and him there was as much difference as between the ocean and the brook, and the eagle and the crow.

Bhaskara Ramayanam shows Sita as saying, 'Rama and you are like the elephant and the mosquito'.

Comparison of Sita-Ravana

Some Ramayana texts say that Sita mocked at Ravana by comparing him with herself:

The jackal that you are, you dare to love me, the lioness. You want to pull out the tooth from the mouth of the lion. You want to survive after consuming potent poison. You want to wipe your eyes with a needle. You want to taste a knife. You want to cross the ocean tying a rock around your neck. You want to carry the blazing flames in your clothes.

Thus **Vanmikam** shows that Sita ridiculed Ravana by comparing herself to Ravana.

Bhagavatam says that Ravana carried off Sita like a wolf stealthily carrying away sheep.

Ramcharitmanas of Tulsidas says Sita told Ravana that he was like a stupid little rabbit desiring a lioness and that he sought his end by his unbecoming desire.

Valmiki has wonderfully depicted the conversation between Ravana and Sita with a literary flourish and by striking similes so that Sita's seething anger, her intelligence and daring are thrown in relief. Kamban's depiction of Sita, as one endowed with the power of logical reasoning and debating skills, arouses wonder and delight.

The Manner of Abducting Sita

Texts such as Vanmikam, Bhagavatam, Bhusundi, Ranganatham, Bhaskaram, Kannassam, Krittibasi Ramayana, Ananda Ramayana, Ezhuthachan Ramayanam, Torave Ramayanam and Ramcharitmanas state that Ravana **physically lifted Sita** and carried her away.

In texts such as Pauma Chariyu, Vasudeva Hindi, Bhattikavyam, Janakiharan, Ramayana Kakawin, Ramakien, Rama Vatthu, and Hikayat Seri Rama it has been said that **Ravana held Sita in his hands**, got on to his chariot and left.

Narasimha Purana says that when Ravana in the disguise

of an ascetic said, 'Rama and others have gone to Ayodhya; they sent me to fetch you', **Sita on her own got on to the chariot,** while Uttara Purana says that when Ravana suggested they could go to Varanasi, Sita boarded the Pushpaka aircraft that looked like a palanquin.

The Tibetan Ramayana Tun Huang (ninth century AD) and other Tibetan commentaries on Ramayana which appeared in thirteenth, fourteenth, and fifteenth centuries say that **Ravana carried off Sita together with the whole plot of ground** on which she was standing. Kamba Ramayanam says that Ravana dug up the soil underneath the hermitage wherein Sita was and carried the whole plot of ground on his shoulders and put it in his chariot. The Sanskrit Adhyatma Ramayana says that Ravana dug up the plot of ground where Sita stood and placed it in the chariot and flew skyward with her.

We can regard Ravana forcibly carrying off Sita as stated in Vanmikam and other texts as the first stage of development of this incident. In Buddhist Ramayanas, this incident of Sita's abduction does not take place at all.

On account of the flowering of devotional sentiments in the country, doctrines of incarnation came up.

When the conception of Sita as an incarnation of Goddess Lakshmi gained momentum, there arose the necessity to state that Sita on her own got on to the chariot and sat on it and that Ravana carried her off, without physically touching her. Narasimha Purana (fifth century AD) was the first text to say so. Following that, we find the trend of reporting this incident thus with just a few changes in Uttara Purana, Tun Huang and Kamba Ramayanam.

As a development of this idea in a different direction, Bhusundi Ramayana set a notion afloat that Ravana carried only the *Maya* (illusory) Sita or the shadowy form of Sita, following which Adhyatma Ramayana as well as Ananda Ramayana present this idea.

Sita's Lament

Sita, when she was being carried away, called out to Lakshmana and Rama to free her. She then addressed the plants and nymphs of the forest on the way and pleaded with them to convey her plight to Rama. Finally, she saw Jatayu perched on a tree and tearfully pleaded with him to report her condition to Rama and Lakshmana. So says Vanmikam.

Sita, who was lifted up together with the hermitage, overcome by grief, addressed the mountain and other objects of nature, and beseeched them to convey her plight to Rama and Lakshmana. Then, calling out to Rama and his brothers, she wailed. So says Kamba Ramayanam.

The Sita depicted by Valmiki laments amidst her wails that 'Kaikeyi along with her kith and kin will be delighted if she comes to know of me being captured'. Such a cry in despair only presses home clearly the hatred that Sita bears towards Kaikeyi and that Sita has not forgotten that Kaikeyi is the root cause of all her misery and their subsequent exile in the forest.

The Sita depicted by Kamban does not express such a sentiment anywhere. On the other hand, Kamba Ramayanam shows her as calling out to all the four brothers saying,

> Oh, the giver of boons! Oh, the younger one,
> Oh, the impeccable Bharata,
> Won't you all become blameworthy?

(77)

Here, Sita calls Bharata 'absolutely unblemished'. Moreover, in Kamban's visualisation, Sita, setting aside her own wretched condition, is seen to be struck with pity for them saying, 'Oh! You princes! You have become vulnerable to the charge of thus losing me'.

Bhaskara Ramayanam says that Sita cried piteously, 'The demon called Ravana carries me off. Oh Lakshmana! I foolishly abused you by uttering improper words. I am facing the consequences of that sin'.

The Sanskrit Adhyatma Ramayana says that Sita, who was being carried away by Ravana, looked at the earth below, and cried out, 'Oh! Rama! Oh! Lakshmana!' and then, 'Oh! Devout Lakshmana! I uttered improper words and hurt you. Please forgive me'.

Bhaskaram and Adhyatmam are the only two texts that show Sita in a spirit of commiseration, deeply regretting her grievous mistake of abusing Lakshmana – the Lakshmana who took up exile in the forest out of love for Rama, the Lakshmana who rendered proper service to Rama and Sita, the Lakshmana who stood guarding her; the very same Lakshmana who exhorted her saying that the golden deer was only the product of trickery perpetrated by the demons. Sita's deep remorse was that she had harshly chastised and charged such a man with an abominably base motive and thus hurt him deeply. The Sita of Kamban expresses such a feeling of commiseration even at the stage when Maricha in Rama's voice cries out desperately. She rues her mistake saying, 'By asking him to capture this deer, I have ruined my life'.

Kamban's subtle art in depicting his Sita as one who did not hurl any charge against Lakshmana has been noted above. It strikes us that the Sita of Vanmikam has not revealed any such sentiment of commiseration while setting forth in detail Sita's unjust charges, levelled furiously in a language absolutely unbecoming.

Some Points for Reflection

Surpanakha, who paved the way for the eventual killing of Ravana, tells him that she had her ears and nose cut off and was thus humiliated by Rama and Lakshmana when, for his sake, she tried to abduct Sita of unparalleled beauty. The flames of lust set ablaze by Surpanakha in Lanka later led to the destruction of Lanka itself.

The flames of lust of the one who set it ablaze, too, did not get extinguished till the end nor did those of the other.

The brothers, not realising the consequences of mocking at Surpanakha's lust, lost their peace of mind as a result and went in search of it; they were never to find it.

Sita, who happened to become the secondary cause for the flames of lust to rage in Ravana, never got back the proud joys of her conjugal life after abusing and sending away Lakshmana.

The life in the forest of Dandaka ended as a punishment for all, the good as well as the wicked. The one who abducted her from there did not prosper either; the one who was abducted and later retrieved too did not live a life of dignity.

What could be the reason for this paradox? Was it an ironic outcome of the blessings of Sage Agastya who selected and suggested Panchavati as the suitable abode? Or is it the tragic predicament of human life?

The Sita who stubbornly went to the forest protesting, 'I will not survive parting from you; therefore I will also go with you to the forest'; the Sita who had insisted on Rama chasing the deer, brushing aside Lakshmana's offer to capture it; the Sita who, doubting Lakshmana who was guarding her, had furiously shouted at him, 'If I part from Rama, I will give up my life; I shall jump into the river Godavari; or hang myself; or consume potent poison; or jump into the fire', and sent him away, as a consequence now had to part from Rama and live in the forest of Ashoka for months together amidst the demonesses, all alone!

Isn't this the tragic predicament of human life?

Reasons for the Abduction of Sita

In the two Buddhist Ramayanas, **Dasaratha Jataka** and **Dasaratha Kathaanam,** the incident of the abduction of Sita has not been narrated. Ravana abducting Sita and consequently getting killed by Rama are contrary to the doctrines of Buddhism. For Rama who is Bodhisattva, killing Ravana would go against the creed of Buddhism. Hence the Buddhist texts do not narrate this incident.

In the story of Ramayana narrated very briefly in Shanti Parva of **The Mahabharata,** the incident of Sita's abduction is not narrated. The reason for not including this incident is not clear when Rama's going for fourteen years of exile in the forest has been narrated.

Excepting these, the other texts that undertook to sing the story of Rama elaborately narrate the abduction of Sita and the consequent battle between Rama and Ravana as an indispensable event of the epic (Bulcke 433).

Disfiguring of Surpanakha

Scholars are generally of the view that it has been stated in Vanmikam that the disfiguring of Surpanakha by Rama and Lakshmana is the root cause for Ravana's abduction of Sita (Bulcke 433).This view is prevalent based on the details in Aranya Kaandam (Sarga 36).

In the Yuddha Kaandam of Valmiki Ramayana, Sarga 9, in the section where Vibhishana is said to be talking to Ravana, there is no reference to Surpanakha:

> You have abducted Rama's wife Sita from Janasthana. What injustice to you has Rama done that should provoke you to act so?
> Khara got killed by Rama for perpetrating limitless cruelties at Janasthana. It is a natural tendency for all living beings to fight against forces of danger whenever they confront them and try to save themselves. What is Rama's mistake in this? (NR+ SR:VI,9:13,14.)

In the above statement of Vibhishana, there is no mention of Surpanakha as the cause for Ravana abducting Sita.

The scholar Camille Bulcke, who has referred to this matter, also mentions another section at the end of Yuddha Kaandam: 'Hanuman briefs Bharata about what happened to Rama during the period of exile in the forest. He gives a detailed account of Rama killing the demons in the Dandaka forest but makes only an incidental reference to the disfigurement of Surpanakha.' The inference is that Ravana was enraged on account of the killing of the demons and hence carried off Sita with the motive of revenge. Vanmikam positions the statement of Hanuman which Camille Bulcke mentions, as follows:

> When Rama was returning after meeting Agastya, a woman called Surpanakha came to Rama. By Rama's orders, Lakshmana cut off the ears and nose of Surpanakha. The 14,000 demons who were the inhabitants of the Dandaka forest and their chief Khara, who came to fight against Rama, were all killed.
> Then the woman (Surpanakha) who was punished by Lakshmana went to Ravana. Ordered by him, Maricha turned into a deer studded with gems and lured Vaidehi (NR. VI.114:16-23; SR.VI.129:16-23).

Hanuman did not start with narrating the killing of the

demons and then come to the details about Surpanakha, as Bulcke holds (434). On the contrary, Vanmikam shows that Hanuman narrated all the incidents in the same sequence as they happened, viz. the disfigurement of Surpanakha (Slokas 16, 17), the decimation of the demons (18,19,20), the killing of Khara and as a consequence Surpanakha complaining to Ravana (22).

While returning home at the end of the battle, sitting on the Pushpaka aircraft, Rama briefly describes to Sita all the routes he traversed and the important incidents which happened on the way. But he omits telling the story of Surpanakha, which happened in Panchavati. This omission is seen in both the Recensions of Vanmikam:

> Oh! Noble woman, this is the hermitage where we stayed, the place where Khara, Dushana and Trisira were killed by my arrows which never miss their mark (43).
>
> Look at our beautiful and auspicious looking hermitage from where Ravana, the king of the demons, stole you (44).

Before these two slokas the spot in Janasthana where Jatayu fought with Ravana (42), and after these slokas, the hermitage of Agastya on the banks of the river Godavari (45), are pointed out by Rama.

In the Yuddha Kaandam of Valmiki there are two synoptic accounts of Rama's story. Of these, the first is the one narrated by Rama to Sita who came with him to the forest and went through much suffering (Sarga III/126). The second is structured as the response of Hanuman to Bharata's request, narrating the incidents that took place during Rama's exile in the forest, though Hanuman did not have first-hand knowledge of them (114/129).

Of the two, the first is the narration by Rama on his own to Sita without Sita asking for it. The second is Hanuman's narration in response to Bharata's request. The first is the narration of all the incidents in the end-to-beginning order, i.e. from the killing of Ravana to the circumstances that led to Rama's heading for the forest. The second synopsis, presented as Hanuman's account, is a narration in the from-beginning-to-end order.

Hanuman, who had grasped the incidents recounted by Rama in Kishkindha Kaandam, does include the matter relating to Surpanakha in his narration in the Yuddha Kaandam; but one can't fathom why Rama, who was the victim of Surpanakha's guile and who had a direct experience of it, left it out in his narration to Sita. It may be because Sita was unaware of the happenings after her abduction; hence he gave a detailed account of them. One can offer an explanation that Rama excluded the Surpanakha matter since Sita already knew about it; however the question arises why Rama narrates to Sita all the happenings before coming to the forest of Dandaka – the incidents that happened when Sita was with him. Rama narrates all about Sage Agastya, Sage Atri, Anasuya, Sarabhangan, Sutikshana and such noble sages. He talks about his friend Guha. He tells her about the killing of Viradha. But it is not clear why he excludes the story of Surpanakha who was the prime cause for the war between him and Ravana, the nucleus of the tale of Sita's sorrow.

The reason for stating this in such detail here arose out of the need to understand and discuss scholar Bulcke's apprehension and surmise, i.e. in the **Aadi Ramayana**, the disfigurement of Surpanakha did not happen. Even in the statement of Vibhishana cited above, this incident is not shown as the cause for the abduction of Sita. But the scholar Bulcke is of the opinion that as time passed, the episode of Surpanakha's disfigurement gained popularity and so probably, it has found a place in the versions of Vanmikam in vogue today (434).

Bulcke's surmise appears to be correct. However, whether the reason given by him is a possibility has to be further analysed. **Aadi Ramayana** is a construct by researchers. Though constructs are acceptable, it is doubtful whether this incident can be taken as one of the bases for it. On the other hand, it has been considered that the story of Rama had gained accretion gradually after the Vedic age. At the time when it got developed according to the doctrines of Buddhism, Aadi Ramayana could have appeared in Sanskrit. As seen above, the Buddhist and Jain Ramayanas have completely set aside the incident of Surpanakha and the abduction of Sita. Therefore, these are not stated in the Aadi Ramayana which came up during that period.

One may think that the Surpanakha episode could have been linked to the killing of Ravana due to the diminishing influence of Buddhist texts at the time when Valmiki Ramayana came up; or as Bulcke thinks, because it would add up to the tempo of the story.

Therefore, according to the existing Vanmikam as well as other Ramayanas in vogue in other Indian languages, the incident of Surpanakha's disfigurement can be considered emerging as a lateral story causally connected to Sita's abduction.

The Killing of Sambukumara

Lakshmana kills Sambukumara (Sambuka), the son of Surpanakha, with his sword. On hearing this, Surpanakha comes to take revenge on Rama and Lakshmana. She sees them and falls in love with them, consequently gets humiliated and complains to Ravana who in turn abducts Sita. Therefore, Vimalasuri's **Pauma Chariyu** says that the killing of Sambukumara became the cause for the abduction of Sita. Telugu Ranganatha Ramayanam, Kannada Torave Ramayanam, Ananda Ramayanam and Siam's Ramakien – all these texts too present this point.

Ravana's Inappropriate Lust

It is worth reflecting a little more on the view that Ravana abducted Sita only with the motive of avenging the humiliation of Surpanakha. The reason is that the Southern Recension of Vanmikam and the Malayala Kannassa Ramayanam show that when Akampana goes and reports to Ravana, he tells him only about the killing of Khara and Dushana but nothing at all about Surpanakha. Encroaching upon the territories under Ravana's reign and killing the demons is an assault on the sovereignty of Ravana; therefore, he says that Rama and Lakshmana should be killed. Yet, since he has personally witnessed the martial valour of Rama and Lakshmana, he suggests that if Ravana abducts Sita by some trickery, Rama will die a natural death unable to bear her separation. Following this, as described above, Ravana goes to Maricha, but gives up the idea of abducting Sita on the latter's advice and goes back to Lanka. In this incident, Ravana's impulse for revenge vanishes the moment he realises that it would cost him his life.

After Akampana, when Surpanakha goes to Ravana and chronicles the happenings at Panchavati, she tells him about the humiliation she suffered and the destruction of Khara and Dushana. She then describes in detail the beauty of Sita with great emotion in fifteen slokas (Sarga 34). Unsettled by Surpanakha's description and overcome by lust, Ravana goes to Maricha *again* and asks him to help him in abducting Sita. Maricha describes in detail Rama's valour, nobility and superhuman qualities and advises Ravana to give up his wicked intention and go back to Lanka. This time, Ravana doesn't heed Maricha's advice. Frightened of Ravana's intimidation, Maricha agrees to help him as per his desire.

The reason for Ravana not accepting the advice of Maricha the second time is his immoral love for Sita. Ravana wanted to abduct Sita by deceit rather than by directly facing Rama in a fight because he was afraid that if he killed Rama and Lakshmana, Sita would give up her life. In other words, the desire to avenge the cruelty to Surpanakha and Khara and Dushana by killing Rama and Lakshmana was *not* present in Ravana's heart; it becomes very clear that to abduct Sita for himself was the paramount motive for Ravana. To put it briefly, as Kamban says,

> Khara he forgot; he forgot the humiliation to his sister; forgot the curse forbidding him even to touch another man's wife; but forget Sita he could not, Sita whom he had not seen, but had just heard of (3:7: 83).

Plays on Rama such as *Mahaveer Charita* point out that Ravana had earlier indeed expressed his desire to marry Sita at the time of her swayamvaram by sending his messengers and that he had gone to the swayamvaram but met with failure, unable to bend the bow of Siva. This matter is talked about in plays such as *Maha Nataka, Bala Ramayana* and *Prasanna Raghava* as well as in Ramayana texts such as Ananda Ramayana, Bhavartha Ramayana, Tulsi's Ramcharitmanas, and Torave Ramayanam. From this, we understand that Ravana had felt unquenchable lust for Sita from the day of her wedding and that when he came to know through Surpanakha that Sita was staying at Panchavati, he simply carried her off. Therefore we come to know from these texts that Ravana's unrequited love for Sita was the cause for abducting her (Bulcke 435-616).

Gunabhadra's Uttara Purana does not speak either about Ravana attending the swayamvaram of Sita or about Surpanakha's disfigurement. Hence, Uttara Purana does not consider these as the cause for the abduction of Sita. On the contrary, Uttara Purana states that Narada approached Ravana after the swayamvaram of Sita and described Sita's beauty in various ways and, consequently, Ravana, struck with desire for Sita, decided to abduct her (Bulcke 435).

When we collate the information presented so far, it becomes clear that the disfigurement of Surpanakha is only an incidental or secondary cause for the abduction of Sita; the primary cause is Ravana's improper love for Sita.

Ravana's Interest in Moksha (Liberation)

Realising that Rama is a divine incarnation, Ravana considers that it is better to turn into an adversary of the divine incarnate than to follow the path of devotion and attain liberation after waiting for thousands of years. Taking this view, texts such as Adhyatma Ramayana (III.5:60;VI.11:80-87), Ananda Ramayana (I.11:244;1.13:120), Padma Purana (VI.269), Bhavartha Ramayana (VI.23), Tulsi Ramayana (III.22:1-3), all of which came up when the Bhakti movement was widespread in society, state that Ravana chose to abduct Sita as a means of getting killed by Rama and thus attaining liberation.

It is in the hymns of Azhwars that we find for the first time the view that on account of his wish to attain liberation, Ravana wanted to die at the hands of Rama and hence he abducted Sita as the first step in his campaign against Rama. Poigai Azhwar, the prime figure among the first Azhwars, who is believed to have lived at the end of sixth century AD, sings of this idea in the following lines:

> Oh, Cosmic Lord! Only to attain your feet
> Did the Ten-headed one choose the way of hatred.
> (Mudhal Thiruvandadhi – 35)

This section, in which the Azhwar offers worship to Lord Vishnu, explains the beauty of God bestowing His grace upon the enemies:

> Oh! Lord! Was not turning into an enemy of yours the means adopted by the ten-headed Ravana to attain your feet easily?

Thus the Ramayana texts cite two chief reasons for Ravana's abduction of Sita. Vanmikam and the Indian Ramayana texts that appeared till the end of twelfth century AD affirm that Ravana's unrequited lust for Sita was the reason.

Adhyatma Ramayana and most of the Indian Ramayanas that came after twelfth century say that Ravana carried off Sita on account of his interest in attaining liberation. **We understand that the motif of *Moksha Prapti* (the attainment of liberation) was first stated by Poigai Azhwar, who lived in the sixth century in the Tamil region.**

Setting Out in Search of Sita

Vanmikam says that Sampaati and Jatayu were the sons born as eagles to a person called Arunan. Jatayu says that Sampaati was elder to him (III.14:33). It has been said that when Rama and the others, after meeting Sage Agastya and, following his advice, were heading to the forest of Dandaka, they met Jatayu and that Jatayu too came to Panchavati and stayed with them. Vanmikam further says that when Sita was being carried off by

Ravana, Jatayu tried hard to prevent it by fighting with Ravana and was lying in the throes of death; and that when Rama and Lakshmana went in search of Sita, they met Jatayu and learnt what happened to Sita.

Texts such as Vanmikam, Narasimha Purana, Kamba Ramayanam, Ranganatha Ramayanam, Bhaskara Ramayanam, Kannassa Ramayanam, Adhyatma Ramayana, Ananda Ramayana, Ezhuthachan's Ramayanam and Tulsidas's Ramcharitmanas say that Rama thus met Jatayu twice.

But some Ramayana texts refer to only one meeting, the one that took place between Rama and Jatayu after the abduction of Sita. For example, Aadhi Ramayana, the Mahabharata (3,263), Bhattikavya (Sarga 5), Ramayana Kakawin (Sarga 5), Udara Raghava (Sarga 8), Molla Ramayanam (43-44,64-69) and Torave Ramayanam (Sandhi/Chapter-12) show Rama as meeting Jatayu only once. The Thai Ramayana Ramakien and other Southeast Asian Ramayanas state similarly that Rama met Jatayu only after the capture of Sita.

The First Meeting of Rama and Jatayu

Most of the Indian Ramayanas narrate the incident of the meeting between Rama and Jatayu. All the Ramayanas state that Rama was initially suspicious on seeing the gigantic figure of Jatayu. Kamba Ramayanam and Thakkai Ramayanam, which follows it, state that Jatayu, on seeing Rama and the others, had some suspicion. Introducing Jatayu as a friend of Dasaratha and engaging him in the task of guarding Sita is an essential element in the development of the epic narrative. Though there are differences in the characters introducing each other, all the texts present in a similar manner the contribution of Jatayu, Rama and others to the development of the plot.

Kamba Ramayanam shows Jatayu introducing himself as a friend of their father. In tune with that, Kamba Ramayanam gives a very moving account of the events such as Dasaratha's passing away, Jatayu's grief, Rama consoling Jatayu, and telling him the reason for going into exile in the forest, and Jatayu appreciating Rama's noble quality of self-sacrifice.

While referring to the lineage of Jatayu, Vanmikam very elaborately presents the evolution of plants, trees, animals, birds, celestials, the Danavas and human beings, starting with the story of Prajapati. While referring to the evolution of human beings, it refers to the four Varnas (castes) and their origin. The Northern and Southern Recensions of Vanmikam too contain this portion. **Other Ramayanas do not present such an account.** Kamba Ramayanam in just one phrase, 'one who appeared during the origin of Varnas', refers to this detail, which Vanmikam presents in about twenty-eight slokas. It is not known why Vanmikam chooses to elaborate these details which are merely *puranic* (legendary) and are irrelevant to the narrative and the structure of the epic.

The Battle between Jatayu and Ravana

Vanmikam

Jatayu, who heard Sita wailing, saw Ravana carrying her off. At once, he addressed him as follows:

> Dasagriva! Sita is the wife of Rama, the champion of righteousness. What harm has Rama done to you? Khara was killed as he fought an unfair battle with Rama on account of Surpanakha. What is the fault of Rama in this matter? Why do you abduct his wife?
> You are carrying a deadly poisonous snake wrapped up in a piece of cloth; you are moving with the rope of Yama (the

god of death) around your neck. You should have only that food which gets digested without causing any illness.
Ravana! If you are a true warrior, stand up and fight with me. It is not proper to run away in dread of Rama and Lakshmana. As long as I am alive, I will not let you abduct Sita (SR III.Sarga 50; NR III.48).

Although Jatayu thus advised Ravana in so many ways, the latter waged war with him with eyes reddened with wrath. Jatayu destroyed Ravana's huge bow and shield; he broke his massive chariot and threw it away. He also killed the mules that were drawing the chariot. He chopped off the head of Ravana's charioteer. Ravana, who lost the bow and the chariot, held Sita, alighted and stood on the ground. Jatayu pounced on Ravana, who was standing on the ground, and pierced him with his talons and beak, injuring him. Enraged by this, Ravana drew Sita close to him with his left thigh and slapped Jatayu with his hand. Since Jatayu attacked him again, he set down Sita, unsheathed his sword and hacked both the wings and legs of Jatayu. When his wings were thus clipped, Jatayu collapsed on the ground, writhing in the throes of death. Sita who was cowering on the ground ran towards Jatayu and hugging him, wailed aloud (SR III.Sarga 51; NR III.49).

Sita, who saw Jatayu writhing in death-throes near the hermitage of Rama, felt very sad and cried, thinking of Rama and Lakshmana. At that time Ravana approached Sita. On seeing him, Sita hugged the huge trees there and cried, 'Please leave me, leave me'. Ravana disregarded her cries and carried her off.

When Ravana thus physically touched and lifted her, all the animate and inanimate things and all the living beings stood dazed, oblivious of their nature; the world was engulfed in utter darkness; the wind ceased to blow; the sun was bedimmed;

Brahma and other sages were grieved by the abduction of Sita and at the same time were happy that Ravana's end was certain (NR III.50:9,10,11; SR III.52:10,11,12,13,14).

When the dark-complexioned Ravana carried Sita away, all the flowers from her hair fell down and scattered. Her anklet dropped down with a mellifluous sound; the chain worn over her bosom slipped down. Thus many of her ornaments dropped down from above like stars that had lost their lustre. In that condition, Ravana, hurtling towards his own doom, stealthily carried off Sita who was crying bitterly with her hair dishevelled, the vermilion mark on her forehead besmeared and her ornaments gone (NR III.50; SR III.52).

As Sita was being carried away by Ravana, she abused and cursed him for his deceit and cowardice in ever so many ways. Not finding a single soul who would save her, she saw on the way five monkeys seated on a mountain peak. On seeing them, she removed her remaining ornaments, wrapped them up in her upper garment and threw them down. Ravana did not notice her act. But those monkeys were watching Sita's crying and all her actions without blinking their eyelids. Ravana crossed the pond Pampa, reached Lanka and confined Sita in his women's quarters (NR III. Sarga 52;SR III.Sarga 54).

Ravana, escorted by the demonesses in his household, took Sita, who was lost in grief, and showed her all the luxuries in his palace and addressed her as follows:

> Sita! You are dearer to me than my life-breath. Become my wife and become the queen of the thousands of my wives here. There is no valiant hero in all the three worlds to match me. What kind of life can you enjoy with Rama, a mere mortal with a short span of life who was prevented

from becoming the king and was exiled, and is now an unmanly human being roaming around as an ascetic? All my heads bow at your feet. I will live as your slave, taking care not to let your mind get upset in the least. Ravana has never bowed to any woman so far. Please bestow your grace on me speedily (NR.III. Sarga 53; SR III.Sarga 55).

Sita, who was disgusted and grieved to hear the words of Ravana overcome by lust, took a piece of darbha grass, dropped it between herself and Ravana and expatiated upon the prowess of Rama. Finally, she said, 'Oh! You wicked demon! Since you defiled me by your touch, the time of ruin has come for yourself and the whole tribe of demons. You have imprisoned only my body, as my mind abides in Rama. If you wish, you can eat up my body. I will not give room for the world to speak ill of me'. So saying, she became quiet.

Ravana heard the harsh words of Sita marked by determination and said, 'Oh! Mythili! You had better yield to my wish within twelve months, failing which my cooks will cut you into pieces for my breakfast', and commanded the demonesses thus, 'Oh! Demonesses! Take this Sita away into the Ashoka grove and guard her closely. All of you together try to persuade her to yield to my ways'. The demonesses who were thus ordered, carried off Sita to the Ashoka grove and kept her confined there. Sita fell into a state of stupor, meditating on Rama and Lakshmana, not knowing what to do, like a female deer caught in the midst of tigers (NR III. Sarga 54; SR III.Sarga 56).

Narasimha Purana

Jatayu hears the distress call of Sita, waylays Ravana, and asks him to leave Sita. When Ravana refuses, he fights a fierce battle with him. However, in the end, Ravana chops off the wings of Jatayu with his sword called Chandrahasa, throws him down and hurries across the sky. On seeing the condition of Jatayu,

Sita sheds tears and wails aloud, 'Oh! King of birds, you are meeting with death for my sake. However, you will reach heaven (Vaikunta) by the grace of Rama. May you be alive till he comes', – thus she blesses him.

Subsequently, she removes her ornaments, ties them up in a piece of cloth and throws them down. Then four monkeys, who were roaming in the forest, pick up the ornaments, hand them over to their king Sugriva and report to him about the battle between Ravana and Jatayu.

When Ravana reaches Lanka with Sita, he keeps her confined in the Ashoka grove, and, after appointing the demonesses to guard her, he returns to his palace. On seeing this, the people of Lanka talk among themselves, 'The wicked-minded Ravana has confined Sita to the city of Lanka. On account of this the entire city will be soon destroyed (49:2-113)'.

Kamba Ramayanam

Jatayu, on seeing Ravana carrying Sita away, admonished him saying, 'Hey! Where are you going? Stop! Stop!' and addressed him as follows:

> Whither art thou fleeing
> Carrying noble Rama's wife
> in the towering chariot of yours?
>
> (III.10:5)
>
> Thou fool! You have committed a grievous mistake.
> Who do you think Sita is?
> One who is like a mother to this vast universe.
> I fear you have acted without thinking.
>
> (10:9)
>
> These two humans are none but the
> Primal source of the Trinity.
>
> (10:14)

> Hence I say unto you,
> thou shalt let go Rama's chaste wife
> Else you are doomed.
>
> (10:8)

Ravana did not listen to Jatayu who thus exhorted him in very many ways; he got angry and said defiantly, 'Eh! Eagle! Leave this place before my arrow pierces your chest'.

> The drop of water that falls over a red hot iron
> may surface again.
> But not she who is in my grip,
> with speech sweet as sugarcane.
>
> (10:18)

Jatayu, on hearing Ravana's refusal, fought a terrible battle with him and broke his bow and flung it off; cut off his breastplate; destroyed the chariot and sixteen of its horses. When Ravana could not find any weapon to hurl at Jatayu who was so powerful, he cut off the wings of Jatayu with his divine sword called Chandrahasa. Jatayu fell to the ground, shorn of his wings.

On seeing Jatayu collapsing, Sita was much agitated:

> Can the noble soul, the one in misery
> Who assured me, 'Fear not'
> Be defeated? Can the devil win?
> Won't such a victory be a scrouge?
> Can the word of the Vedas go wrong?
> Whither Dharma? Thus rued she.
>
> (10.46)

> To uphold chastity is but my duty;
> But haven't I brought disrepute to the
> bow of invincible Rama?
> Haven't I cast a stigma upon the clan of
> my geniture by my act?
> Thus lamented she in anguish.
>
> (10:48)

Kamban describes Ravana carrying Sita off as she was lamenting helplessly, in the following manner:

> The demon noted her helpless plight
> and the mortal condition of Jatayu with his wings clipped off.
> He lifted up Sita along with the plot of land
> over his shoulders,
> set it down on the chariot and flew aloft.
> (10:50)

The demon departed; the King of birds poured out his heart thus:

> Alas! The fence of righteousness has been demolished.
> Who knows, what more is in store?
> (10:53)
>
> This Rama is none but the dark-hued Vishnu
> who reposes on the snake-bed.
> Hence can the wrathful demon conquer him?
> Never!
> (10:55)

Reflecting along these lines, even while a river of blood was flowing from where the huge wings were chopped off, Jatayu felt helpless. Deeply regretting, 'I couldn't retrieve the lady' and filled with this sense of shame, feeling weighed down, he fell into deep slumber. The deceitful demon too feared to touch her directly, says the poet. Therefore, Ravana kept her in confinement in the Ashoka grove amidst the demonesses who were deadly as poison (10:58,59).

Telugu Ramayanas

Hearing Sita lamenting and crying for help when she was captured and being carried off, Jatayu resolved, 'I will kill Ravana and redeem Rama's wife Vaidehi. Or else, I will fight with him and die', and he fought with Ravana. Ranganatha

Ramayanam says that at the end of the battle, with his wings cut off by Ravana, he collapsed on the ground, lay gasping in a pool of blood and grieved (pp.156-158). Bhaskara Ramayanam (pp.116-120;366-375) and Molla Ramayanam (43-44;64-69), narrate this incident more or less in a similar manner.

Ananda Ramayana

Jatayu waylaid Ravana, who was carrying Sita away, and fought a fierce battle with him. He broke and smashed his chariot and killed the mules. Then he broke his bow; cut off his crowns. Enraged, Ravana fought with Jatayu, made him collapse on the ground, then carried Sita and proceeded to Lanka.

When Jatayu fell down injured, Sita cried out, 'Rama, Rama' and looked below. Then she spotted five monkeys at the top of a mountain. At once, she tore off a piece of her upper garment, tied up her ornaments in a bundle and threw it down. In a short while, Ravana reached Lanka with Sita, where he kept her confined in the Ashoka grove amidst a thousand demonesses (I.7:107-116).

Tulsi Ramayan

Jatayu, on seeing Ravana carrying off Sita, shouted at him and ordered him sternly, 'Oh! Wicked demon, stop!' Ravana turned in the direction from where the voice came. Identifying Jatayu, he said 'Oh! Decrepit Jatayu! Do you wish to die at my hands?' Jatayu, who heard this, advised him, 'Oh! Ravana! Do not, like the moth, needlessly go to your doom along with your entire clan into the fire of Rama's wrath. Let Sita go free'. When Jatayu noticed that Ravana was ignoring his advice, he waged war with him. After a fierce battle, Ravana took a keen sword and cut off the wings of Jatayu. Then he hurriedly carried away Sita to

Lanka and kept her confined in the Ashoka grove (III.29a:3-10).

Ramakien

As a friend of Sita's father-in-law, Jatayu fought against Ravana, who was carrying her away. Ravana could not kill Jatayu even after a protracted battle.

Then Jatayu turned to Ravana and said, 'You cannot kill me with your sword or arrow or with any other weapon. It is possible for you to kill me only with Siva's ring which Sita is wearing on her finger'. Ravana at once pulled out the ring from Sita's finger and threw it at Jatayu. The moment the ring hit Jatayu, he fainted and collapsed on the ground.[20]

Summary

Most of the Ramayana texts narrate the battle between Ravana and Jatayu in the same manner. Vanmikam elaborately narrates in seven sargas all the incidents after Jatayu's fall such as Ravana carrying off Sita to Lanka, first keeping her in the inner quarters in his palace, and later, realising her unwillingness to yield, confining her to the Ashoka grove. Other Ramayanas do not narrate this incident in such an elaborate manner.

We can put down the differences found in the references to Jatayu's battle (with Ravana) and the wretched state of Sita as follows:

- After the fall of Jatayu, when Ravana lifted her up by physically touching her, all the objects of nature and the five elements and the two luminaries lost their respective functions. So says Vanmikam. However, Vanmikam does

---

20 *Sri Ramakirti Mahakavyam.* Trans. Satyavrat Shastri, pp. 252 – 253.

state that even in the first instance, when he abducted her at Panchavati, Ravana physically touched her while lifting her. Even when he fights with Jatayu, too, he keeps holding her physically. The question arises why there was no mention of such ill-omens earlier and why Valmiki has chosen to state them at this juncture. The slokas stating it are found in the Northern and Southern Recensions of Vanmikam.

- Vanmikam refers to Ravana as **dark-complexioned** several times, directly as well as through similes. Such a description is not found in other texts.

- Vanmikam says that when Ravana pleaded with Sita to yield to his wishes, he placed his (ten) heads at her feet and bowed to her.

- Vanmikam says that after the fall of Jatayu, when Ravana was carrying away Sita in the sky, she was crying. Looking below, she saw five monkeys on the ridge of a mountain. Ananda Ramayana too states this. But only Narasimha Purana says she saw four monkeys. This number is not very important. However, the reason for such a difference in a very old text is perplexing.

- All the Ramayanas say that when Sita noticed the monkeys, she tied up her ornaments in a piece of cloth and threw the bundle down. All the texts, more or less in a similar manner, say that the monkeys looked up when they heard the wailing voice of Sita, saw Ravana carrying her away and that they picked up the ornaments.

- All the texts, from Vanmikam onwards, say that, when Ravana could not vanquish Jatayu even after a long struggle, he cut off his wings with a divine sword called Chandrahasa; at once Jatayu fainted and fell down. The implication of this happening is that Jatayu's life breath was in his wings and hence he was vanquished. However, the texts do not state this directly. But this matter is found in the Southeast

Asian Ramayanas. For example, the Thai Ramayana known as Ramakeerthi or Ramakien says that Jatayu himself told Ravana that it was possible to kill him only with the ring on the finger of Sita and that Ravana, on hearing that, wrested the ring from Sita's finger, threw it at Jatayu who collapsed on the ground. This too is an evidence of puranic features being superimposed on the epic.

- Narasimha Purana states that the citizens of Lanka, who witnessed the abducted Sita being imprisoned by Ravana in Lanka, became worried, fearing: 'The evil-minded Ravana has imprisoned Sita in our city. On account of this, the entire city might get destroyed.' From the fact that this text, which has left out many incidents of Rama's story, has referred to this elaborately, we infer that there were many noble-minded demon folks like Vibhishana in Lanka.

In the Tamil devotional literary tradition, Thirumangai Azhwar, in twenty verses, movingly sings of the citizens grieving that they were meeting with their destruction on account of Ravana's atrocity (Periya Thirumozhi 10: 2,3):

> Oh! Look how our Ravana's act of capturing the goddess Sita and keeping her in a strictly guarded grove has itself become a sin. Didn't his own brother warn him that this lady would prove to be the poison for the demons? The one endowed with ten heads and firm shoulders turned his attention upon women and got ruined. We, poor people, do not know what to do. Oh Lord! do spare us; we dread the worst. We dance to the beat of the drums lamenting as one who is defeated (*thadam pongatham pongo*). Oh Leader of monkeys! Oh Lakshmana, the younger Prince! Oh Rama, holding the beautiful and mighty bow! We, the demons, are cowering in fright. We dance to the beat of the drums lamenting as one who is defeated (*thadam pongatham pongo*).

The manner or style in which the Azhwar has cast this matter as *Pongatham*, which belongs to the genre of Nattar street play, depicting the fear and trepidation of the demon public that they would become the victims of Ravana's evil deed, is worth being compared with what the Narasimha Purana has to say, and reflected upon.

The Second Meeting of Rama and Jatayu

Rama and Lakshmana, while searching for Sita in all the caves, underground springs and valleys in Janasthana, happened to come across Jatayu who was lying, with his body soaked in blood. Immediately, mistakenly thinking, 'Here lies the demon in an eagle's form, who has killed and eaten up our Sita', Rama got ready to shoot an arrow at him.

Then Jatayu turned to Rama: 'Rama! I saw Ravana carrying away Sita, whom you are searching for, and strove to put up a fight against him to prevent him from doing so. Behold his chariot, parasol, shield, bow and the charioteer, strewn all over here. At the end of the battle, he chopped off my wings and has gone southwards. He is the son of Visravasu and Kubera's younger brother'. Saying so, Jatayu breathed his last.

Rama, who felt sad about the plight of his father's friend Jatayu, held him tight and grieved. Then with the help of Lakshmana, he lit the funeral pyre and performed the last rites for Jatayu and immediately started walking southwards again, resuming the task of searching for Sita (NR 63, 64; SR 67,68).

Summary

- While coming towards Panchavati after killing Maricha, Rama happened to come across several inauspicious signs. So say Vanmikam and all other Indian Ramayanas.

- All the texts say that Rama became apprehensive after hearing the distress call of Maricha while dying and therefore he rushed back in trepidation.

- Many of the Ramayanas state that when Rama met Lakshmana on the way and heard of the happenings at Panchavati through him, Rama rebuked him for leaving Sita alone. But Kamba Ramayanam alone says that Rama chastised himself in disgust,

    > It was not your fault; you warned me.
    > Not forestalling it, I took the wrong step.
    > Alas! It has brought upon us disaster.
    >   (III. 10:69)

- Shocked at not finding Sita at Panchavati, Rama and Lakshmana went all over in search of her, but could not find her. All the Ramayanas describe how Rama was heartbroken and low in spirits as a result, and kept lamenting while Lakshmana tried to console him. However, it is only Vanmikam that elaborately describes this in seven sargas. Kamban, too, sings of Rama's lamentation and fury in some detail. Vanmikam and Kamba Ramayanam show that though in one or two places Rama and Lakshmana talk in a tone reflective of superhuman nature, they act mostly as human beings. Bhusundi and Telugu Ramayanas too more or less narrate it in the same manner.

- In Adhyatma Ramayana, Rama is shown to be thinking that though he knew pretty well that it was the Sita in illusory form who had been captured, Lakshmana did not know it. And therefore, Rama had to feign thus before Lakshmana.

- Vanmikam and other texts say that Lakshmana counselled Rama and pacified him when the latter rose in fury and swore that he would destroy all the worlds. Kamban alone says that it was Jatayu who performed this task of pacifying Rama.

- All the texts, almost without any striking difference, narrate in the same manner the series of incidents such as meeting Jatayu who was gasping for breath after fighting with Ravana, getting information about Sita, Jatayu dying, and Rama and Lakshmana performing the last rites for Jatayu.

- Rama chased the illusory deer mistaking it to be a true deer though Lakshmana had warned him; later he decides to kill Jatayu mistaking him to be a demon in disguise. Both betray his weaknesses. The former is the result of his bravado in trying to please the whim of a woman; the latter, the fear caused by suspicion as the saying goes, 'Everything appears to be a phantom in the eyes of one in fright'.

- Weaknesses – the deluded states of humans to whom paradoxically, truth appears as illusion and illusion as truth. Aren't these but natural to human beings? We know not.

The Story of Ayomukhi

Vanmikam

Rama and Lakshmana, after performing the last rites for Jatayu, embarked on the journey to the south; they crossed the Dandaka forest and entered the forest of Krouncha. Searching for Sita, they were moving towards the hermitage of Sage Matanga. Then out of a cave came a demoness who drew Lakshmana close to her and said, 'I am the famous woman Ayomukhi. You are fortunate to be loved by me, be my husband and live in this beautiful forest happily'. Enraged on hearing this Lakshmana drew his dagger and cut off her ears, nose and both her breasts. Thus humiliated, the demoness Ayomukhi cried out loudly and ran in the direction from which she had come.

Kamba Ramayanam gives a similar account of Ayomukhi with a few additional details. Rama asked Lakshmana to fetch some water. When he went to fetch water, he came across the demoness Ayomukhi. She coveted him and tried to carry him away skyward. Then Lakshmana cut off her ears and nose. When Rama came in search of Lakshmana, apprehensive of the delay in fetching water, Lakshmana met him and told him about what he had done to the demoness Ayomukhi. Rama appreciated his magnanimity in just disfiguring her and letting her off without killing her.

The texts that narrate the story of Ayomukhi are all those that were composed in Southern India: i.e. the Southern Recension of Vanmikam. So they were written in Telugu, Malayalam, Kannada and Tamil. Even though Champu Ramayana was written in Sanskrit, we understand that it was composed in the south, i.e. by a Sanskrit scholar in the Kannada region as an example for a literary genre called 'Champu', as a synopsis of the story of Ramayana.[21] Therefore, one is inclined to view the story of Ayomukhi as an interpolated tale in the southern region.

The Story of Kabandhan
Vanmikam
After the demoness Ayomukhi ran away, Rama and Lakshmana continued their search for Sita. At that time a demon called Kabandhan who had no head and neck, with his mouth in the stomach and with his yojana-long (miles long) arms, held Rama and Lakshmana tightly in his hands and threatened to make a meal of them. Rama and Lakshmana cut off his hands. Kabandhan fell down unconscious.

---

21 'Champu form of composition flourished in Southern India; and the Bengal Vaishnava school and the Jaina writers (Karnataka) made use of this kind of literature for religious propaganda.' Gourinatha Sastri, *A Concise History of Classical Sanskrit Literature*. Delhi: Motilal Banarsidass, rpt. 1998; p. 140.

Then recovering, he asked them who they were. Lakshmana gave a brief account of themselves; they in turn asked him who he was. He said that a sage called Sthulasirasa cursed him with that monstrous shape and that he would get back his shape once Rama cut off his hands and cremated him. He requested them to give him a proper cremation and assured them of providing some information about who could help them. They accordingly gave him a proper cremation. Kabandhan rose from the burning fires with an effulgent appearance. Then he suggested that Sugriva, the King of monkeys on Mount Rishyamukha, could help them find out the whereabouts of Sita. Thus the story of Kabandhan is related to the incidents that make the plot in the story of Rama.

Kamba Ramayanam follows Vanmikam and narrates the incidents related to the story of Kabandhan. However Kamban has used the story of Kabandhan to express the bond of love and affection between Rama and Lakshmana. When Rama spoke in despair that he could not save Sita and was prepared to become a meal for the demon, Lakshmana assured him that they would find some means to kill the demon.

Other texts do not set these accounts as a means of foregrounding this emotional bond of affection between them. In Ramopakhyanam of Mahabharata, Adhyatma Ramayana, Ananda Ramayana, Krittibasi Ramayana and Ramcharitmanas, the story of Kabandhan is narrated following Vanmikam with a few changes.

The Story of Sabari

The story of Sabari is narrated in Vanmikam. Rama and Lakshmana went in search of Sugriva in the forest of Matanga. They reached the hermitage of a female ascetic by name Sabari.

Sabari fell at the feet of Rama and also paid obeisance to Lakshmana. She treated them with a variety of vegetables, fruits and roots. Then she expressed her wish to reach the heavenly abode of the sages and sought the blessings of Rama. Rama blessed her accordingly. Then Sabari jumped into the fire, shuffled off her mortal coil, acquired an effulgent body and reached heaven.

Kamba Ramayanam states that the celestial gods such as Brahma had told Sabari that the time for the completion of her penance had come. They told her to worship Rama and thus she would reach their celestial abode. Sabari, then telling Rama how to find Sugriva, cast off her body and reached heaven.

The story of Sabari is an episode which remains loose and not much related to the plot of Rama's story.

The story of Sabari is not narrated in Mahabharata (Bulcke 428). Hence scholars consider that this episode could not have been found even in Aadi Ramayana and that it must have been an interpolation in the later-day texts. The story of Sabari is not found in Bhagavata Purana either.

The reference to Vibhishana giving a letter to Sabari to be passed on to Rama when he comes to the hermitage of Sage Matanga, as stated in Mahaveer Charita (eighth century AD), is not found in any of the other texts.

Kamban's point about Brahma and others inviting Sabari to their world is not found in Vanmikam. Kamba Ramayanam states that Sabari gave Rama directions to reach Sugriva; but its source text says that it was Kabandhan who did this act of kindness. Vanmikam mentions Sabari jumping into the fire and reaching heaven. Kamban, on the contrary, says that Sabari, by virtue of her power of penance, cast off her body and reached heaven. This section (padalam) with just nine verses unfolding the story of Sabari turns out to be by far the shortest in Kamba Ramayanam.

As far as Indonesia is concerned, Ramayana Kakawin is the first text to narrate the story of Rama in the Javanese language. However, the temples of Parampana in central Java reveal that the details of Ramayana had begun to be depicted in stone sculptures as early as ninth century AD. The sculptures in the inner precincts of these temples were called Lara Jonggrang. These bear the entire story of Ramayana from Bala Kaandam to Uttara Kaandam. We cannot find references to Ramayana displayed as sculptures in any other part of the world during this period (ninth century AD).

As far as the Tamil region is concerned, Ramayana sculptures are found in the temples in the Chola areas of Kumbakonam and Pulla Mangai which were built around tenth century AD. However, these differ from Parampana sculptures in two respects. One is that the sculptures in the Tamil region are found in miniature forms at the bottom portion of the temple while the Parampana sculptures are found to be large in size, sculpted along the *praakaram*s (the paved ways around the sanctum) so as to be clearly visible to people during circumambulation. Secondly, while there are depictions of Uttara Kaandam in the Parampana sculptures, there are no sculptures pertaining to Uttara Kaandam in the temples of the Chola region cited above.

The story of Sabari inscribed in the Parampana temple sculptures and the story of Sabari as shown by Ramayana Kakawin are highly innovative, not found in other Ramayanas. Researchers are of the view that the folklore or stories spread through hearsay by immigrants such as warriors from other countries or traders must be the reason for these innovations.[22]

---

22   Malini and Khanna, *The Ramayana in Indonesia*, pp. 32-33; 51, 101.

In the Southern Recensions of Vanmikam, Sabari worships Rama as a divine incarnation (74:12). Rama too regards himself as a divine incarnation, appreciates her devotion and blesses her (74:13). The Northern Recension too presents it thus. Such a slant is not found in the Eastern and North-western Recensions of Vanmikam. The Rama of Kamba Ramayanam too does not conduct himself as a divine incarnation. But the highly influential Ramayanas which appeared after Kamban such as Adhyatma and Ramcharitmanas have depicted Rama ipso facto as a divine incarnation.

In **Champu** Ramayana, the detail about Sabari jumping into the fire and reaching heaven after extending hospitality to Rama has not been stated.

In **Bhusundi** Ramayana, many details are mentioned for the first time as listed below.

Sabari, who was awaiting the arrival of Rama, had gathered various kinds of fruits, and had kept apart the very tasty ones after tasting them. Rama, who relished those fruits, praised her profusely.

The sages of Matanga forest, who saw Rama accepting the hospitality of Sabari, got jealous of her, and complained to Rama about her many flaws. As a consequence, they underwent various kinds of punishment. Being upset by this, they went to Agastya and following his advice, sought the forgiveness of Sabari and then returned to their routine in the hermitage.

Rama advised Sabari to continue to follow her ascetic life until she attained him in the next *yugam* (era). Hence, in Bhusundi Ramayana, the incident of Sabari immolating herself and reaching heaven does not take place. Agastya coming to the hermitage of Matanga, referring to the objective of Rama's divine incarnation, and praising Sabari are innovations not found in other texts.

The first two Telugu Ramayanas narrate the story of Sabari in tune with Vanmikam. In Assamese Ramayana, the detail about Sabari jumping into the fire is not found. In Bhaskaram and Molla Ramayanam, Sabari's end has not been mentioned.

Adhyatma Ramayana and Molla Ramayanam state that Rama, on seeing Sabari worshipping him, briefed her about his exile in the forest and requested her to enlighten him on the whereabouts of Sita and the means of retrieving her. That Rama himself asked Sabari about it is not mentioned in the other texts.

Krittibas's Bengali Ramayana does not mention the name of Sabari anywhere in the text. On the other hand, it uses terms such as *kanni, kanya* (virgin) and 'little girl' to refer to the woman ascetic. Of the texts taken up for study, Krittibasi Ramayana alone does not mention the name of Sabari; nor does it show the female ascetic as an aged woman.

That Sabari, the huntress, along with her husband met Rama and Lakshmana, that Rama happily relished the fruits she offered by way of hospitality after tasting them herself first, that Sabari went to Mount Rishyamukha following the advice of Rama and from there reached heaven are all new details that Balaram Das's Oriya Ramayan presents.

In many of the Southeast Asian Ramayanas such as Ramakien, the story of Sabari has not been narrated.

Content Variations in Aranya Kaandams

The following are the differences between the texts of Vanmikam of Northern, North-western, Eastern Recensions and the Southern Recension of Vanmikam.

Akampana, who is one of the spies of Ravana, tells him about the killing of Khara and Dushana in Janasthana and asks him to carry off Sita to take revenge on Rama. Accordingly, Ravana goes to Maricha and seeks his help to abduct Sita. Maricha explains the divinity of Rama in great detail to Ravana and sends him back to Lanka. Sarga 31 of the Southern Recension presents this information. But this detail is not found in the Northern, North-western and Eastern Recensions of Vanmikam. These three texts say that it is only Surpanakha who first narrates the killing of Khara and Dushana to Ravana.

In the other Ramayanas and in Southeast Asian Ramayanas such as Ramayana Kakawin, the subject of Akampana's acting as a spy and reporting to Ravana is not found. Therefore, scholars consider that the entire Sarga 31 (50 slokas) of the Southern Recension must have been an interpolation (Bulcke 413).

In Sargas 61 and 63 of the Southern Recension, we find Rama, greatly distressed by the disappearance of Sita, addressing objects of nature and lamenting. Moreover, many of the details of Sarga 60 are found to be repeated in these Sargas. These are not found in the Northern, North-western and Eastern Recensions of Vanmikam.

The story of the disfiguring of the demoness Ayomukhi narrated in slokas 11-18 in Sarga 69 of the Southern Recension is not found in the other Recensions of Vanmikam.

Aadi Ramayana states that the three of them, Rama, Lakshmana and Sita left Chitrakootam and straightaway came to Panchavati. Therefore, the scholar Jacobi considers that the eleven Sargas in between found in the existing Vanmikam of today and the narration of the killing of Viradha, the visit of Rama to the hermitages of Sarabhanga, Sutikshana and Agastya, could be interpolations. It is obvious that these incidents are not indispensable to the plot of the Ramayana epic. Rama meeting Jatayu before the capture of Sita stated at the end of these Sargas cited above is also not found in the other Ramayanas.

Some scholars are of the view that the important incidents of Aranya Kaandam such as the arrival of the illusory deer and the capture of Sita are not found in the source text of Ramayana. Though such a view is not readily acceptable, it cannot be dismissed as entirely wrong.

The source text or Aadi Ramayana is a hypothesis. It has not been retrieved and given an authentic form. Until we get such an account, these basic questions or doubts will continue to remain as uncertainties to be explored further.

Sloka variations in the Aranya Kaandams

Table 5 illustrates how the Northern and the Southern recensions of Vanmikam are different in terms of number of slokas.

Table 5
Valmiki Ramayanas
ARANYA KAANDAMS

Sarga	Sloka Critical edition	Sloka Gorakhpur edition	Sloka Dharmalaya edition	Sarga	Sloka Critical edition	Sloka Gorakhpur edition	Sloka Dharmalaya edition
1.	22	23	23	25.	24	47	49
2.	24	26	26	26.	20	38	39
3.	27	26	26	27.	30	20	21
4.	36	34	32	28.	28	33	33
5.	21	43	40	29.	35	28	30
6.	22	26	26	30.	22	41	42
7.	18	24	24	31.	23	50	50
8.	29	20	20	32.	24	25	25
9.	21	33	33	33.	38	24	24
10.	92	22	23	34.	22	26	28
11.	34	94	95	35.	23	42	42
12.	25	37	40	36.	28	24	24
13.	36	25	65	37.	20	25	26
14.	29	36	37	38.	21	33	33
15.	39	31	32	39.	20	25	25
16.	25	43	44	40.	32	27	28
17.	26	29	32	41.	49	20	20
18.	21	26	26	42.	21	35	35
19.	25	26	28	43.	37	51	50
20.	18	25	27	44.	36	27	28
21.	26	22	22	45.	45	40	41
22.	34	24	26	46.	23	38	38
23.	27	34	35	47.	36	50	52
24.	28	36	36	48.	27	24	24

Sarga	Sloka			Sarga	Sloka		
	Critical edition	Gorakhpur edition	Dharmalaya edition		Critical edition	Gorakhpur edition	Dharmalaya edition
49.	40	40	42	63.	26	20	20
50.	42	28	28	64.	36	77	76
51.	25	46	47	65.	31	16	19
52.	29	44	46	66.	15	21	20
53.	35	26	27	67.	31	29	29
54.	32	30	29	68.	22	38	42
55.	20	37	38	69.	36	51	51
56.	20	36	37	70.	27	19	20
57.	25	23	25	71.	26	34	34
58.	35	20	20	72.		27	31
59.	29	27	27	73.		46	46
60.	52	38	40	74.		35	37
61.	16	31	32	75.		30	31
62.	20	20	21		2059	2473	2540
						+414	+481

Total number of Sargas/Slokas in Aranya Kaandam	Sargas	Slokas
Critical Edition:	71	2059
Gorakhpur Edition:	75	2473
Dharmalaya Edition:	75	2540

Glossary

Adisesha: In Hindu mythology Adisesha, sometimes also known as 'Ananta' (The Endless One), is the thousand-headed ruler of the Nagas, the serpent race that is thought to guard the hidden treasures of the earth. Vishnu is often depicted as resting on Adisesha.

Aditya Hrudayam: The Aditya Hrudayam is a hymn in glorification of the Sun or Surya and is believed to have been imparted by the great sage Agastya to Lord Rama on the battlefield before fighting with Ravana.

Agamas: The Agamas are the primary source and authority for rituals, yoga and temple construction. The Sanskrit term literally means tradition or 'that which has come down'.

Akam tradition: Akam is one of two genres of Classical Tamil poetry which deals with the subject of love.

Ashvamedha Yagam:	The Ashvamedha Yagam is a horse sacrifice ritual followed by the srauta tradition of Vedic religion. It was used by ancient Indian kings to prove their imperial sovereignty.
Azhwars:	The Azhwars were Tamil poet-saints of South India who espoused bhakti (devotion) to the Hindu god Vishnu or his avatar Krishna in their songs of longing, ecstasy and service.
Braj Bhasha:	Braj Bhasha is a western Hindi language. Along with Awadhi (a variety of eastern Hindi), it was one of the two predominant literary languages of North-Central India before the switch to Khari Boli in the 19th century.
Darbha grass:	Darbha is a tropical grass considered a sacred material in Vedic scriptures and is said to purify the offerings during such rituals.
Gandharvas:	Gandharva is a name used for a distinct class of heavenly beings in Hinduism and Buddhism; it is also a term for skilled singers in Indian classical music.
Homam:	Homam refers to a ritual, wherein an oblation or any religious offering is made into fire.
Itihasa:	An Itihasa is a religious story that tells about what happened in the past. Itihasas are usually epic poems.
Iyaibu-t-totai:	Term in Tamil poetics, meaning 'concatenation', a verse form in which the last letter of each line is the same, creating a sound pattern.
Kaandam:	Part or section.
Kandam:	Continent.

Glossary

Kavya:	Kavya refers to the Sanskrit literary style characterised by abundant usage of figures of speech, metaphors, similes, and hyperbole to create emotional effects. 'Kavya' can refer to the style or the completed body of literature.
Koormavataram:	The second incarnation of Vishnu – Koorma, the giant tortoise. When the devas and asuras were churning the Ocean of Milk in order to get Amrita, the nectar of immortality, the Mount (Mandaara) they were using as the churning staff started to sink and Vishnu took the form of a tortoise to bear the weight of the mountain.
Kothandam:	The celestial bow of the Hindu God Vishnu, in his incarnation as Rama.
Mahapurana:	The major puranas (epics).
Marudam:	One of the Thinais (land forms) in Sangam poetry. Marudam refers to the plains and adjoining lands.
Nagastra:	A weapon that took on the form of a snake, proving deadly upon impact.
Neithal:	A thinai in Sangam Tamil poetry describing the land and life near the sea shore.
Paalai:	One of the Thinais (land forms) in Sangam poetry. Paalai refers to the desert region, Kurinji to mountains and adjoining lands and Mullai to forests and adjoining lands. Kurinji and Mullai lands rendered arid by drought were referred to as Paalai. In fact these lands are mentioned as 'naduvunilai', meaning 'in between'. The term 'Paalai' was coined later by the commentators.
Paripadal:	It is a classical Tamil poetic work. It is the fifth book in the Eight Anthologies

	(Ettuthokai), a Sangam literature anthology. Paripadal contains seventy poems on various deities of the Hindu pantheon.
Pongatham:	The term 'pongatham' is a sound symbolic of the fear of the surviving demon population during the Lankan war. The term 'thadam' denotes the lofty victorious status of Rama hailed by the demons. The term 'pongatham pongo' indicates the increasing fear of the demons with the rise of Rama's strength.
Puranas:	The word Purana literally means 'ancient, old'; it refers to a vast genre of Indian literature about a wide range of topics, particularly myths, legends and other traditional lore.
Riti:	It means style or fashion in Vedic Sanskrit.
Sargas:	A section or a canto.
Shankaye:	From Sanskrit 'shankaya', meaning 'doubt'; 'shankayeva' suggesting 'out of fear' or 'apprehension'.
Sutras:	Sutra in Indian literary traditions refers to an aphorism or a collection of aphorisms in the form of a manual or, more broadly, a condensed manual or text. Sutras are a genre of ancient and medieval Indian texts found in Hinduism, Buddhism and Jainism.
Swayamvaram:	In ancient India, swayamvaram was a practice of choosing a husband, from an assembly of suitors, by a girl of marriageable age belonging to a royal family.
Thiruvonam:	One of the twenty-seven stars in Indian astrology. This star is ruled by Vishnu.

Vayu:	It refers to air. It also means wind, and also refers to the Wind God.
Visishtadvaita:	Literally, 'Advaita with uniqueness; qualifications'. It is a non-dualistic school of Vedanta philosophy. It is non-dualism of the qualified whole, in which Brahman alone exists, but is characterised by multiplicity.
Yagam, Yagna:	A Hindu ritual of sacrifice using fire.
Yojana:	It is a Vedic measure of distance that was used in ancient India. A yojana is about 12-15 km.

BIBLIOGRAPHY

I Primary Sources

Adhyatma Ramayana, ed. Swami Tapasyananda (with English Translation), Madras: Sri Ramakrishna Math, 1985.

Ananda Ramayanam, ed. Pt. Ramteja Pandeya. Delhi: Chaukhambha Sanskrit Prathishthan, rpt. 2003.

Ayodhi Kathai (Folk Epic) ed. VT Natarajan. Nagercoil: Rajeswari Publication, 1987 (Tamil).

Bhaskara Ramayanam. Chennapuri: Vavilla Ramaswamy Sastrulu and Sons, 1941.

Bhavartha Ramayana (Critical edition) ed. BG Ghate et al. Bombay: Government of Maharashtra, 1981-1982.

Bhusundi Ramayanam (Purab Kandam) ed. Bhagawat Prasad Singh. Varanasi: Vishwa Vidyalaya Prakashan, 1975.

Champu Ramayana. Varanasi: Krishnadas Academy, 1998.

Ezhuthachan Ramayanam ed., Hari Sarma, Kottayam: Sahitya Pravarthaka Cooperative Society, rpt 1977.

Gvay Dvorabhi ed. Sachchidananda Sahai (with an English translation), 1976.

Hikayat Seri Ram ed. Reverend WG Shellabear, Singapore: Malaysia Publishing House Ltd. 1964.

Janakiharan (with Hindi Trans.), Allahabad: Mitra Prakashan, 1967.

Kamba Ramayanam.
Chennai: Kamban Kazhaga Pathippu, 1976 (Tamil).

Kamba Ramayanam. Paada Bedha Pathippu (Variorum edition). Annamalai Nagar, South India: Annamalai University, 1952-1970 (Tamil).

Kannassa Ramayanam ed. RS Varmaji.
Thiruvananthapuram: Prakati Publishers, 1993.

Kashmiri Ramayan (Persian script).
Srinagar: Pratap Steam Press, 1910.

Kashmiri Ramayan (Devanagari) (with Hindi Trans.) Shiban Krishnan Raina, 1975.

Krittiibasu (Valmiki) Ramayana ed. Jayagopal Tarkalankar, Serampore Mission Press, 1802.

Kritivasa Ramayanam (14th Edition) ed. Dinesh Chandra Sen. Calcutta: Bhattacharya & Sons, 1955.

Molla Ramayanam.
Chennapuri: Vavilla Ramaswamy Sastrulu, 1917.

Narasimha Purana, ed. KL Shastri and Bindiya Trivedi.
Delhi: Parimal Publications, 2003.

Pauma Chariyam (Cariyu) ed. Jacobi. Bhava Nagar, 1914.

Phra Lak Phra Lam (in Laotian language) ed. Sachchidananda Sahai. Laos: ICCR (Vientiane), 1973.

Rama Carita of Abhinanda, edited in the GOS (xlvi, 1930).

Ramacharita Manas, Gorakhpur: Gita Press, Sixth edition, 1991.

Ramacharitamanasa. SP Bahadur (ed. & English translation), New Delhi: Munshiram Manoharlal Publishers Pvt. Ltd. 1994.

Ramakien (The Thai Ramayana). Bangkok (Thailand): Patamini Ltd, Naga Books, Chorakaebua, 1993.

Ramayana Kakawin, Indonesian Ramayana. (ed. trans) Soewito Santoso. New Delhi: 1980.

Ramayana Manjari. Bombay: Kavyamala Publication, 1903.

Ranganatha Ramayanam. Chennai: Vavilla Ramaswamy Sastrulu, 1941.

Srimad Bhagavata (with Eng. Trans.). Swami Tapasyananda. Madras: Sri Ramakrishna Math, (1980), 1996.

Srimad Kambaramayanam, Ayodhya Kaandam (First Part) Chennai: Dr U Ve Sa Nool Nilayam, 1972 (Tamil).

Srimad Valmiki Ramayana (with English translation), (Southern Recension). Gorakhpur: Gita Press, 4th edition, 1995.

Srimad Valmiki Ramayana (Southern Recension), Dharmalaya Edition. rpt. Coimbatore: Arsha Vidya Ashram, Anai Katti, 1993.

Sri Ramakirti Mahakavyam, Satya Vrat Shastri (Trans.) Bangkok: Moolamal & Amarnath Sachdeva Foundation, 1990.

Takkai Ramayanam. (vols. 1, 2) ed. K Arunachala Gounder, Chennai: Tamil Nadu Government Archaeology Department 1983.

Tamil Villupattugal, ed., TC Gomathi Nayagam. Chennai: Tamil Publishing House 1979 (Tamil).

Thai Ramayana by King Ram I of Siam. Bangkok: Chalermnit Book Shop, 1982.

The Mahabharata. Critical Edition. Pune: Bhandarkar Oriental Research Institute, 1918-1966.

The Valmiki Ramayana (Northern Recension), Critical Edition.
Baroda: Oriental Research Institute, MS University, 1951-1971.

The Valmiki Ramayana. Critical Edition, Vol.I, Balakanda ed.
GH Bhatt, 1959.

Torave Ramayanam, vol.1.
Bangalore: Kannada Sahitya Parishad, 1977.

Uttara Puranam. Kashi: Bharatiya Gnanapith, 1954.

II (a) Secondary Sources (Tamil)

Akananuru. Chennai: Murray and Co. First Edition, 1958.

Manimekalai ed., UVe Swaminatha Aiyyar.
Chennai: Thyagaraja Vilas Publication, Sixth Edition, 1965.

Nalayira Divya Prabandham, ed., K Venkatasami Reddiar.
Chennai: Thiruvengadathan, Fifth Edition, 2000.

Paripadal. Text and Parimelazhagar's Commentary, ed.
UVe Swaminatha Aiyyar, 1935.

Pathinen Keezhanakku. Chennai: Murray & Co. First Edition, 1959.

Purananuru. Chennai: Murray and Co. First Edition, 1958.

Silappathikaram ed. Na Mu Venkatasami Nattar.
Chennai: Saiva Siddhanta Publishing House, Fifth Edition, 1956.

Thevara Thirupathigangal, ed. AS Gnanasambandan. Chennai:
Gangai Book Society, 1998.

II (b) Secondary Sources (English)

A Sanskrit-English Dictionary, ed. Sir Monier Williams.
London: OUP, 1976.

Bhayani, HC 'The Prakrit and Apabhramsa Ramayanas', *Asian Variations in Ramayana,* ed. KR Srinivasa Iyengar.

New Delhi: Sahitya Akademi, 1983, pp. 77-82.

Bijoya Das. *A Comparative Study of Krittibasa Ramayana and Kambaramayana*. Unpublished PhD Thesis, Jadavpur University, Calcutta, 1988.

Biswanarayan Shastri. 'Ramayana in Assamese Literature', *The Ramayana Tradition in Asia*, ed.,V Raghavan.
New Delhi: Sahitya Akademi, (1980) 1989, pp. 583-594.

Bizot, F. *The Reamker. Asian Variations in Ramayana*, ed. KR Srinivasa Iyengar. New Delhi: Sahitya Akademi, 1983, pp.263-275.

Bulcke, Camille. *Ram Katha* (Origin and Development), (Hindi). Allahabad: Allahabad University, (1950) 1971.

Bulcke, Camille. 'Ramacaritamanasa and its Relevance to Modern Age'. *The Ramayana Tradition in Asia*, ed. V Raghavan.
New Delhi: Sahitya Akademi, pp.58-75.

Das, AK. 'Notes on the Emperor Akbar's Manuscript of the Persian Ramayana'. *Asian Variations in Ramayana*, ed. KR Srinivasa Iyengar.
New Delhi: Sahitya Akademi, 1983, pp. 144-153.

De Jong, JW. 'The Story of Rama in Tibet'. *Asian Variations in Ramayana*, ed. K R Srinivasa Iyengar.
New Delhi: Sahitya Akademi, 1983, pp.163-182.

De Jong, JW, 'The Story of Rama in Tibet'. *A Critical Inventory of Ramayana Studies in the World*, Vol. II.
New Delhi: Sahitya Akademi, 1993, pp. xxxviii-lvii.

Francisco, Jaun, R. 'The Ramayana in the Philippines'. *A Critical Inventory of Ramayana Studies in the World*, Vol. II.
New Delhi: Sahitya Akademi, 1993, pp. cxix-cxl.

Garg, SK, 'Ramakatha Variegations and Negations'. *Kalyana-Kalpataru*. Rama Number, 1996, pp.111-125.

Godakumbura, CE. 'Ramayana in Sri Lanka...' *A Critical Inventory of Ramayana Studies in the World*, Vol. II.

New Delhi: Sahitya Akademi, 1993, pp. xcv-cxviii.

Goswami, Niranjan. 'A folk painted manuscript of the Ramacarita manasa'. *Asian Variations in Ramayana*, ed., KR Srinivasa Iyengar. New Delhi: Sahitya Akademi, 1983, pp. 108-123.

Gnanasundaram D. *Kamban Malar* Coimbatore: Kamban Kazhagam, 1991, pp.21-22 (Tamil).

Hara, Minoru. 'Rama stories in China and Japan: A Comparison'. *Asian Variations in Ramayana*, ed., KR Srinivasa Iyengar. New Delhi: Sahitya Akademi, 1983, pp. 348-356.

Jacobi, H. *Das Ramayana*. Bonn: 1893.

Jani, AN. 'Different Versions of Valmiki's Ramayana in Sanskrit'. *Asian Variations in Ramayana*, ed., KR Srinivasa Iyengar. New Delhi: Sahitya Akademi, 1983, pp. 29-56.

Jegavira Pandian. *Pulavar Ulagam* (Kamban Kalai Nilai).Part 4, Madurai: Varadarajulu Naidu Press, 1945 (Tamil).

Kamban Malar. Coimbatore: Kamban Kazhagam, 1998.

Kathleen M. Erndl. 'The Mutilation of Surpanakha'. *Many Ramayanas*, ed. Paula Richman. Oxford India Paperback, 1992, pp. 67-88.

'Kaandam Structure of Ramayana', *Purana Bulletin*, Ayodhya Special Issue, vol. xxxiii No.2, Varanasi, July 1991.

Krishnamoorthy, K. *A Critical Inventory of Ramayana Studies in the World* (Vols. I & II). New Delhi: Sahitya Akademi (1991, 1993).

Kaul, Omkar. *A Comparative Study of Kashmiri and Hindi Ramayanas*. (Hindi). Chandigarh: Bahri Publication, 1974.

Manasa, Piyush. *Ayodhya Kaandam*, (Hindi) ed. Anjani Nandan Sharan. Gorakhpur: Gita Press, Fourth Edition, 1967.

Mishra, Nilamani. 'Ramayana in Oriya Literature'. *The Ramayana Tradition in Asia*, ed. V Raghavan.
New Delhi: Sahitya Akademi, (1980), 1989, pp. 617-635.

Misra, Vidya Nivas. 'The Rama Story in Indian Folklore'. *Asian Variations in Ramayana,* ed., KR Srinivasa Iyengar. New Delhi: Sahitya Akademi, 1983, pp. 100-107.

Naidu, Shankar Raju. *Kamba Ramayana and Tulasi Ramayan.* Madras: University of Madras, 1971.

Narayana Rao, Velcheru. 'The Politics of Telugu Ramayanas...' *Questioning Ramayanas,* ed., Paula Richman. New Delhi: Oxford University Press, (2000) 2003, pp. 159-185.

Natesa Sastriyar. *Srimad Adhyatma Ramayanam.* Chennai: Balaji & Co. Second Edition, 1914.

Pande, CR Desh. *Transmission of the Mahabharata Tradition.* Simla: IIAS, 1978.

Pushp, PN, 'Ramayana in Kashmiri Literature and Folk-lore'. *The Ramayana Tradition in Asia,* ed., V Raghavan. New Delhi: Sahitya Akademi, (1980), 1989, pp.534-545.

Puranic Encyclopaedia, ed., Vettam Mani. New Delhi: Motilal Banarsidass, 1975.

Raghavan, V. 'The Ramayana in Sanskrit Literature'. *The Ramayana Tradition in Asia,* ed.,V Raghavan. New Delhi: Sahitya Akademi, (1980), 1989, pp. 1-19.

Raghavan, V. *Ramayana in Classical Sanskrit and Prakrit Literature.* Chennai: 2004.

Ratnam, Kamala. 'Socio-Cultural and Anthropological Background of the Ramayana in Laos'. *Asian Variations in Ramayana,* ed. V Raghavan. New Delhi: Sahitya Akademi, 1983, pp.230-251.

Richman, Paula,ed. *Many Ramayanas.* Oxford India Paperback, 1992.

Richman, Paula, ed. *Questioning Ramayanas: A South Asian Tradition.* New Delhi: Oxford University Press, 2003.

Sahai, Sachchidananda, 'The Khvay Thuaraphi'. *The Ramayana*

Tradition in Asia ed., V Raghavan.
New Delhi: Sahitya Akademi, (1980) 1989, pp. 282-300.

Sankalia, HD. *Ramayana: Myth or Reality?* New Delhi: People's Publishing House, 1991.

Saran, Malini & Khanna, Vinod C. *The Ramayana in Indonesia.*
New Delhi: Ravi Dayal, 2004.

Sarma, CR. *Ramblings in Telugu Literature.* Madras, 1978.

Sarma, CR. *The Ramayana in Telugu & Tamil.* Madurai, 1994.

Seetharamachar, H. *Kumaravanmiki- A Study.*
Mysore: Mysore University, 1976.

Sen, DC. *The Bengali Ramayans.* Calcutta: 1920.

Shah, UP. 'Ramayana Manuscripts of Different Versions'. *The Ramayana Tradition in Asia* ed., V Raghavan. New Delhi: Sahitya Akademi, (1980) 1989, pp. 93-102.

Shah, UP. 'Ramayana in Jaina Tradition'. *Asian Variations in Ramayana* ed., KR Srinivasa Iyengar.
New Delhi: Sahitya Akademi, 1983, pp.57-76.

Singaravelu, S 'Tulasidas… Valmiki… Kamban… and Thai version…' *The Ramayana Tradition in Asia* ed., V Raghavan.
New Delhi: Sahitya Akademi, (1980) 1989, pp. 455-474.

Singaravelu, S. 'The Literary Version of the Rama Story in Malay.' *Asian Variations in Ramayana* ed., KR Srinivasa Iyengar. New Delhi: Sahitya Akademi, 1983, pp. 276-295.

Singh, Bhagawati Prasad. 'Bhusundi Ramayana…' *The Ramayana Tradition in Asia*, ed., V Raghavan.
New Delhi: Sahitya Akademi, (1980) 1989, pp. 475-504.

Smith, WL. *Ramayana Traditions in Eastern India.*
New Delhi: Munshiram Manoharlal Pvt. Ltd. 1995.

Sorensen, S. *An Index to the Names in the Mahabharata.*
New Delhi: Motilal Banarsidass, rpt. 1978.

Sitapathi, PC. *Vanmiki – Kamban Maatrangal Bala Kaandam.*
Coimbatore: Kamban Kazhagam, 1984 (Tamil).

Sitarama Sashtrigal. *Valmiki Munihrdaya Tattuvacharaprakasika.*
Trichy: United Printers Ltd.,1943 (Sanskrit).

Suman, Amba Prasad. *Tulsi Kavya Chintan.* (Hindi).
Aligarh: Grantayan, 1982.

Thampi, Padmanabhan, P. *Ramayanas of Kampan and Eluttacchan.*
Trivandrum: University of Kerala, 1996.

'The Tun-huang manuscripts of the Tibetan Ramayana Story.'
Indo-Iranian Journal, 19, pp. 37-88.

Toru, Ohno. *A Comparative Study of South East Asian Ramayanas,*
Part II.1999.

U Thein Han and Ukhin Zaw. 'Ramayana in Burmese Literature and Arts'. *The Ramayana Tradition in Asia,* ed., V Raghavan.
New Delhi: Sahitya Akademi, (1980) 1989, pp. 301-314.

Weber, Albrecht. *Uber Das Ramayana.* Berlin: 1870, pp. 1-80,
English Translation by DC Boyd. Bombay, 1873.

Whaling, Frank. *The Rise of the Religious Significance of Rama.*
Delhi: Motilal Banarsidass, 1980.

II(c) Other Reference Works

Chennai Palkalaikazhagam Tamil Peragaradhi. (Tamil Lexicon).
Madras: University of Madras, Volumes 1-7, 1982 (Reprint) (Tamil).

Gaurinath Sastri. *A Concise History of Classical Sanskrit Literature.*
Delhi: Motilal Banarsidass, 1998.

Giriprakash, TS and Anadakumar P. *Telungu Illakiya Varalaru.*
Madurai: Parthiban Pathipakam, 1986 (Tamil).

Gurusamy, Ma Ra Po. *Kasil Kotram.*
Coimbatore: Narendrasivam Pathippakam, 2002 (Tamil).

Manavalan, AA. *Epic Heroism in Milton and Kamban*. Coimbatore: Kamban Trust, 1984.

Manavalan, AA. 'Ramayana Bala Kaandangal – Oru Oppiyal Aayvu'. *Kamba Ramayanam – Bala Kaandam (With Commentary)*. Coimbatore: Kamban Trust, 1993 (Tamil).

Manavalan, AA. 'Ramayana Ayodhya Kaandangal – Oru Oppiyal Aayvu', *Kamba Ramayanam – Ayodhya Kaandam (With Commentary)*. Coimbatore: Kamban Trust, 1994 (Tamil).

McGregor, RS. *The Oxford Hindi-English Dictionary*. New Delhi: Oxford University Press, 1993.

Naarla Venkateswara Rao, Manuel Ra. (Tamil Translation). *Sitai Josiyam*. (Telugu Play). New Delhi: Sahitya Akademi, 2001.

Padmanabhan Thampi, P. *Kamban Ezhuthachan Ramayangal*. Chennai: International Institute of Tamil Studies, 1993 (Tamil).

Parameshwaran Nair, PK Rama Gopinathan (Tamil Translation). Gopinathan. *Malayala Illakiya Varalaru*. New Delhi: Sahitya Akademi, 1995.

Pandurangan, A. *Kambarum Valmikiyum*. Pondicherry: Tamizharangam, 2003 (Tamil).

Pathak, RC. *Bhargava's Standard Illustrated Dictionary*. (Hindi-English). Varanasi: Bhargava Book Depot, 2002.

Ramakrishnan, S. *The Epic Muse: The 'Ramayana' and 'Paradise Lost'*. New Delhi: People's Publishing House, 1977.

Singaravelu Mudaliyar, A. *Abhidhana Chintamani*. New Delhi: Asian Educational Services, 1986.

Sivakami, Sa. *Kamban Aayvadangal*. Chennai: Tamizh Padippakam, 1978 (Tamil).

Srinivasa Iyengar, PT. *History of the Tamils*, (From the Earliest Times to 600 AD). New Delhi: Asian Educational Services, 1995.

Thilakam, Ch. *Kusa-Lavan Kathai*.

Thanjavoor: Thanjai Saraswati Mahal Publication, 1983 (Tamil).

Trilokinath Raina. *A History of Kashmiri Literature.*
New Delhi: Sahitya Akademi, 2002.

Varadharasan. Mu. *Tamil Ilakkiya Varalaru.*
New Delhi: Sahitya Akademi, 2003 (Tamil).

Vayyapuri Pillai, S. *Tamizhar Panpaadu – Kamban Kaaviyum.*
Chennai: Vayyapuri Pillai Ninaivu Mandram, 1993 (Tamil).

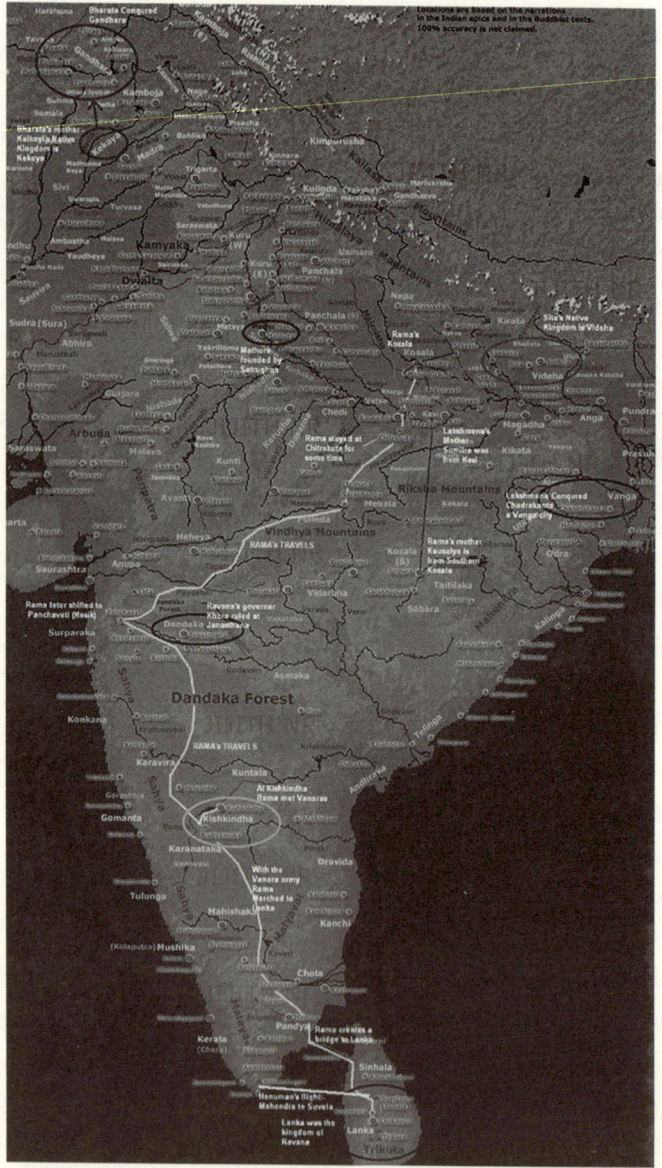

Map of Rama's Travels: The reader is cautioned against regarding this map as either exact or universally acceptable. This map is representational and is included here to facilitate the modern-reader's understanding of the mythical geography of the Ramayana, as it is a travelogue in some sense and is in no way claimed to be factual. The locations are according to what is mentioned in the epic and its various renditions. The map is available in Creative Commons.

—Publishing Editor.

Translators' Acknowledgements

To translate *Ramakaathaiyum Ramayanangalum* by Professor A A Manavalan has been an enriching experience intellectually, academically as well as spiritually. The contents of the book enhanced our knowledge of the epic and it was interesting to note several variations of the text rendered in different languages at different periods of time. It was an informative and delightful experience. The author's language, closely following classical texts, posed certain challenges to us as translators with regard to the syntax as well as the vocabulary in many an instance. However, we strove hard to resolve the problems to the best of our abilities. It took two years for us to complete the task with liberal help from many a good heart.

We would like to thank all those who provided typing assistance to us: Dr Nandini Iyengar who was kind enough to key in a basic draft of about fifty pages to begin with and R Sumathy for sparing her time to give us a typed rough draft of the text of nearly 250 pages. Then Kalpana stepped in and generously helped us to complete our revision and editing of the text. Annapoorani willingly helped us when we were in dire need of technical support. We wish to place on record our sincere gratitude to Dr Sumathi Shivakumar for sparing her time to key in the contents before each Kaandam and coming to our rescue every now and then.

There are three scholars and generous souls who travelled with us in different phases and periods in this journey covering many Ramayanas, who joyfully pulled us out of the 'Slough of Despond', to use Bunyan's profound phrase, when we faced the wall in critical situations. Our debt of gratitude to them is immense and in each case very special. Professor T Sriraman, formerly of the English and Foreign Languages University, Hyderabad, took upon himself the onerous task of bringing the syntax in the translated version closer to normal English structure when we were having 'an intolerable wrestle' with the language, in the words of T S Eliot. He patiently read through the entire text in Tamil and our translated version and meticulously edited it to facilitate unimpeded reading. Despite his marathon efforts, if the work suffers from faults, the blame entirely falls on us. Next in the horizon appears another enthusiastic scholar and workaholic – Uma Rajagopal. With a post-graduate degree in Vaishnavism from the University of Madras and exposure to Hindu Thought and Literature, not to mention her knowledge of Sanskrit and Hindi and her keen sense of English vocabulary and syntax, Uma too went through our entire translation and edited it with consummate skill and enviable ease. Having herself translated devotional works and doctrinal discourses from Tamil to English, she also explained many a recondite item to us. It was for her a labour of love as an earnest scholar who is also a devotee of Lord Narayana.

The one who appears next came last in our map, but she is not the least – Malini Ravindran, M A B Ed, formerly Head of the Department of Tamil, Sir Sivaswamy Kalalaya, Chennai. She is a much-loved Tamil teacher and is much sought after by dance gurus, performers and professionals. Professor Manavalan has cited scores of passages from classical and folk literary works throughout his book, most of them being from *Kamba Ramayanam* and Azhwars' hymns and Tamil bow-songs. We, as translators, postponed the task of confronting them in our English translation till the very end. It was providence that brought Malini into our ken in the very last stage, literally in the last few weeks. Being an ardent admirer of Kamban whose poetry runs in her blood and bones, very knowledgeable in Tamil Literature, Malini explained every passage, its context, linguistic and tonal features with amazing alacrity and spontaneous involvement. The Vindhya mountain was subdued, we must say! In a trice Malini was able to help us scale it. Malini thought she was the squirrel in the Ramayana; but we think, she was like Hanuman who not only crossed the ocean, but carried us across too. To use Milton's paradoxical way of conveying gratitude in *Paradise Lost, Book IV*, 'A grateful mind by owing owes not, but still pays at once indebted and discharged'. A note of caution, however, may be in place. We have not attempted to render the verse passages exactly in a poetic mode. We would be happy if they are regarded as verse paraphrases which would help lay readers to comprehend the meaning in the context.

The same is the case with a couple of Telugu passages which were translated for us by Dr Shanthilakshmi, Dean, MGR-Janaki College of Arts and Science for Women, Chennai, after consulting a few Telugu scholars in Hyderabad. We thank her too, most heartily. We wish to state, however, that not all passages so translated find a place in this edited version of the work. We record our special appreciation and gratitude to two scholars of immense erudition, one in Sanskrit and the other in Tamil, Prof K Srinivasan, currently Sri Anna Subrahmanya Iyer Chair in Kuppuswami Sastri Research Institute, Chennai, and Dr P R Subramanian, Director, MOZHI, Chennai. They readily helped with clarifications in the very last stage of checking.

We would like to thank Dr N Govindarajan of American College, Madurai for clarifying doubts in Kamba Ramayanam while reading the proofs.

We are grateful to Dr Meenakshi Hariharan for helping us to check the proofs of the copy-edited version.

Above all, this academic exercise would not have been possible if Professor Manavalan had not chosen to give us this wonderful opportunity to translate his award-winning text and enable us to traverse the length and width of the epic narrative which was a journey into all the regions connected with the narrative. At the time of this work getting published, Professor Manavalan is sadly not with us any more.

We also thank the publishers of the Tamil work, Institute of South Indian Studies, for giving us permision to publish this English rendition of Professor Manavalan's epic work, *Ramakaathaiyum Ramayanangalum*.

By divine will operating through us, we hope that the text will get a wider readership through translation and reach not only the avid but the discerning researchers of the Indian epic.

About Professor A A Manavalan

Professor A A Manavalan (1935-2018) taught in the Tamil Language Department of University of Madras, Chennai, and retired as Professor and Head. He was proficient in Telugu and Hindi also. His doctoral research was on the epic poetry of Kamban and Milton. He was a Visiting Professor for Comparative Literature in the Universities of Indiana, Columbia and New York, USA, under the Indo-American Cultural Exchange programme (1988-89). He has published research works on *Tolkappiyam*, Tamil Bhakti Literature, twentieth-century literary theories, comparative literary studies in epics, Sangam Tamil Literature, and world Tamil literary history. The book translated here, *Ramakathaiyum Ramayanangalum (vol. 1)*, published in Tamil in 2005 by the Institute of South Indian Studies, Chennai, was awarded the Saraswati Samman by the KK Birla Foundation, Delhi, in 2011.

TRANSLATOR-EDITOR C T INDRA

C T Indra taught at the University of Madras (1976-2008) and served as Professor and Head of the English Department from 1995 to 2007. She was also Chair of the School of English and Foreign Languages for some time. She was a Fulbright post-doctoral Fellow at Harvard University (1980-81) and American Research Fellow at the University of California, Santa Barbara (1990). Her publications in the area of translation include *The Legend of Nandan* (OUP, 2003, Indira Parthasarathy's Tamil play *Nandan Kathai*), Indira Parthasarathy's *Three Plays*, with T Sriraman (Authors Press 2019), *Cross Section*, in collaboration with Prema Jagannathan (Sahitya Akademi 2014, P Sivakami's Tamil novel *Kurukku Vettu*), translation of critical articles by P Sivakami and Thenmozhi, jointly with Meenakshi Hariharan in *Oxford Anthology of Tamil Dalit Writings* (OUP, 2012), *Internal Colloquies* (trans. from Tamil into English of selected poems of Thamizhachi Thangapandian's *Vanapechi*, Rubric Publishing, 2019) and *The Solitary Sprout, Selected Stories of R Chudamani* with T Sriraman (Orient BlackSwan 2019). With R Rajagopalan she has contributed to and edited *Language, Culture and Power: English-Tamil in Modern India: 1900 CE-Present Day* and *Culture, Language and Identity: English-Tamil in Colonial India: 1750-1900* (London: Routledge, 2018) a British Council project.

TRANSLATOR-EDITOR
PREMA JAGANNATHAN

Prema Jagannathan is an Associate Professor of English (retired) and former Dean of Academic Affairs, Stella Maris College, Chennai. Her areas of interest include Indian Fiction, Bhakti Literature, Translation Studies and Communicative English. She is the author of *The Mahabharata and Contemporary Indian Fiction,* published by Prestige Books, New Delhi (2010). She has translated a few short stories, plays and non-fictional works from Tamil into English and vice versa. A few to name are translation of P Sivakami's *Kurukku Vettu* along with CT Indra, Sahitya Akademi, New Delhi (2014) and translation of S Ramakrishnan's *Urulum Paaraikal* in **Four Tamil Plays** published by Orient BlackSwan and Stella Maris College 2014.

Among her published work is also the *Key to JC Nesfield's English Grammer and Composition,* co-authored by Sharada Bhanu and published by Macmillan India.

श्री राम श्री राम श्री राम श्री राम श्री राम श्री राम श्री राम श्री राम श्री
श्री राम श्री राम श्री राम श्री राम श्री राम श्री राम श्री राम श्री राम श्री
श्री राम श्री राम श्री राम श्री राम श्री राम श्री राम श्री राम श्री राम श्री
श्री राम श्री राम श्री राम श्री राम श्री राम श्री राम श्री राम श्री राम श्री
श्री राम श्री राम श्री राम श्री राम श्री राम श्री राम श्री राम श्री राम श्री
श्री राम श्री राम श्री राम श्री राम श्री राम श्री राम श्री राम श्री राम श्री
श्री राम श्री राम श्री राम श्री राम श्री राम श्री राम श्री राम श्री राम श्री
श्री राम श्री राम श्री राम श्री राम श्री राम श्री राम श्री राम श्री राम श्री
श्री राम श्री राम श्री राम श्री राम श्री राम श्री राम श्री राम श्री राम श्री
श्री राम श्री राम श्री राम श्री राम श्री राम श्री राम श्री राम श्री राम श्री
श्री राम श्री राम श्री राम श्री राम श्री राम श्री राम श्री राम श्री राम श्री
श्री राम श्री राम श्री राम श्री राम श्री राम श्री राम श्री राम श्री राम श्री
श्री राम श्री राम श्री राम श्री राम श्री राम श्री राम श्री राम श्री राम श्री
श्री राम श्री राम श्री राम श्री राम श्री राम श्री राम श्री राम श्री राम श्री
श्री राम श्री राम श्री राम श्री राम श्री राम श्री राम श्री राम श्री राम श्री
श्री राम श्री राम श्री राम श्री राम श्री राम श्री राम श्री राम श्री राम श्री
श्री राम श्री राम श्री राम श्री राम श्री राम श्री राम श्री राम श्री राम श्री
श्री राम श्री राम श्री राम श्री राम श्री राम श्री राम श्री राम श्री राम श्री
श्री राम श्री राम श्री राम श्री राम श्री राम श्री राम श्री राम श्री राम श्री
श्री राम श्री राम श्री राम श्री राम श्री राम श्री राम श्री राम श्री राम श्री

श्री राम श्री राम श्री राम श्री राम श्री राम श्री राम श्री राम श्री राम श्री राम